# *Camping*
# Colorado

**Melinda Crow**

FALCON®

Helena, Montana

*CAUTION*

Outdoor recreational activities are by their very nature potentially hazardous. All participants in such activities must assume the responsibility for their own actions and safety. The information contained in this guidebook cannot replace sound judgment and good decision-making skills, which help reduce risk exposure, nor does the scope of this book allow for disclosure of all the potential hazards and risks involved in such activities.

Learn as much as possible about the outdoor recreational activities in which you participate, prepare for the unexpected, and be cautious. The reward will be a safer and more enjoyable experience.

♻ Text pages printed on recycled paper.

*To Gary and Alyssa. None of this makes any sense
without the two of you.*

# Contents

**Public**

## Area 18: Castle Rock

**Commercial**

**Public**

## SOUTHWEST

### Area 19: Montrose

**Commercial**

**Public**

### Area 20: Gunnison

**Commercial**

## Area 26: Pagosa Springs
### Commercial

### Public

## Area 27: South Fork and Platoro
### Commercial

### Public

## SOUTH CENTRAL
### Area 28: Buena Vista
### Commercial

### Public

### Area 29: Colorado Springs
### Commercial

### Public

# Acknowledgments

The people who helped make the research of this book an easier task are, unfortunately, too numerous to mention all by name. The list includes RV park owners and managers who took the time to either fill out a questionnaire or talk to me in person. Thanks also to the camp hosts and rangers across the state who fielded questions. I know your time is valuable; thank you for sharing it.

I am also indebted to Mark Hassell who happily went along for the ride when he could, and loaned us his truck and took care of our cats when he could not. We'd never have made it beyond the Eisenhower Tunnel in our Toyota. Thanks Mark. I owe you yet another cheesecake.

Other camping companions included Chelsea Sissom and my parents, Bill and Louise West and JoAnn and Ramon DeLano. I know it was harder work than you all thought it would be, but you managed to keep the complaints mostly to yourselves. Thanks for sharing the campfire at the end of each day; your help and companionship are always appreciated.

Friends and family members helped at home by running errands, cooking meals, providing computer assistance when my hard drive crashed, and supplying a generous amount of sympathy when I whined. Thanks Mother, Sugar, Cindy, Chuck, and Steve.

My daughter Alyssa earned the title of Photographic Assistant this year by hauling equipment, changing lenses, labeling slides, and even shooting a few of the pictures that appear in the book. Thank you A.J.

Final and most heartfelt thanks go to my partner on this project as in life, my husband Gary. Thank you for all the miles, for all the golf courses you drove past rather than on, for all the pictures you took or reminded me to take, and for all the times you've encouraged my dreams to soar higher than the Rockies.

# About This Book

When I set out to write this book, I realized that the first order of business wasn't researching the campgrounds, but rather researching the campers. Before I could write about the places, I had to know the people who would visit them.

What I found was a mix of people from across this continent and beyond, with one thing in common: the people who journey to Colorado's campgrounds are seekers. Some seek heart-pounding excitement running the rapids or climbing soaring peaks. Some seek physical challenges like pedaling some of the steepest bike trails in the country. Others come looking for fish to catch, birds to watch, waterfalls to photograph. Still others come seeking nothing more than the solitude of the wild.

Perhaps the most incredible thing is that Colorado can satisfy all of these travelers. But could this book? My own version of the ideal campground involves a quiet place to stretch out in a lounge chair, and a couple of easy hiking trails nearby, with a hot mineral pool and maybe a golf course down the road. I don't ride dirt bikes anymore, but I knew I must find campgrounds suitable for you if that's what you like to do, just as I knew I had to find camping destinations for people who like to fish, hike, bike, climb, ride horses, swim, ski, bird watch, gamble, or just park.

The second task at hand was how to narrow the choices. You will find more than 800 camping facilities listed in this book, and there are probably some that got overlooked. But only about half are described in detail. Knowing that a good guidebook should be more than just a directory, I had to decide which places you most wanted to know about. The following criteria were used to determine which campgrounds would get more than a simple listing: popularity of the destination, in case you want to follow or avoid the crowds; accessibility, because most people choose the easy road; and availability of reliable information, because accuracy was the number one goal.

The descriptions provide facts important to your travel planning, like elevation, road conditions, and activities, plus contact information in case you need to know even more. Also included is a brief narrative based on my own observations of the site. Interestingly enough, I found that when I viewed each campground with you and your needs in mind, I found an exciting array of choices that I might have otherwise overlooked.

It's important to remember that the sites listed as Additional Campgrounds weren't judged as poor choices, only *other* choices that fell outside the realm of the criteria. Location and contact phone numbers are provided so you can decide for yourself if they might better suit your camping desires.

My strongest hope is that somewhere between these pages you will find that one spot that begs you to air out the sleeping bags and hit the road. And when you arrive, I hope it's everything you dreamed of and stirs a song in your soul that will keep you coming back.

# How to Use This Guide

As you begin looking at the campground descriptions, you will notice a few differences between the heading information provided for privately owned parks and those that are public. Private or commercial camp listings include affiliations, such as Good Sam or KOA, which indicate the possibility of discounts for members or, in some cases, a monitoring of standards. Many parks offer multiple ways to contact them, including phone, fax, or e-mail. If a toll-free number is available, it is usually for reservations only and is listed separately in the descriptions for your convenience.

The price per night information provided in commercial campground listings depends upon the chosen site. The price is usually for two people and does not include tax. All prices are subject to change. Since accessibility to commercial campgrounds is rarely a problem, road conditions are not provided for these operations.

Activities at the private campgrounds are not listed separately. Instead, look for amenities, such as fishing ponds or stables, included in the list of on-site facilities. Some indication of nearby activities is usually provided in the campground description, and further information can be found on the introductory page for the area in which the park is located.

Opening and closing dates at both commercial and public campgrounds are often affected by weather. You can assume a May opening and a September or October closing unless the season is noted as year-round. The descriptions of public campgrounds include a phone number to call for further information. Many national forest camps are operated by concessionaires under the supervision of the U.S. Forest Service. These individual companies are not listed because they change from year to year.

Fees listed for the public camps are based on 1997 prices and are subject to change. Many campgrounds have restrictions on the number of people per campsite. When in doubt, call the managing agency.

Camping facilities, both public and private, change frequently. The information in this book was current at the time of publication, but it may be slightly outdated by the time you use it. If you would like to share information about changes you encounter, please send it to the author, care of Falcon Publishing, P.O. Box 1718, Helena MT 59624.

# Camping Choices

Colorado offers a wide variety of camping choices to suit every taste. Because the level of development is one of the most important factors people use when choosing a destination, this book is arranged by those levels as well as geographically.

Within each of five geographic regions are thirty-four areas in which camping choices are listed as follows: the commercial campgrounds are first (in alphabetical order), then national parks, state parks, city or county parks, national forest campgrounds, and Bureau of Land Management camps. Listed last are state wildlife areas, which are least developed. In general, the farther down each area's list you go, the fewer amenities you can expect to find. The following descriptions of these classifications should help in your planning.

### Commercial Campgrounds and RV Parks

In many areas of the country commercial campgrounds consist mainly of roadside parking lots designed for people who are just passing through. You will find those in Colorado, but the overwhelming majority of commercial operations here offer much more. Many use the word resort in their names, and they mean it. Among the choices you will find working ranches, fishing camps, and white-water rafting resorts.

Most commercial facilities offer such amenities as hot showers, flush toilets, and public phones. All provide drinking water, and there is usually a choice of other hookups, such as sewer, electricity, and even phone and cable TV. Don't be surprised to find video gamerooms, gift shops, or tour services at many of these operations.

Commercial campgrounds are often an ideal choice for active families. Some facilities can keep older kids busy around the clock, allowing parents time to relax. If this is your vacation plan, look for destinations with swimming pools, stables, movies, hayrides, bike rentals, and family meals.

Other places cater more to retired travelers, offering potluck socials and evening card games. A good indicator of these parks is the ratio of sites with full hookups to sites with no hookups. The reason is simple: retirees are more likely to travel in RVs that use the hookups.

A growing trend at many commercial campgrounds in Colorado is the addition of sleeping cabins. These are usually nothing more than four walls and a bare bed. They sometimes have electricity inside, but they don't have plumbing. They make a nice compromise between camping and staying in a motel.

With a few exceptions, the commercial campgrounds in Colorado are below 9,000 feet in elevation. This makes them attractive to people who are susceptible to altitude sickness or anyone with heart or lung disorders that would make camping at higher altitudes uncomfortable.

Seasons of operation for these privately owned campgrounds are dictated by location and elevation. You will find a few mountain parks open year-round, primarily near ski resorts. But unless otherwise noted, you can assume that seasonal openings and closures apply.

All of these conveniences do come with a price tag. You should expect to pay anywhere from $15 to $35 per night (plus taxes) for a site occupied by two people. It is customary throughout the state to charge extra ($2 average) for each additional person, including children. The other price you pay is usually in lack of privacy. Even in the nicest parks space is a premium, so expect to be close to your neighbors.

With only one or two exceptions, these operations take and encourage reservations. Popular destinations like those near the Royal Gorge, the Arkansas River, or Rocky Mountain National Park are booked well in advance, so planning ahead is essential.

## National Parks and Monuments

Colorado has two national parks, four national monuments, and one national recreation area with camping facilities. From dinosaur bones to ancient cliff dwellings to fascinating geologic formations, these destinations offer incredible educational opportunities for travelers of every age. If the idea of spending the night in a living museum tickles your fancy, then these are ideal destinations for you.

Physical activity at the national parks and monuments usually centers on hiking, but there are also places to fish, four-wheel drive, or go whitewater rafting. For campers who need even more stimulation, all but one of the parks are located close enough to other attractions to make day trips outside the park an additional bonus.

The terrain in this category is diverse, but with the exception of Rocky Mountain National Park, don't plan trips to these spots expecting a campground in pine-covered, snowcapped mountains. In general, think desert beauty, not mountain beauty. As with the previous category, campgrounds remain below the 9,000-foot mark, making them accessible to a great number of campers.

The campgrounds themselves are all well designed. They are tightly spaced to conserve precious land resources, but there are usually vegetation screens between campsites to provide a bit more privacy than you would find at a commercial campground. Facilities vary from camp to camp, even within a single park. There are primitive camps at some locations, but the usual amenities include tables, toilets, fire rings, and drinking water. Additional services found at some locations include public phones and rental stables.

With the exception of Mesa Verde National Monument, the campgrounds in this category are currently operated by the national parks system. You can expect cleanliness, strict enforcement of rules concerning water and ground fires, and ranger involvement, in the form of nightly visits and scheduled presentations.

The massive Morefield Campground at Mesa Verde is operated by a concessionaire, which provides services not found at the other parks, including a cafe, showers, and laundry. The trade-off is cost. A night at Mesa Verde can run as high as $19, plus the $10 per vehicle gate fee.

Camping fees at the other parks range from $3 to $14 per night, plus the entrance fee. The fees are discounted for Golden Age and Golden Eagle Passport holders. System-wide, reservations are possible only at two of Rocky Mountain National Park's campgrounds, currently without an additional fee. All other campgrounds are first come, first serve.

Seasons of operation vary within the system, often depending on weather and road conditions, but there are some year-round choices. For more information, call the National Park Service at 800-365-CAMP (2267).

## State Parks

Colorado has thirty-one state parks with camping facilities. They are a diverse group of destinations, with water being the primary focus at most. The amenities vary from park to park, but you can almost always plan on having drinking water, picnic tables, and vault toilets. Fourteen parks also offer electricity at some campsites, seventeen offer hot showers, and thirteen have on-site laundry facilities.

Activity is the keyword when you think of the state parks. They are busy places, attracting busy people. Water sports like swimming, skiing, sailing, wind surfing, and jet skiing reign at warm-water parks, while fishing, hiking, and biking facilities are found at almost all parks. The parks with large lakes have marinas, with most offering boat rentals.

Other attractions found at various parks include waterslides, golf courses, riding stables—even flying fields for model airplanes and launch pads for hot-air balloons.

A bonus throughout the system is that most of the large state parks offer regularly scheduled interpretive programs ranging from campfire talks to wildflower discovery hikes. The rangers are always eager to share knowledge about their parks.

Campgrounds at the state parks generally offer a bit more space per site than you would find at commercial campgrounds, but you can expect little in the way of privacy. One thing you can expect is cleanliness. Facilities at the state parks are well maintained and usually spotless.

State parks are open more months of the year than any other camping category in the state, with twenty-five parks offering winter camping. These parks usually have facilities for winter sports, such as snowmobiling, ice skating, ice fishing, and cross-country skiing. Twenty-nine of the parks allow seasonal hunting.

As with the private campgrounds and those in national parks, state park campgrounds are typically located below 9 thousand feet so that the largest number of visitors can enjoy them.

Camping fees at the parks range from $2 for primitive sites to $12 a night for sites with electricity. An additional $4 per day is charged on each vehicle entering the park (whether camping or not). A $40 annual pass eliminates this additional charge. All rates are subject to change.

A statewide reservation system operates from the first of April to early fall, allowing you to reserve specific sites at any park. There is a non-refundable fee of $7 per reservation for this service. Even with that added, on a two-day trip your maximum camping cost is still below $20 per day per site. You can call each park directly to check availability of open sites before you decide whether or not to make a reservation and incur the fee. As a general rule, reservations are recommended if your stay includes a weekend. The reservation number is 800-678-CAMP(2267), outside the Denver Metro area. In Denver, call 470-1144.

## City and County Parks

This is a relatively small category of campgrounds, but one worth mentioning because it includes some very nice campgrounds. Facilities typically include toilets, picnic tables, drinking water, fire rings, and occasionally even showers. Because these campgrounds are often located in city parks, recreational opportunities include golf, tennis, swimming, and sometimes fishing.

The cost is usually much lower, anywhere from free to $10 per night. It is always a good idea to call the recreation office in charge of the park before planning your trip around this type of stop.

## National Forests

The national forest campgrounds offer the most sites, the most diversity, and the greatest array of recreational opportunities in Colorado. From roadside stopovers to primitive, near-wilderness camps, you can choose from hundreds of campgrounds across the state.

The two things almost all national forest campgrounds have in common are toilets and concrete picnic tables. Most also have drinking water and fire rings with a grill attached. Many now sport level tent pads and paved parking spaces. A select few have electrical hookups and two or three even have flush toilets and hot showers. There are camps with corrals for pack-and-saddle livestock, double-wide parking for large families, and wheelchair-accessible sites, restrooms, and boardwalk trails.

Most of the national forest campgrounds are now operated and maintained by concessionaires. These companies supply camp hosts who are responsible for collecting fees, maintaining order in the camp, and cleaning the facilities. The hosts also usually sell firewood in small bundles.

Elevation is a critical factor when deciding on a national forest campground. Choices range from around 5,800 feet to just over 11,000 feet, with the average running around 9,000. Higher elevations mean cooler temperatures. It doesn't make sense to choose a campground perched at the tree line if you don't have adequate equipment to protect you from the elements.

Altitude sickness affects many first-time visitors to Colorado's national forest campgrounds. Though individual susceptibility varies greatly, it can usually be avoided by allowing your body time to adjust gradually to higher elevations. Try to spend the first few days of your stay at elevations below 8,000 feet, then move up. If that isn't possible, try to avoid strenuous activities during the first day or two. Anyone with symptoms of nausea, debilitating fatigue, headache, shortness of breath, or palpitations should move to a lower elevation, where symptoms should quickly disappear.

The cost of camping in the national forests ranges from $4 to $14 per night for a site that will accommodate as many as five people and two vehicles. Sites for as many as ten people are available at some campgrounds for a double fee. A few camps with space limitations also charge a second vehicle fee that is equal to half the camp fee. All fees are subject to change.

Reservations are available by site at many national forest campgrounds for a non-refundable fee of $8.65. If reservations are possible at a campground, they are probably necessary, at least on weekends. Most of these campgrounds set aside a limited number of sites as non-reservable, but you can be assured that they will fill by early Friday afternoon.

More and more campgrounds are being added to the reservation system each year, so if you wish to stay in a particular campground that is not listed as reservable, it can't hurt to double check. When you make reservations, you will need know the campground name and the national forest and state in which it is located. Be sure to verify all three. You'd hate to discover upon arrival in Colorado that you reserved a site in a campground of the same name in California. For reservations, call 800-280-CAMP (2267). Or go to www.nrrc.com on the Worldwide Web.

## Bureau of Land Management

These rare gems are an interesting mix of campgrounds that range from high mountain camps to rugged canyons. The two things they all have in common is that they are small and hard to find. Facilities vary, from none at all to tables, toilets, and fire rings. The fact that they are located on BLM land means fewer restrictions on land usage, making them attractive to ATV enthusiasts. Many are also located near trailheads that see lower usage than national forest trails.

Only a couple of BLM camps are described in detail in this book, but if you are looking for a rugged, isolated camping spot, scour the lists of additional campgrounds for others.

## State Wildlife Areas

These areas offer the least amount of development you can find in the state and still camp with your vehicle. There are more than fifty wildlife areas across the state that allow camping. The heaviest concentration is in the east, but they can be found in every region. Most have water as a focal point, so anglers should pay particular attention.

Facilities are almost nonexistent, with most areas offering only dispersed camping. Toilets are usually available and occasionally drinking water, but not much else.

Seasons of operation are limited only by road conditions, making some locations ideal for ice fishing. There currently is no charge for using the wildlife areas, but you should read and follow any posted regulations.

*Elk are among the most commonly observed large animals in Colorado.* MICHAEL SAMPLE PHOTO

# Travel Tips

Though greatly improved in the last quarter century, the roads of Colorado can sometimes inadvertently create adventures all their own. Here are a few tips to make those adventures a little less troublesome.

— **There are no shortcuts in this state.** You shouldn't automatically assume that fewer miles means a shorter trip. Get in the habit of comparing elevations if you have a choice of routes. Higher roads involve switchbacks that are impossible to detail on most maps, adding miles and driving time. Road conditions must also be considered. Twenty-five miles of dirt road over a 12,000-foot mountain pass will take three times longer to drive than a 50-mile route around the mountain on pavement.

— **Use detailed maps.** This point cannot be stressed strongly enough. The maps in this book are simplified and intended only for the purpose of helping you locate the campgrounds. Unless you are just passing through on the interstate, it is very difficult to navigate in Colorado using only a single-page highway map. There are several map books that you can purchase at your local bookstore, and any one of them is a good investment.

— **A pass is a pass is a pass.** When you see the word "pass" on your map, picture pioneers struggling against snow and ice, hunger and hardship to make it over the Rockies. Paved passes are a bit easier to navigate now, but not a lot. And you might be better off with a pack mule than a motorized vehicle on some of the unpaved passes. On either, be prepared for steep grades, narrow curves, and heartstopping drop-offs, most without guard-rails or even shoulders. If you or your vehicle isn't up for the challenge, find an alternate route.

— **Know your vehicle's limitations.** Don't risk your life and the lives of other travelers by pushing the limits. If you know that your brakes or trans-mission are on the short side of perfect, stay off steep roads. If your vehicle can barely haul your trailer across the prairie, don't expect it to suddenly improve in the mountains. Travel with good tires, properly maintain all fluid levels, and don't try to tackle four-wheel-drive roads in a two-wheel-drive passenger vehicle.

— **Read the signs.** Colorado road crews are particularly good at provid-ing signs that warn about steep grades, sharp curves, and worsening road conditions. Look for them. Read them. Live by them.

— **Be prepared for construction delays.** Because the work season is short here and because most roads are only two lanes, repairs usually in-volve halting traffic. Pilot vehicles lead one direction of traffic through the construction at a time, causing delays of up to thirty minutes. Build an extra half hour into your plan on every trip off the interstate during the summer.

— **Expect poor roads from September to June.** Travel in Colorado anytime other than summer is difficult at best. Many minor roads close for the entire season, others only when conditions are at their worst. But major roads aren't exempt from the foibles of Mother Nature; even the interstates can close for days at a time in Colorado. If you do not have adequate snow tires, tire chains are required on most passes when they are open. To travel safely, always know the weather forecast, check road conditions before setting out, never go around a road closure barrier, and be prepared for trouble by carrying tire chains, snack food, water, and blankets.

# Colorado Wildlife

The wildlife population in Colorado is as diverse as the terrain. Since many of the camping options in the state put you in prime wildlife habitat, it is up to you to educate yourself about the local fauna. You need to know what creatures live here and how to enjoy or, in some cases, avoid them.

### Birds and Bees

Watching Colorado's migrant and resident bird population is the sole reason some people come to the state. For most however, sharing camp with a Stellar's jay is just icing on the cake. What are you likely to see here? Everything from hummingbirds to California seagulls, from great-horned owls to mountain bluebirds. There are turkeys, ptarmigans, towhees, pipits, prairie chickens, and even white pelicans.

To best enjoy the winged parade, carry along a small pair of binoculars and spend time listening to interesting calls and songs. Give all birds their space and never approach a nesting bird. Check with rangers regarding feeders; these may attract bears and discourage the birds from finding more reliable food sources.

Where there are wildflowers there will be bees, and Colorado overflows with wildflowers. Most bees aren't aggressive unless you threaten them. People are most commonly stung while cutting dead wood, in which many species make their homes. The best advice is to be conscious of your surroundings in the woods and tune in to any conspicuous buzzing before you cut.

### Small Mammals

Colorado is home to an enormous number of small mammals: rabbits, squirrels, shrews, bats, otters, ferrets, badgers, chipmunks, skunks, coyotes, foxes, weasels, marmots, raccoons, mice, gophers, porcupines, opossums, and beavers, just to name a few. Of course, you won't likely see most of these critters. Visitors to your camp will probably include Colorado chipmunks, golden-mantled ground squirrels, as well as red and gray tree squirrels. You may discover evidence of night raiders, such as coyotes, skunks, and raccoons. Just outside camp you will likely see timid cottontail rabbits. All the rest are seen only in rare glimpses, usually in such a flash of fur that you won't even know for sure what you've seen. A good field guide (try Falcon's *Scats and Tracks of the Rocky Mountains*) that includes drawings of tracks will increase your chances of identification.

All of these animals are best enjoyed by observing them in their wild state. Do not use food to tempt any of them into your camp, either intentionally or by accidentally leaving food out where they can get to it. Ground squirrels and chipmunks are adorable, especially when they beg. But they are like miniature bears; they quickly become a nuisance to all campers when fed by a few. They can chew through almost anything: sleeping bags, soft-sided coolers, tents, and grocery bags. Do you really want one to run up your leg to get a closer look at your breakfast? Neither does the camper who stays in your campsite next after you've spent a week feeding them.

## Hoofed Animals

These include deer, bighorn sheep, pronghorn antelope, elk, moose, and bison. All have been known to charge at tourists who get a little too close. They are best viewed with strong binoculars, spotting scopes, or telephoto camera lenses.

Hoofed animals pose a hazard when they cross roads. Striking a deer while driving at sixty or seventy miles an hour can be deadly for all involved. When you drive at or after dusk, you need to pay particular attention to activity along the sides of the road, but be aware that deer feed at all hours. Always slow down when you spot a deer because you can never be certain which direction it may leap. There are small inexpensive devices that can be mounted to the front of your vehicle that produce a high-pitched sound, supposedly with the effect of scaring away the deer. Many people swear by them, but they should not be considered fail-safe.

## Bears

Bears are probably the most awesome, yet feared, members of Colorado's wildlife community. It is sad but comforting to campers that the only bear remaining in the state is the black bear. There are no grizzlies; bears with brown coloration are simply black bears with cinnamon coloration.

Bears create a nuisance in many camping areas, but unprovoked attacks on humans are rare. Still, there are things you need to know when camping in the neighborhood of these beautiful beasts. The Colorado Department of Parks and Outdoor Recreation provides the following tips for vehicle campers:

— Follow all posted regulations concerning where you camp. Backcountry camping is often prohibited in areas with bear problems.

— Store all food and food containers inside a closed, hard-sided vehicle. This includes canned food, beverages, pet food, coolers, and water containers.

— Store all cooking utensils in the same manner. This includes coffee pots, stoves, silverware, and dishes, no matter how clean you think they are.

— **Do not** bring food, cosmetics, or other toiletries into your tent or pop-up camper. Eliminate everything that smells!

— **Do not** sleep in the same clothes you cook in. Change into clean clothes and store cooking clothes inside a closed, hard-sided vehicle.

— Immediately dispose of all trash in dumpsters or bear-proof containers.

Also, hummingbird feeders are prohibited in some areas; in others, they should be stored with all other scented items at night. Additional information for hikers, even those just out for a stroll, is as follows:

— Hiking at dusk or dawn increases your chances of encountering a bear.

— Use extra caution in places with limited visibility, such as brushy areas or bends in the trail.

— Try not to hike alone.

— Make sure children stay within your sight at all times.

— Don't take pets into the backcountry.

— Clap your hands, sing, or make other noise as you hike and stay alert.

— Watch for signs of bear activity, such as scat, scratch marks on trees, tracks, and overturned logs.

If you encounter a black bear, you and your children need to know how to handle the situation. The old advice of playing dead applies only to situations in which you are actually attacked. Your goal is to avoid this by giving the bear a way out of the confrontation. If that fails and an attack does occur, and if you have nerves of steel, lying motionless may discourage a continued attack. For a simple encounter:

— **Stay calm.** Leave the area if the bear has not detected you.

— If detected, stop and slowly back away while facing the bear, but without direct eye contact. Give the bear plenty of space to escape, by stepping off the trail if necessary. Remember that a charge is not necessarily an attack; startled bears may attempt to bluff.

— **Speak softly** to the bear.

— **Never run!** Always walk away. Running may trigger a bear's predatory instinct to give chase.

Spotting a bear will give you a story to tell for the rest of your life, and educating yourself about how to handle the situation is your best assurance that you will live to tell it a thousand times over. A good additional source of information is *Bear Aware* by Falcon Publishing.

## Mountain Lions

It comes as a surprise to many Colorado visitors that they will be sharing a habitat with lions. The fact is, mountain lions have been here for ages. Population estimates from 1997 run from around 1,500 to 3,000 lions, far fewer than estimates of black bears. The lion's habitat is widely varied, both subalpine and desert. You will find them most plentiful in areas with large deer populations.

Though attacks on humans are rare in Colorado, they do occur, often without provocation. Educating yourself on the habits of mountain lions is your best protection. Lions are most active during the night, but they do travel and even hunt during daylight hours. Lions prefer a diet of deer, but they also prey on elk, small mammals, livestock, and pets. After spotting prey, a lion will usually stalk silently, then attack in a rush, often from behind. Lions that are feeding can be dangerous to people, and a seemingly tame lion fed by humans is the worst hazard of all. Tips for camping in lion country provided by the Colorado Division of Wildlife include:

— Make lots of noise if you are out between dusk and dawn.

— Closely supervise children and teach them what to do if they see a lion.

— Keep pets under control and don't take them on hikes.

— Don't feed any wildlife.

— Hike with a sturdy stick that can be used for defense in the event of an attack.

While bear encounters in the state are relatively common, lion encounters are rare enough to warrant reporting them. First you must know how to handle the encounter. The overall object is to appear large and threatening, while giving the lion a route for escape.

— **Stay calm.**

— **Talk softly, yet firmly.**

— **Stop and back away** only if it appears you can do so safely.

— **Never run!** This activates a cat's natural instinct to give chase. (Think about a house cat chasing small moving objects; it's automatic.)

— Do everything you can to appear larger and more intimidating. Raise your arms; open your jacket. Pick up or shield children.

— If the lion is behaving aggressively, throw things, wave your arms slowly, and speak in a firm voice.

— Do not crouch down or turn your back. That is the animal's cue to pounce.

— If you are actually attacked by a lion, DO NOT PLAY DEAD. Fight back in any way you can. If possible, remain standing or get back up. A good additional source of information is *Mountain Lion Alert,* by Falcon Publishing.

*Mountainous areas of Colorado often resound with the chattering call of the chickaree.*
Michael Sample photo

# Camping Etiquette

You are no longer at home. You're not even on your own turf. Camping is a foreign world where strangers may be sleeping on the ground under the stars 50 feet away. It's a world where the choices you make can make a difference from the top of the food chain to the bottom. And it's a world where respect for your fellow man and beast is of utmost importance if we are all to continue to enjoy our natural resources.

The first sign of that respect is in knowing the camping rules that apply to your destination. The rules may seem arbitrary to you, but respect the fact that they have been placed into effect for good reason. Some examples of rules you should know include:

— **Maximum number of people per campsite.** This varies between five and fifteen, but in general, fewer is better. Fewer people means less impact on the campsite and less impact on neighboring campers.

— **Maximum number of vehicles per campsite.** The reasons are the same as for people per campsite, plus, by requiring additional vehicles to pay for additional space, the facility gains needed revenue.

— **Campfire restrictions.** Always find out whether or not fires are allowed at the time of your stay. You don't want to be the one responsible for the next forest fire.

— **Maximum number of nights.** Commercial operations rarely impose a maximum, but all public facilities do. Campgrounds in state parks and national forests are not second homes. They are for the enjoyment of all. Popular areas may limit stays to as few as three days, while secluded destinations may allow up to 14 or 21 days. (Campgrounds restricted to fewer than seven are so noted in the book.)

— **Quiet hours.** All campgrounds place people a little closer together than we would like. Quiet hours are to ensure everyone's enjoyment and are usually strictly enforced. The normal times are between 10 P.M. and 8 A.M., but you will occasionally find places that are more strict.

— **Checkout time.** You've paid your money and you intend to stay all day, right? Wrong. What you paid for was the previous night. Staying past your welcome cheats fellow campers out of a campsite. Even the national forest campgrounds have checkout times around noon. If for some reason you must stay longer, be sure to contact the camp host or a ranger about whether or not you need to pay for another night.

— **No picnicking in campgrounds.** This is one of the most ignored rules in national forest campgrounds, but in areas where campgrounds stay filled, it is an important rule. You wouldn't dream of pulling into a commercial campground just to spread out a blanket for lunch. You would be cheating fellow campers in need of a place to sleep out of a good site and the state or federal agency running the campground out of revenue.

— **Don't pollute other people's senses.** Specifically, consider the impact on other people of every noise you make, every flashlight you shine, and every smelly pile your dog leaves behind.

— **Share space graciously.** Campgrounds force us to share everything from toilet facilities to parking spaces, from waterspouts to boat ramps. A good rule of thumb is to never use more than your neighbor does. Don't take up extra parking. Don't spread your camp right up to the next one. Don't hang buckets or towels from or leave hoses attached to shared water faucets. And where showers are available, don't hog the hot water. There's always a limited supply.

— **Leave your campsite better than you found it.** Do more than clean up after yourself. Pick up trash left behind by others and leave a stick or two of firewood for the next guy.

— **Learn how to camp lightly.** Camping lightly means having the least amount of impact on the environment as possible. Little things, like pitching your tent in a grassy spot rather than on already hardened ground, cause damage that lasts far beyond your stay. The next camper sees that the grass is matted down where your tent was and decides to try that spot himself. In a very short time, that spot of grass no longer exists; it is now hardened earth that may be subject to erosion. There are good books written entirely about this subject, but they tend to be overlooked by vehicle campers who think those camping techniques apply only to wilderness campers. Many of them apply to anyone who sets foot in the forest. One of the best guides available is *Wild Country Companion,* by Falcon Publishing.

It all boils down to respect—for each other and for nature. If you lack either, you simply are not welcome as a fellow camper.

# Camping with Kids

Kids need to camp. All kids, whether they are raised on the farm or in the city, benefit from the experience of family camping. Group camping with organizations, such as Girl Scouts and Boy Scouts, can provide some of the same benefits, but the memory of helping Dad build a campfire can outshine even the glitter of a trip to Disney World.

And, a camping vacation generally doesn't break the bank or require years of saving to accomplish. The average cost of accommodations per night for a family of four camping in Colorado is somewhere around $25. There are pricier spots, but there are also hundreds more that are considerably less. Also, take into consideration that camping allows you to eat all or part of your meals at camp rather than at high-priced restaurants, and the savings grow even larger. In most cases, even if you rent equipment, camping is the best travel bargain to be found.

Camping is the perfect opportunity for your children to develop an appreciation of nature. Ever see a kid at the deer and elk exhibit at the zoo? It's a big yawn. But let those same kids spot one grazing in the meadow beside their campground and you'll see real excitement. And, if they spot a moose or a bear? They'll tell the story for years. Kids today are bombarded with television shows about nature, but knowing the facts about the world around them isn't enough. Camping takes the passivity out of learning about nature. Only by stepping into the wild themselves will children feel the awe.

Likewise, history, archeology, and paleontology are brought to life when children spend time living on the same piece of land where dinosaurs or ancient peoples once roamed. Indian paintings on a cliff wall have a much stronger impact than pictures in history books. And, camping down the road from a rock wall containing thousands of dinosaur bones beats any museum trip.

Even if your family camping trip doesn't bring you into contact with any of the above, it will bring you into closer contact with each other. While the close quarters in the car driving to the campground may be a little too much togetherness for some families, those same families will often find that a tent or trailer parked in a small campsite is just the right amount of space. There are no bedrooms for teenagers to hide out in and few closed doors that have to be yelled through. There are probably scientific studies that supply facts and statistics about the comfort derived in being close to the people you love, but why not just test the idea yourself?

Camping skills are wonderful confidence builders for kids of all ages. Learning to build a fire is a big step for eight- to twelve-year-olds. For a teenager who is doubtful about handling the challenges that adulthood will bring, the accomplishment of hiking a difficult trail may spur confidence that might not be gained in any other way. Younger children show off skills, such as jumping over rocks near camp or helping wash the dishes. It's all about pushing their comfort zones just a little. It may be scary, but there's something primeval about knowing that you can take care of yourself in the wild.

So how do you go about planning a family camping trip? And how do you ensure that the trip will be a success? First of all, know your family. Pick a spot close to the kinds of things your kids are interested in. Don't drag a three-year old who is terrified of *Tyrannosaurus rex* to see Dinosaur National Monument. Seek out activities that he or she will enjoy. If your kids have always harbored a love of horses, find a campground with a rental stable close by. If they love to swim, make sure there's a pool or swim beach available. Finding what suits your family is the most important key to success.

The second key is to ease into camping. Don't plan a two-week unguided wilderness expedition if your family has never camped, and certainly don't rush out and buy thousands of dollars of equipment for that first trip. Borrow or rent what you need, or consider trying a commercial campground with rustic sleeping cabins for the first time out. Then, if camping suits your family, buy a few things and branch out into the woods a little farther.

How old should children be before you consider camping? There's no easy answer. It depends a lot on your own adaptability, as much as that of the child. Many parents take infants camping, while others wouldn't dream of taking a child under the age of four or five. Again, the best advice is to take small steps. If you are determined to take a very young child, try a one-night trip close to home first.

Here are a few tips to make camping with kids all that you want it to be:

— Expand comfort zones, but don't make the trip uncomfortable. This applies to everything from the length of the trip to the food. A camping trip is not the time to try new camp foods or to break in new hiking boots. Simple things, like making sure kids are warm, well fed, and comfortably dressed, go a long way toward making the trip more pleasant for everyone.

— Don't forget to make the trip comfortable for Mom and Dad, too. All that companionship goes down the drain if you can't get a good night's sleep. Don't leave home without a well-stocked first-aid kit, either. There will be bumps, scratches, bites, and upset stomachs, so be prepared for them.

— Keep attention spans in mind. Parking a lawn chair beside the lake and waiting for the fish to bite might seem like a relaxing way to spend the day to an adult, but a busy four-year-old will be throwing rocks in the water and scaring away the trout before the first minute has passed. Likewise, a half-day trail ride would push the limits for even a horse-loving eight-year-old. (Not to mention the comfort of all concerned. Being saddle sore will not add to anyone's enjoyment.)

— Include physical activities. Children have energy to burn, and that energy often increases proportionally with stressful situations. Forgetting that simple fact can make or break your trip. Find opportunities for them to run or jump or swim or bicycle—anything, as long as they are moving at their pace. A leisurely stroll around the lake at your pace is not what their bodies need. On smooth trails you can let them run ahead of you as long as they stay within your sight. Older children and teenagers may seem to prefer a slower pace, but making sure they spend time moving is important too.

— Choose your rules. Because camping involves a new set of rules—some of which can mean the difference between life and death—figure out which of your usual rules from home can be relaxed just a bit. This way you aren't put into the tyrant role with more rules than can be obeyed, and the new rules take on a greater significance. Possibilities include slight modifications of bedtimes, food and beverage restrictions, and cleanliness. So what if they play in the dirt? It's part of being outside.

— Let them help. If children are allowed to help with things, such as gathering wood, preparing meals, or baiting hooks, the experience becomes more real. This isn't just a ride at an amusement park where they settle back in their seats and wait for the action. Make them part of the trip.

Camping with children takes patience, careful planning, and an adventurous spirit on everyone's part. It's hard work, and the rewards are hard to measure. They come in little things like seeing your teenager's face without a telephone attached to it or watching the firelight dance in your child's eyes while she roasts marshmallows for the first time. It's about laughing through fish stories where the fish get bigger with every retelling. It's about just being a family.

# The Campgrounds

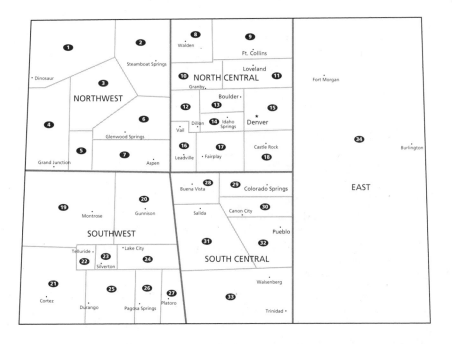

Map regions and campground locations: NORTHWEST, NORTH CENTRAL, EAST, SOUTHWEST, SOUTH CENTRAL

Cities and towns shown: Walden, Ft. Collins, Steamboat Springs, Loveland, Dinosaur, Granby, Fort Morgan, Boulder, Glenwood Springs, Dillon, Vail, Idaho Springs, Denver, Grand Junction, Aspen, Leadville, Fairplay, Castle Rock, Burlington, Buena Vista, Colorado Springs, Montrose, Gunnison, Salida, Canon City, Telluride, Lake City, Pueblo, Silverton, Walsenberg, Cortez, Durango, Pagosa Springs, Platoro, Trinidad

# Map Legend

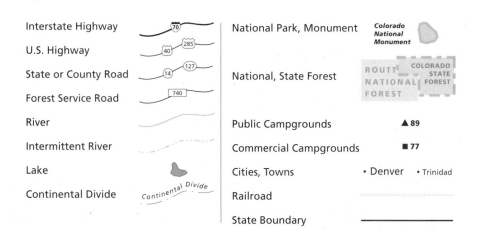

| | |
|---|---|
| Interstate Highway | National Park, Monument — Colorado National Monument |
| U.S. Highway | |
| State or County Road | National, State Forest — ROUTT NATIONAL FOREST, COLORADO STATE FOREST |
| Forest Service Road | |
| River | Public Campgrounds — ▲ 89 |
| Intermittent River | Commercial Campgrounds — ■ 77 |
| Lake | Cities, Towns — • Denver • Trinidad |
| Continental Divide | Railroad |
| | State Boundary |

# Key to Abbreviations

## Campground types

| | |
|---|---|
| **BLM** | Bureau of Land Management |
| **CP** | city park |
| **DSP** | Dispersed camping without designated "sites"; vault toilets are usually the only amentities. |
| **NF** | National Forest |
| **NWR** | National Wildlife Refuge |
| **P** | privately-owned commercial campgrounds |
| **SP** | State Park |
| **SWA** | State Wildlife Area |
| **Water Dist.** | Reservoir and campground operated by a local water district |

## Road Types

| | |
|---|---|
| **FSR** | Forest Service Road |
| **CR** | County Road |
| **CO** | Colorado Highway |

# Northwest

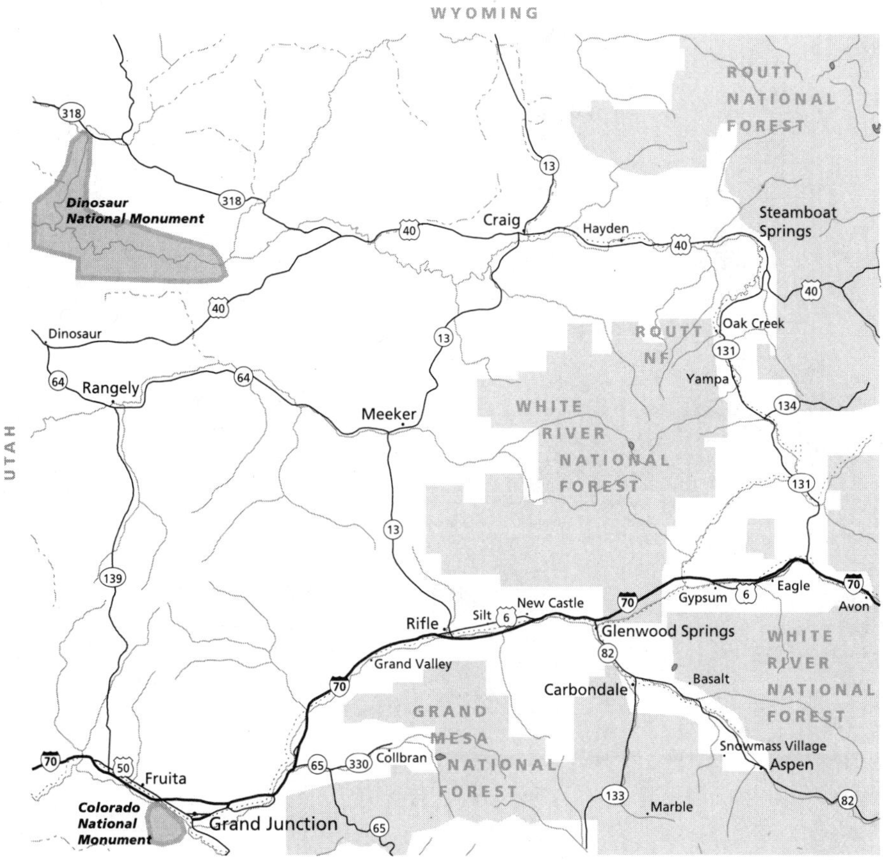
WYOMING
UTAH
ROUTT NATIONAL FOREST
Dinosaur National Monument
318
13
Craig
Hayden
40
Steamboat Springs
Dinosaur
Oak Creek
ROUTT NF
131
Yampa
64
Rangely
Meeker
WHITE RIVER NATIONAL FOREST
134
139
Rifle
Silt
6
New Castle
70
Gypsum
Eagle
Avon
Glenwood Springs
82
Grand Valley
Carbondale
Basalt
GRAND MESA NATIONAL FOREST
Snowmass Village
Aspen
50
Fruita
65
330
Collbran
133
Marble
Colorado National Monument
Grand Junction

# Area 1: Dinosaur National Monument

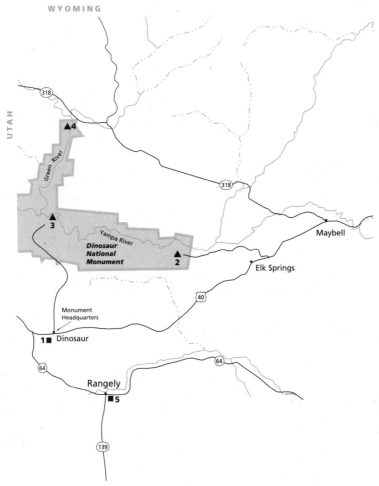

WYOMING

UTAH

318

318

Green River

Yampa River

3

Maybell

Dinosaur
National
Monument

2

Elk Springs

40

Monument
Headquarters

1 Dinosaur

64

64

Rangely

5

139

## DINOSAUR NATIONAL MONUMENT

The landscape of the far northwestern corner of the state is not what comes to mind when most people think about Colorado. The terrain consists of dry rolling hills crumbled by the ages and broken by the sharp-edged canyons carved by the Yampa and Green rivers. In summer, it's hot. If the pavement seems to give slightly beneath your tires, it isn't your imagination. Temperature extremes and tons of oilfield equipment moving through the area contribute to short lives for roadbeds.

The big attraction in this area is Dinosaur National Monument, which straddles the Colorado/Utah border. But don't come here looking for pretty, because it's not. Come looking instead for adventure in the form of intense whitewater. Raft trips are offered by various outfitters on both the Green and Yampa rivers. If you are in the area for only a day or two, book your trip well ahead of arrival. The best source of information on these outfitters is the monument headquarters at the address and phone listed below.

Come looking also for a fascinating tour of a dinosaur quarry so full of fossil remains that they put a building over it and named the monument after it. Though more than 15 tons of bone have been excavated from the site, there are still plenty to see. One wall of the quarry exhibit building consists of rock layers with hundreds of exposed fossils. The quarry is open year-round. It is located on the Utah side of the monument, near Jensen.

This is an ideal area if you crave solitude. Hike into the wild far reaches of the park or stake out a spot near the river. Then listen. The silence is worth every hard mile you had to drive to get here.

Camping choices in the area are limited but still adequate. There is currently only one full-service RV park in operation in the town of Dinosaur, Colorado. Other camping facilities include three small campgrounds on the Colorado side of the monument, but the bulk of the campsites in the vicinity are in Utah. The park headquarters can provide additional information about Utah campsites. Many visitors choose to stay elsewhere, driving to the monument for day trips. But be warned that it's a long way from anywhere and a long way back at the end of the day.

For More Information:

Dinosaur National Monument Headquarters
P.O. Box 210
Dinosaur, CO 81610
970-374-3000

Colorado Welcome Center
101 E. Stegosaurus Street
Dinosaur, CO 81610

## Commercial

### 1 Blue Mountain Village

**Location:** Dinosaur.
**Affiliations:** None.
**Contact:** 970-374-2747.
**Amenities:** Wheelchair-accessible restrooms, showers, public phone, laundry, grills.
**Sites:** 100, all full hookups.
**Price per night:** $15.50.

**Elevation:** 5,900 feet.
**Finding the campground:** From the junction of U.S. Highway 40 and Colorado Highway 64, go half a mile east on CO 64, then 500 feet west on Seventh Street. The entrance is on the left.

**The campground:** Camping choices near Dinosaur National Monument are scarce, but this RV park in the town of Dinosaur offers all the amenities. The quarry (the only place to view the dinosaur bones) is a 20-mile drive into Utah. Whitewater rafting tours can be arranged in town. Rockhounds will enjoy exploring the area outside the monument. Fossil and agate collecting is possible on Bureau of Land Management land near Elk Springs to the west.

| Public |
| --- |

| 2 | Dinosaur National Monument: Deerlodge Park |
| --- | --- |

**Location:** East end of the national monument, north of Elk Springs.
**Facilities:** Fire rings, picnic tables, vault toilets, no water.
**Sites:** 8.
**Fee:** None for camping; $10 per vehicle park entrance.
**Elevation:** 4,800 feet.
**Road conditions:** two lane, gravel.
**Management:** National Park Service, 970-374-3000.
**Activities:** Fishing, hiking, rafting, wildlife viewing.
**Finding the campground:** From Elk Springs, travel east on U.S. Highway 40 about 5 miles to Twelve Mile Gulch Road. Turn right and go about 8.2 miles to the campground.

**The campground:** Deerlodge is a primitive campground situated in a cottonwood grove on the Yampa River as it enters the canyonlands. It is one of the most scenic spots at the monument. Hiking trails abound in the area, and backcountry camping areas are accessible via the river west of this point. Keep in mind that none of the campgrounds on the Colorado side of the monument are close to the dinosaur quarry, which is the main reason many visitors come here. If you're planning a trip to hike and enjoy the stunning canyons, any of the Colorado campgrounds will suit you. If your interest lies mainly in the quarry, try the Green River campground on the Utah side.

| 3 | Dinosaur National Monument: Echo Park |
| --- | --- |

**Location:** Echo Park Road.
**Facilities:** Central water, fire rings, picnic tables, vault toilets.
**Sites:** 9, tent only.
**Fee:** $5 per night; $10 per vehicle park entrance.
**Elevation:** 4,800 feet.

**Road conditions:** One-and-a-half lane, steep, dirt; impassable when wet.
**Management:** National Park Service, 970-374-3000.
**Activities:** Hiking, fishing, rafting.
**Season:** Summer only.
**Finding the campground:** From the monument headquarters on U.S. Highway 40, west of Dinosaur, travel north about 25 miles to Echo Park Road. Travel east about 8 miles to the junction with Yampa Bench Road. Bear left at the fork and continue about 5 miles north to the campground.

**The campground:** The setting for this campground is magnificent if you can get to it. Four-wheel-drive and high-clearance vehicles are recommended. You are required to check with park rangers about road conditions before setting out.

## 4 | Dinosaur National Monument: Gates of Lodore

**Location:** Northern tip of the national monument, off Colorado Highway 318.
**Facilities:** Central water, fire rings, picnic tables, vault toilets.
**Sites:** 17.
**Fee:** $5 per night; $10 per vehicle entrance fee.
**Elevation:** 4,800 feet.
**Road conditions:** two lane, gravel.
**Management:** National Park Service, 970-365-2267.
**Activities:** Fishing, hiking, rafting.
**Finding the campground:** From the junction of U.S. Highway 40 and Colorado Highway 318 in Maybell, travel west on CO 318, about 44 miles to Moffat County Road 34. Travel north 7 miles to the campground.

**The campground:** The Gates of Lodore is probably the most popular campground on the Colorado side of the monument. The views are outstanding, and backcountry camping and hiking opportunities are almost limitless. The Gates of Lodore Trail is an easy 1.5-mile hike to a vantage point from which you can see the Green River as it enters the canyon.

## 5 | Rangely Camper Park

**Location:** Rangely.
**Facilities:** Electricity, restrooms, showers, central water.
**Sites:** 25.
**Fee:** $10 per night with electricity, $5 without.
**Elevation:** 4,800 feet.
**Road conditions:** Paved.
**Management:** Town of Rangely Recreation Center, 970-675-8211.
**Activities:** Rock collecting, hiking in Utah.
**Finding the campground:** One block north of Colorado Highway 64 in Rangely. Follow the signs.

**The campground:** This shady campground offers a quiet stopover if you need one. For those headed south or east, the next available campgrounds are more than 50 miles away. This campground is also a great place for rockhounds to use as a home base while scouring the area for fossils and agate. Fossil collectors can try the Bureau of Land Management land south of town off CO 139 for finding fossils. Agates are abundant to the east near Elk Creek.

## Additional Campgrounds in the Far Northwest

| | Type* | Contact | Location |
|---|---|---|---|
| Brown's Park | NWR DSP | 970-365-3663 | 59 miles NW of Maybell on CO 318 |
| Brown's Park | SWA DSP | 970-248-7175 | 41 miles NW of Maybell off Moffat County Road 72 |
| Irish Canyon | BLM | 970-824-4441 | 53 miles N of Maybell on Moffat County Road 19 |
| Little Snake | SWA | 970-248-7175 | 17 miles N of Maybell on Moffat County Road 19 |

*See "Key to Abbreviations" p.22.

# Area 2: Steamboat Springs

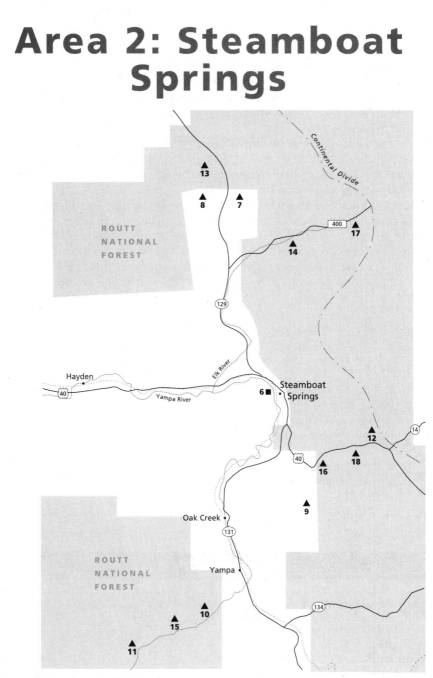

## STEAMBOAT SPRINGS

Tucked away beneath the western slope of the Continental Divide is an area of incredible beauty and diversity. The town of Steamboat Springs is noted for its steaming hot springs. It is also a retreat for the wealthy and the hometown of numerous Olympic skiers. With golf, chair-lift rides, weekly rodeos, hot-air ballooning, and horseback riding to choose from, there is no shortage of activity right in town.

But to fully appreciate the splendor of this area, head north or southwest into the Routt National Forest. To the north lie green peaks begging to be climbed, roaring rivers coursing with trout, and crystalline lakes reflecting a sapphire sky. There are plenty of activities to engage your every whim, usually without a crowd to keep you company.

To the southwest are the extraordinary Flat Top Mountains. These aspen-covered mesas soar well over the 10,000-foot mark and are dotted with fishing lakes that few people seem to know exist. Time it just right and you may only have to share a lake with a beaver or two.

Deciding where to camp in the area is a pleasant but difficult dilemma. There are a couple of RV parks to choose from, one of them right in Steamboat Springs. There are three state parks and numerous national forest camps. The difficulty comes from having to decide between bustling activity and quiet solitude. Either way, a visit to this area leaves your heart wide open for an attack of Never-wanna-leave-itis. Go home if you must, but know that you are destined to return.

**For More Information:**

Steamboat Springs Chamber Resort Association
P.O. Box 774408
Steamboat Springs, CO 80477
970-879-0882
www.steamboat-chamber.com
e-mail: info@steamboat-chamber.com

Steamboat Health & Recreation Association
(hot-springs pool)
970-879-1828

# Commercial

## 6  Steamboat Springs KOA

**Location:** West of Steamboat Springs.
**Affiliations:** KOA.
**Contact:** 970-879-0273; fax 970-879-0283.
**Amenities:** Cabins with or without kitchens, city bus stop, dump station, game room, laundry, mini golf, playground, pool, hot tub, public phone, showers, store.
**Sites:** 135, 47 full hookups.
**Price per night:** $17 to $23.
**Elevation:** 6,900 feet.

**Season:** Year-round.
**Finding the campground:** From Steamboat Springs, go about 2 miles west on U.S. Highway 40. Entrance is on the left.

**The campground:** You won't have a hard time selecting an RV park in Steamboat, because this is the only one in town. It offers all of the usual KOA amenities, including a friendly staff and clean facilities. The list of activities in the area includes fishing (on-site), golf, hot-air ballooning, scenic driving, horseback riding, tennis, hiking, biking, river rafting, weekly summer rodeos, and of course, skiing. This abundance of fun is combined with the beauty of the western slope of the Rockies to create a near-perfect vacation destination.

# Public

## 7 | Pearl Lake State Park

**Location:** North of Steamboat Springs.
**Facilities:** Boat ramp, central water, fire rings, picnic tables, vault toilets.
**Sites:** 39, some pull-throughs.
**Fee:** $6 plus $4 daily or $40 annual vehicle pass.
**Elevation:** 8,000 feet.
**Road conditions:** two lane, gravel.
**Management:** Colorado Department of Parks and Outdoor Recreation 970-879-3922.
**Reservations:** 800-678-CAMP, $7 fee.
**Activities:** Fishing, hiking.
**Season:** Camping in summer only, but winter sports available.
**Finding the campground:** From Steamboat Springs go 2 miles west on U.S. Highway 40 to County Road 129. Travel north 23 miles to Pearl Lake Road. The campground is about 2 miles east.

**The campground:** Stunning is too weak a word to describe this high-mountain lake and the heavily wooded campground on its shore. Only trophy-sized fish—18 inches and longer—may be taken from the lake. There is a two-fish-per-day limit. Some of the campsites are lakeside (sites 28,31,32,34,35,36), but there isn't a bad site in this campground. Rehabilitation was under way in 1997, which may bring some changes in campground layout. This is one of Colorado's most beautiful campgrounds, so plan to stay long enough to settle into the peace and quiet.

## 8 | Steamboat Lake State Park

**Location:** North of Steamboat Springs.
**Facilities:** Amphitheater, boat ramp, central water, dump station, fire rings, laundry, marina, picnic tables, public phone, snack bar, showers, swim beach,

vault toilets, visitor center.
**Sites:** 200, some with electricity (sites 116-165).
**Fee:** $7 to $10, plus $4 daily or $40 annual vehicle pass.
**Elevation:** 8,000 feet.
**Road conditions:** Paved.
**Management:** Colorado Department of Parks and Outdoor Recreation, 970-879-3922.
**Reservations:** 800-678-CAMP, $7 fee.
**Activities:** Fishing, water sports, hiking, horseback riding, cross-country skiing.
**Season:** Year-round.
**Finding the campground:** From Steamboat Springs, travel 2 miles west on U.S. Highway 40 to County Road 129. Go north 26 miles to the park entrance.

**The campground:** Much larger than its neighbor, Pearl Lake, Steamboat Lake offers similar mountain beauty coupled with the bustle of outdoor activity. Fishing for rainbow and cutthroat trout is only one of many attractions here. Horseback riding is available nearby, and various types of watercraft can be rented at the marina (970-879-7019). Rangers present daily interpretive activities, from quiet wildflower walks to cowboy sing-a-longs. The campground has been recently updated and offers a mix of wooded and meadow sites, many with beautiful views of the lake and surrounding mountains.

## 9 | Stagecoach State Park

**Location:** South of Steamboat Springs.
**Facilities:** Boat ramps, central water, dump station, fire rings, hiking/biking trails, marina, picnic tables, public phone, showers, swim beach, vault toilets.
**Sites:** 92, some with electricity.
**Fee:** $4 to $10, plus $4 daily or $40 annual vehicle pass.
**Elevation:** 7,210 feet.
**Road conditions:** Paved.
**Management:** Colorado Department of Parks and Outdoor Recreation, 970-226-6641.
**Reservations:** 800-678-CAMP, $7 fee.
**Activities:** Fishing, water sports, wildlife viewing.
**Season:** Year-round (limited winter camping).
**Finding the campground:** From Colorado Highway 131, south of Steamboat Springs, turn onto County Road 14. Follow the signs to the park entrance.

**The campground:** For those who love wide, open spaces, this is a perfect camping destination. The reservoir is nestled in open parkland bordered by Oak Ridge to the west and Green Ridge to the east. Water-oriented activities are the main attraction, but the wetland habitat preserve at the southwest end of the lake offers outstanding wildlife viewing. Serious hikers will want to consider the nearby Service Creek Trail, which traverses the Gore Range, reaching elevations of more than 9,000 feet before winding around to Buffalo Park.

## 10 | Bear Lake/Routt

**Location:** Southwest of Yampa.
**Facilities:** Central water, fire rings, picnic tables, vault toilets.
**Sites:** 29 trailer sites; 32 dispersed sites with fire rings only.
**Fee:** $4 to $7.
**Elevation:** 9,600 feet.
**Road conditions:** two lane, gravel.
**Management:** Routt National Forest, 970-638-4516.
**Activities:** Fishing, hiking.
**Finding the campground:** Yampa is located 31 miles southwest of Steamboat Springs on Colorado Highway 131. In Yampa, turn onto Routt County Road 7, which becomes Forest Service Road 900. The dispersed camping begins about 10 miles from Yampa. The improved campground is about 2 miles farther.

**The campground:** Bear Lake is the first campground along a series of reservoirs near the Flat Tops Wilderness. The area surprises many who see it for the first time. Situated on the far western slope of the Colorado Rockies, the Flat Tops present an imposing line of mesas that rise to more than 12,000 feet. The campground is a combination of open meadows and dense forest; from some sites it is impossible to see neighboring sites. Like most western slope campgrounds, usage is fairly low. Watercraft are limited to those that are hand propelled. This is the kind of campground that makes you want to hang the hammock and stay awhile.

## 11 | Cold Springs/Routt

**Location:** Southwest of Yampa.
**Facilities:** Boat ramp, central water, fire rings, picnic tables, vault toilets.
**Sites:** 5, short trailers only.
**Fee:** $5.
**Elevation:** 10,200 feet.
**Road conditions:** One-and-a-half lane, gravel, winding.
**Management:** Routt National Forest, 970-638-4516.
**Activities:** Fishing, hiking.
**Finding the campground:** Yampa is located 31 miles southwest of Steamboat Springs on Colorado Highway 131. In Yampa, turn west onto Routt County Road 7, which becomes Forest Service Road 900. The campground is about 16 miles from Yampa.

**The campground:** If you want to get a little farther off the beaten path than most people, this is the perfect place to go. Cold Springs is the uppermost campground along Forest Service Road 900. It sits at the eastern edge of Stillwater Reservoir. The trailhead to the Flat Tops Wilderness is nearby, as are several other trails leading to the small lakes on top of the mesa.

## 12 | Dumont Lake

**Location:** West of Rabbit Ears Pass Summit.
**Facilities:** Boat ramp, central water, fire rings, picnic tables, vault toilets.
**Sites:** 22.
**Fee:** $7.
**Elevation:** 9,508 feet.
**Road conditions:** Paved.
**Management:** Routt National Forest, 970-879-1870.
**Activities:** Fishing, four-wheel driving, hiking.
**Finding the campground:** On U.S. Highway 40, travel 22 miles southeast of Steamboat Springs or 1 mile west of Rabbit Ears Pass. Turn north onto Forest Service Road 316. The campground is about 1 mile off US 40.

**The campground:** The sites here are widely spaced across an open meadow, though most abut pine forest. The lake is a short hike from the campground, which is surrounded by mountain vistas. Numerous hiking and jeep trails branch out into the Gore Range near the campground. Proximity to the highway makes this an ideal stopover between Kremmling and Steamboat Springs, or an easily accessible weekend destination.

## 13 | Hahns Peak

**Location:** Northwest of Steamboat Springs.
**Facilities:** Boat ramp, central water, fire rings, picnic tables, vault toilets.
**Sites:** 26.
**Fee:** $7.
**Elevation:** 8,500 feet.
**Road conditions:** one lane, gravel with turnouts, well maintained.
**Management:** Routt National Forest, 970-879-1870.
**Reservations:** 800-280-CAMP, www.nrrc.com, $8.65 fee.
**Activities:** Biking, fishing, hiking, horseback riding.
**Finding the campground:** From Steamboat Springs, travel 2 miles west on U.S. Highway 40 to County Road 129. Travel about 28 miles to Forest Service Road 486 (about 2 miles north of Steamboat Lake State Park). Turn west. The campground is on the northwest side of Hahns Peak Lake.

**The campground:** Hahns Peak is an outstanding high-country, lakeside choice for camping. In addition to fishing and the usual array of hiking trails, the trailhead for the Hahns Peak/Nipple Peak Mountain Bike Loop is less than a mile north on Forest Service Road 129. Electric motors are allowed on the lake. The campground offers sites to suit different tastes. Sites 1-11 are heavily wooded with pine and spruce, and are widely spaced. Sites 12-26 are somewhat closer together but are nearer the lake. With so many other camping choices in the surrounding area, this campground tends to attract the quiet crowd.

## 14 | Hinman

**Location:** Northwest of Steamboat Springs.
**Facilities:** Central water, fire rings, picnic tables, vault toilets.
**Sites:** 13.
**Fee:** $7.
**Elevation:** 7,600 feet.
**Road conditions:** two lane, gravel.
**Management:** Routt National Forest, 970-897-1870.
**Activities:** Biking, fishing, hiking, playground, horseback riding.
**Finding the campground:** From Steamboat Springs, go 2 miles west on U.S. Highway 40 to County Road 129. Travel north approximately 16 miles to Forest Service Road 400. Turn east. Travel about 4 miles to FSR 440. The campground is about half a mile down this road.

**The campground:** The only sounds heard here are likely to be the rush of Hinman Creek and the Elk River. No motorized traffic is allowed on the trail closest to the campground, and this is a rather isolated area so even the road noise from FSR 400 is slight. Campers looking to stay awhile aren't likely to be disturbed.

## 15 | Horseshoe

**Location:** Southwest of Yampa.
**Facilities:** Central water, fire rings, picnic tables, vault toilets.
**Sites:** 7.
**Fee:** $7.
**Elevation:** 10,000 feet.
**Road conditions:** One-and-a-half lane, gravel, winding.
**Management:** Routt National Forest, 970-638-4516.
**Activities:** Fishing, hiking.
**Finding the campground:** Yampa is located on Colorado Highway 131 about 31 miles southwest of Steamboat Springs. In Yampa, turn west on Routt County Road 7, which becomes Forest Service Road 900. The campground is about 15 miles from town.

**The campground:** Horseshoe is the middle campground at the Stillwater Lakes complex. It is small and tightly spaced but offers a more centralized base for fishing all three of the main lakes, as well as trails to several of the smaller lakes. The campground sits atop a hill, providing captivating views of Flat Top Mountain.

## 16 | Meadows

**Location:** Southeast of Steamboat Springs.
**Facilities:** Central water, fire rings, picnic tables, vault toilets.
**Sites:** 30.

**Fee:** $9.
**Elevation:** 9,300 feet.
**Road conditions:** Paved.
**Management:** Routt National Forest, 970-879-1870.
**Activities:** Fishing, hiking.
**Finding the campground:** From Steamboat Springs, travel southeast on U.S. Highway 40, about 15 miles to the campground.

**The campground:** Meadows is a pretty campground and an ideal stopover along U.S. Highway 40. Weekday travelers should find open sites throughout the season. Weekend travelers without reservations might find the campground full, but there are a total of 66 sites in the three campgrounds along the highway (Dumont Lake, Meadows, Walton Creek), all of which are excellent places to spend a night or two.

## 17 | Seedhouse

**Location:** Northwest of Steamboat Springs.
**Facilities:** Central water, fire rings, picnic tables, vault toilets.
**Sites:** 24.
**Fee:** $9.
**Elevation:** 8,000 feet.
**Road conditions:** One-and-a-half lane, gravel.
**Management:** Routt National Forest, 970-879-1870.
**Activities:** Fishing, four-wheel driving, hiking, motor biking.
**Finding the campground:** From Steamboat Springs, go 2 miles west on U.S. Highway 40 to County Road 129. Travel north about 16 miles to Forest Service Road 400. Turn east. Travel about 7 miles to the campground.

**The campground:** Seedhouse is an ideal home base for exploring the Elk River Valley and the Mount Zirkel Wilderness. The scenery is spectacular, the fishing is top notch, and the crowd is thin. The campsites are moderately spaced and lightly wooded. Some of the nearby trails are open to motor bikes and ATVs, but not all, so check posted regulations carefully.

## 18 | Walton Creek

**Location:** Southeast of Steamboat Springs.
**Facilities:** Central water, fire rings, picnic tables, vault toilets.
**Sites:** 14.
**Fee:** $9.
**Elevation:** 9,400 feet.
**Road conditions:** Paved.
**Management:** Routt National Forest, 970-879-1870.
**Activities:** Fishing, hiking.
**Finding the campground:** From Steamboat Springs, travel southeast on U.S. Highway 40 about 17 miles to the campground.

**The campground:** Another perfect stopover, Walton Creek is nicely wooded and quiet. If you are traveling either early or late in the season, be sure to call ahead to make sure the campgrounds are open. This area can get a lot of snow, forcing shutdown of the water system or complete closure of the campground.

## Additional Campgrounds in the Steamboat Springs Area

| | Type* | Contact | Location |
|---|---|---|---|
| Sawmill Creek | NF (6) | 970-879-1870 | 25 miles NE of Craig |
| Blacktail Creek | NF (8) | 970-638-4516 | 13 miles E of Toponas on CO 134 |
| Chapman Reservoir | NF (5) | 970-683-4516 | 11 miles SW of Phippsburg |
| Dry Lake | NF (8) | 970-879-1870 | 6 miles NE of Steamboat Springs |
| Freeman | NF (17) | 970-879-1870 | 22 miles NE of Craig |
| Gore Pass | NF (12) | 970-638-4516 | 16 miles E of Topoas on CO 134 |
| Lyx Pass | NF (11) | 970-638-4516 | 21 miles E of Yampa on FSR 270 |
| Rock Creek | SWA DSP | 970-248-7175 | 20 miles NW of Kremmling on FSR 205 |

* See "Key to Abbreviations" p.22—(# of sites)

# Area 3: Meeker

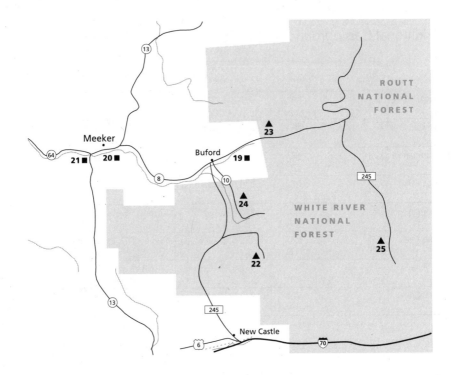

## MEEKER

With a vast, dry desert on one side and the rich green mesas of the White River National Forest on the other, Meeker is a good place to go seeking peace and quiet. The crowds are all on the other side of the mountains, unless of course you come during hunting season, when a deluge of elk hunters pours through the area.

Besides being home to the world's largest herd of elk, the Flat Top Mountains can also boast of the largest known aspen grove and an average of 8,000 trout per mile. The area is also home to the biggest, most vicious mosquitoes in the state during early summer.

Need more to do than fishing and hunting? Hundreds of miles of hiking and pack/saddle trails will take you through this country where the "Wilderness Area" concept first took root. If that's not enough, there are always the four-wheel-drive roads to keep you bumping happily along.

Camping choices include several RV parks, plus a vast array of national forest and State Wildlife Area camps. Any one of them is an outdoor enthusiast's dream. Pack your insect repellent and try not to get lost.

**For More Information:**

Meeker Chamber of Commerce
710 Market Street
P.O. Box 869
Meeker, CO 81641
www.colorado-west.com

# Commercial

## 19 Pollard's Ute Lodge

**Location:** East of Meeker.
**Affiliations:** Colorado Association of Campgrounds, Cabins, and Lodges.
**Contact:** 970-878-4669.
**Amenities:** Dump station, picnic tables, grills, showers, restrooms, cabins.
**Sites:** 12, all full hookups.
**Price per night:** $20.
**Elevation:** 6,200 feet.
**Finding the campground:** From the junction of Colorado Highways 64 and 13, travel north 4.25 miles through Meeker. Turn east onto County Road 8 and go about 26 miles, then 1 mile southeast on CR 12 and 2 miles south on CR 75.

**The campground:** Well off the main roads, Pollard's is nestled on the western side of the Flat Top Range amid a pine and spruce forest. With fishing, hiking, mountain biking, and horseback riding to pass the time, this makes for a peaceful and fun getaway.

## 20 Rimrock Campground

**Location:** Meeker.
**Affiliations:** Colorado Association of Campgrounds, Cabins, and Lodges.
**Contact:** 970-878-4486.
**Amenities:** Laundry, public phone, picnic tables, grills, dump station, showers, cabins.
**Sites:** 33, all full hookups.
**Price per night:** $14.
**Elevation:** 6,200 feet.
**Finding the campground:** From the junction of Colorado Highways 64 and 13, go 0.75 mile on CO 64. The entrance is on the right.

**The campground:** Meeker serves as the perfect stopover between Interstate 70 and the northwestern corner of the state, and Rimrock Campground provides comfortable accommodations. Activities for those wanting to spend time in the area include hiking, mountain biking, golf, and four-wheel driving.

## 21 | Stagecoach RV Resort

**Location:** Meeker.
**Affiliations:** Colorado Association of Campgrounds, Cabins, and Lodges.
**Contact:** 800-878-4334.
**Amenities:** Cabins, dump station, laundry, picnic tables, fire rings, showers, playground.
**Sites:** 50, 26 full hookups.
**Price per night:** $15 to $18.
**Elevation:** 6,200 feet.
**Finding the campground:** At the junction of Colorado Highways 13 and 64.

**The campground:** Fishing is an easy way to pass the time at this park, which spreads along a half mile of the White River. Many sites are shaded; all are grassy. This is a convenient stopover on the way to Dinosaur National Park. It also makes a comfortable home base from which to enjoy the unique beauty of the White River National Forest.

# Public

## 22 | Meadow Lake

**Location:** Northwest of New Castle.
**Facilities:** Boat dock, central water, fire rings, picnic tables, vault toilets.
**Sites:** 10.
**Fee:** $7.
**Elevation:** 9,600 feet.
**Road conditions:** One-and-a-half lane, gravel, rough, and winding.
**Management:** White River National Forest, 970-625-2371.
**Activities:** Fishing, hiking, four-wheel driving.
**Finding the campground:** From Exit 105 on Interstate 70 in New Castle, travel northwest on County Road 245 for about 9 miles, at which point the road becomes Forest Service Road 245. Continue north for about 20 miles to FSR 601. Turn east and travel about 4 miles to FSR 823. The campground is about 3 miles south.

**The campground:** This is about as far off the beaten path as you can get while still safely pulling a trailer. Forest Service information states trailers up to 36 feet, but that will be difficult. It may be a hard road in, but once you get here, you will appreciate the solitude and rugged beauty of this region. If the fish aren't biting, jeep trails spread out in every direction, begging you to wander. It is strongly advised that you call the ranger station to check road conditions before setting out on the 30-mile trek to the campground, and don't attempt it without detailed maps.

## 23 | North Fork

**Location:** Northeast of Buford.
**Facilities:** Central water, fire rings, picnic tables, vault toilets.
**Sites:** 40.
**Fee:** $9.
**Elevation:** 7,750 feet.
**Road conditions:** two lane, gravel.
**Management:** White River National Forest, 970-878-4039.
**Activities:** Fishing, hiking, horseback riding.
**Finding the campground:** Buford is located on County Road 8, east of Meeker. From Buford, the campground is about 20 miles east on CR 8.

**The campground:** North Fork is the only easily accessible campground on the western side of the Flat Tops. Numerous trails branch out in this area, which attract relatively few people but clouds of mosquitoes. As you swat at the buzzing pests, it sometimes helps to keep in mind that they add considerably to the size of the trout in the White River. The campground is on the North Fork of the White River, so catching those fat trout should be easily accomplished.

## 24 | South Fork

**Location:** Southwest of Buford.
**Facilities:** Central water, fire rings, wheelchair-accessible sites, picnic tables, vault toilets.
**Sites:** 18, plus 2 hike-in.
**Fee:** $7.
**Elevation:** 7,600 feet.
**Road conditions:** One-and-a-half lane, gravel, rough.
**Management:** White River National Forest, 970-878-4039.
**Activities:** Fishing, hiking, horseback riding.
**Finding the campground:** Buford is east of Meeker on County Road 8. From Buford, travel about 10 miles south on CR 10 to the campground.

**The campground:** You can't get any closer than this to the Flat Top Wilderness by vehicle. The campground graces the banks of the winding South Fork of the White River at the base of the 10,000-foot White River Plateau. If the fish aren't biting or you prefer lake fishing, a drive back to Buford and Lake Avery should allow you to satisfy your daily limit in a hurry. Motor boats are allowed. Don't forget the insect repellent.

## 25 | Trappers Lake

**Location:** Southeast of Buford.
**Facilities:** Central water, dump station, fire rings, picnic tables, vault toilets.
**Sites:** 50.
**Fee:** $10.

**Elevation:** 9,750 feet.
**Road conditions:** One-and-a-half lane, gravel, winding.
**Management:** White River National Forest, 970-878-4039.
**Activities:** Fishing, hiking, horseback riding.
**Finding the campground:** Buford is east of Meeker on County Road 8. From Buford, continue about 21 miles east on CR 8, then turn south on Forest Service Road 205 and go about 10 miles to the campground.

**The campground:** The campsites here are broken into four named campgrounds: Bucks, Cutthroat, Sheppards Rim, and Trapline. All can accommodate trailers up to 22 feet long. The scenery is beautiful and the mosquitoes vicious, so take your camera and your insect repellent. Only non-motorized boats are allowed, but they can be rented at the lodge. Fishing is limited to artificial flies and lures, with catch and release only under 16 inches on the native cutthroat trout.

## Additional Campgrounds in the Meeker Area

|  | Type* | Contact | Location |
|---|---|---|---|
| East Marvine | NF (7) | 970-878-4039 | 7 miles SE of Meeker on CR 12 |
| Hill Creek | NF (10) | 970-878-4039 | 30 miles SE of Meeker on CR 10 |
| Himes Peak | NF (11) | 970-878-4039 | 48 miles E of Meeker on FSR 205 |
| Marvine | NF (18) | 970-878-4039 | 35 miles SE of Meeker on CR 12 |
| Indian Run | SWA DSP | 970-248-7175 | 18 miles SE of Hamilton |
| Jensen | SWA DSP | 970-248-7175 | 9 miles NE of Meeker on CO 13 |
| Oak Ridge | SWA DSP | 970-248-7175 | SW of Buford on CR 8 |
| Piceance | SWA DSP | 970-248-7175 | 29 miles SW of Meeker on CR 5 |
| Rio Blanco | SWA DSP | 970-248-7175 | 20 miles W of Meeker off CO 64 |

* See "Key to Abbreviations" p.22—(# of sites)

# Area 4: Grand Junction

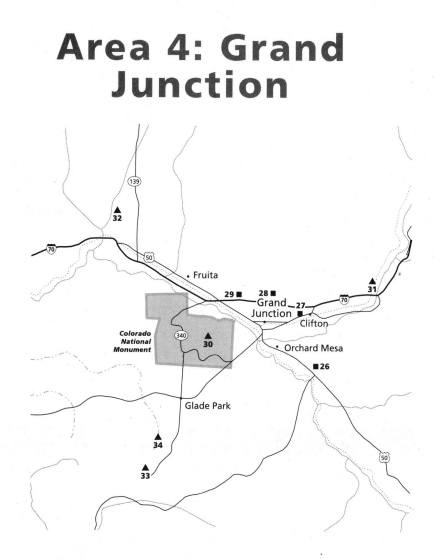

## GRAND JUNCTION

The town of Grand Junction sprawls in an oasis along the Colorado River. Beyond the green boundaries lies a no-man's land of stark cliffs and mesas, into which intrude, here and there, the pine and aspen forests found elsewhere in the state.

Nowhere is this dichotomy more obvious than east of town along Interstate 70. From the river, you can look to the south and see vast, green orchards and vineyards taking life. But turn your head north and you are greeted with the haunting, gray Book Cliffs upon which nothing dares grow.

What all of this means to travelers in the area is an incredible array of activities that cannot be found elsewhere in the state. Museums and dig sites offer a chance to dabble in geology and paleontology. Stretches of BLM land await those wanting to do a little off-road exploring. There are golf courses, winery tours, fine restaurants, history museums, tennis courts, public swimming pools, white-water rafting trips, and, in the winter, skiing.

And then there's Colorado National Monument. This is your chance to see unusual twisting, red and orange rock formations like those found in southern Utah and Arizona. Bring your camera. You can see plenty from Rimrock Drive, which snakes through the monument, but for a closer look, pack your hiking boots.

Camping in the area is a pleasure. As with most interstate locations, there is a good selection of RV parks. If you prefer to rough it a bit but still want to stay close to the action, try either the Highline or Colorado River state parks. To really lose yourself, there are a few national forest and BLM camps worth trying. To the southeast is the Grand Mesa Plateau, which offers so many campgrounds that it warrants its own section in this book.

The best news for campers here is that the crowds are far behind you now, squashed together like sardines in less tranquil campgrounds. You can laugh at them as you enjoy this oasis in the badlands.

**For More Information:**

Grand Junction Visitor and Convention Bureau
740 Horizon Drive
Grand Junction, CO 81506
970-244-1480 or 800-962-2547
www.grand-junction.net

# Commercial

## 26 Big J RV Park

**Location:** Grand Junction.
**Affiliations:** Good Sam.
**Contact:** 970-242-2527.
**Amenities:** Grills, ice, laundry, playground, public phone, showers, store, swimming pool, picnic tables.
**Sites:** 110, all full hookups; no tents.
**Price per night:** $14 to $18.
**Elevation:** 4,650 feet.
**Season:** Year-round.
**Finding the campground:** From Interstate 70, take Exit 26. Travel 7.25 miles east on U.S. Highway 50. The entrance is on the right.

**The campground:** Big J offers easy access to the amenities of Grand Junction and nearby attractions such as Colorado State Monument. It also makes an ideal stopover on US 50 between Grand Junction and Delta.

## 27 Grand Junction/Clifton KOA

**Location:** Clifton.
**Affiliations:** KOA.
**Contact:** 970-434-6644.
**Reservations:** 800-562-0898.
**Amenities:** Picnic tables, grills, laundry, cabins, public phone, store, movies, swimming pool, dump station, café, playground.
**Sites:** 102, 80 full hookups.
**Price per night:** $17 to $21.50.
**Elevation:** 4,600 feet.
**Season:** Year-round.
**Finding the campground:** Take Exit 37 from Interstate 70. Travel about 1 mile southwest on Business I-70.

**The campground:** This award-winning KOA campground offers a comfortable place to stay near Grand Mesa National Forest. Other nearby activities include golf, horseback riding, and whitewater rafting and kayaking on the Colorado River.

## 28 Junction West RV Park

**Location:** Grand Junction.
**Affiliations:** Colorado Association of Campgrounds, Cabins, and Lodges.
**Contact:** 970-245-8531.
**Amenities:** Store, tables, grills, sports, showers, laundry, dump station.
**Sites:** 51, 42 full hookups.
**Price per night:** $15 to $18.
**Elevation:** 4,600 feet.
**Season:** Year-round.
**Finding the campground:** Take Exit 26 from Interstate 70. Travel 4 blocks west to County Road 22. Turn north and travel another 4 blocks.

**The campground:** Junction West is a convenient stopover without all the road noise of parks closer to the highway. It's close to necessities in town and offers easy access to Colorado National Monument.

## 29 Mobile City RV Park

**Location:** Grand Junction.
**Affiliations:** Good Sam; Colorado Association of Campgrounds, Cabins, and Lodges.
**Contact:** 970-242-9291.
**Amenities:** Dump station, laundry, showers, public phone.
**Sites:** 30, all full hookups.
**Price per night:** $10 to $16.
**Elevation:** 4,600 feet.

**Season:** Year-round.
**Finding the campground:** From Interstate 70, take Exit 26. Go west 2 miles on U.S. Highway 50/6.

**The campground:** Mobile City is just 1 mile from the largest mall in western Colorado. There is an excellent selection of restaurants nearby, as well as golf, fishing, winery tours, hiking and biking trails, and ski resorts.

# Public

## 30 | Colorado National Monument: Saddle Horn

**Location:** West of Grand Junction.
**Facilities:** Central water (summer only), fire rings, picnic tables, vault toilets.
**Sites:** 80.
**Fee:** $5, plus $10 per vehicle entrance fee.
**Elevation:** 5,800 feet.
**Road conditions:** Paved.
**Management:** National Park Service, 970-858-3617.
**Activities:** Biking, hiking, photography.
**Finding the campground:** From Interstate 70, take Exit 19 at Fruita. Travel south on Colorado Highway 340 to the park entrance.

**The campground:** The prospect of waking to a sunrise mirrored on towering red stone walls is enough to make anyone want to spend the night here. The place looks like the backdrop of a Roadrunner-Coyote cartoon. The red and orange rock formations are so fantastic that they seem to have sprung from an illustrator's imagination.

The camping facilities are minimal, with little to block your view but a few scattered junipers. You can see much of the beauty by driving through the monument on Rim Rock Drive, but the best way to really experience it is on foot. The selection of trails ranges from moderate to difficult. The visitor center is the best place to get information regarding individual trails. Never set out hiking here without adequate water (a gallon per person per day), and always notify someone of your route.

## 31 | Colorado River State Park: Island Acres

**Location:** East of Grand Junction.
**Facilities:** Central water, dump station, wheelchair-accessible sites, swim beach, picnic tables, restrooms.
**Sites:** 60.
**Fee:** $7, plus $4 daily or $40 annual vehicle pass.
**Elevation:** 5,000 feet.

**Road conditions:** Paved.
**Management:** Colorado Department of Parks and Outdoor Recreation, 970-434-6862.
**Reservations:** 800-678-CAMP, $7 fee.
**Activities:** Hiking, fishing, swimming, non-motorized boating, bird watching.
**Season:** Year-round.
**Finding the campground:** From Interstate 70, take Exit 47. The park is on the northwest side of the highway.

**The campground:** Island Acres is the only camping area in Colorado River State Park. The campground is situated around a string of four small lakes created by a dam built in the 1950s. Sites are clustered around these lakes, affording visitors the opportunity to enjoy the scenic beauty of DeBeque Canyon, formed by the river. Sites are grassy and some offer shade trees. This campground makes a wonderful stopover, especially for families. The kids can burn off excess energy splashing in the water, while road-weary parents relax and enjoy the red-rock beauty.

## 32 | Highline State Park: Bookcliff

**Location:** Northwest of Grand Junction.
**Facilities:** Boat ramp, central water, designated wheelchair-accessible campsites, dump station, fire rings, hiking trails, laundry, pay phone, picnic tables, restrooms, showers, swim beach.
**Sites:** 25.
**Fee:** $7, plus $4 daily or $40 annual vehicle pass.
**Elevation:** 4,697 feet.
**Road conditions:** Paved.
**Management:** Colorado Department of Parks and Outdoor Recreation, 970-585-7208.
**Reservations:** 800-678-CAMP, $7 fee.
**Activities:** Fishing, water sports, hiking, winter bird watching, rock collecting.
**Season:** Year-round.
**Finding the campground:** Take Interstate 70 west from Grand Junction to the Loma exit (Colorado Highway 139). Go north 6 miles to Q Road. Go west 1.2 miles to 11.8 Road. Turn right, and then go north 1 mile to the park entrance.

**The campground:** In this small state park, you will see a prime example of the diversity of the park system in Colorado. Campsites are widely spaced in an oasis of shade trees in a grassy park. A swim beach is a short walk from camp. Two lakes within the park provide ample opportunity for both anglers and water-sports enthusiasts. Highline is an ideal base camp from which to tour the geological wonders of northwest Colorado. BLM land surrounding Douglas Pass (on your way to or from a visit to Dinosaur National Monument) is known for a rich supply of leaf and insect fossils.

## 33 | Hay Press

**Location:** South of Colorado National Monument.
**Facilities:** Picnic tables, vault toilets, no water.
**Sites:** 11.
**Fee:** $6.
**Elevation:** 9,300 feet.
**Road conditions:** one lane, rocky, some washboarding.
**Management:** Uncompahgre National Forest, 970-242-8211.
**Activities:** Fishing, four-wheel driving, hiking, wildlife viewing, rockhounding.
**Finding the campground:** From Interstate 70, take the Fruita exit onto Colorado Highway 340. Follow the signs to the Colorado National Monument. At the monument entrance, tell the attendant that you are going through to the campground on the other side of Glade Park (unless you plan to stop in the monument, for which you must pay the $10 entrance fee). Stay on Rim Rock Drive until it splits. Go right on 16.50 Road. Stay on 16.50 Rd. through Glade Park, continuing about 10 miles to the campground. Stay to the right at all forks.

**The campground:** If you're looking for a destination way off the beaten path, this is it. Hay Press sees very little use, but only because no one seems to know it's here. The road to the campground will leave you wondering if you're ever going to find the place, but relax and enjoy the lush meadows and pristine aspen forests along the way. The entire area overflows with wildflowers during most of the summer. Columbine and lupine spill right into the campsites. Fishing in the nearby Fruita Reservoirs is iffy, but in this beautiful setting, who cares? An additional bonus are the agate and petrified-wood specimens, which are likely to turn almost anyone into a true rockhound.

## 34 | Mud Springs

**Location:** South of Colorado National Monument.
**Facilities:** Central water, fire rings, wheelchair-accessible sites, picnic tables, vault toilets.
**Sites:** 12.
**Fee:** $7.
**Elevation:** 8,000 feet.
**Road conditions:** one lane, rocky, some washboarding.
**Management:** Bureau of Land Management, 970-945-2341.
**Activities:** Hiking, four-wheel driving, wildlife viewing, rockhounding.
**Finding the campground:** From Interstate 70, take the Fruita exit onto Colorado Highway 340. Follow the signs to the Colorado National Monument. At the monument entrance, tell the attendant that you are going through to the campground on the other side of Glade Park (unless you plan to stop in the monument, for which you must pay the $10 entrance fee). Stay on Rim Rock Drive until it splits. Go right on 16.50 Road. Stay on 16.50 Rd. through Glade Park. From there, the campground is about 4 miles south. Stay to the right at all forks.

**The campground:** Mud Springs is another little-known haven in the center of an aspen and scrub-oak glade dotted with wild pink roses. The oaks provide a privacy screen between the widely spaced sites, but it isn't even necessary since most of the other sites will likely be empty. The camp is accessible to trailers up to 30 feet long. This is the kind of place that begs you to stretch out and do a whole lot of nothing. The magic of the aspens is a surefire cure for the daily grind.

## Additional Campgrounds in the Grand Junction Area

| | Type* | Contact | Location |
|---|---|---|---|
| Monument RV Park | P (112) | 970-858-3155 | CO 340 in Fruita |
| Rabbit Valley | BLM (8) | 970-945-2341 | 2 miles E of Utah off Interstate 70 |
| Horse Thief Canyon | SWA DSP | 970-248-7175 | 5 miles S of Fruita off CO 340 |

* See "Key to Abbreviations" p.22—(# of sites)

# Area 5: Grand Mesa

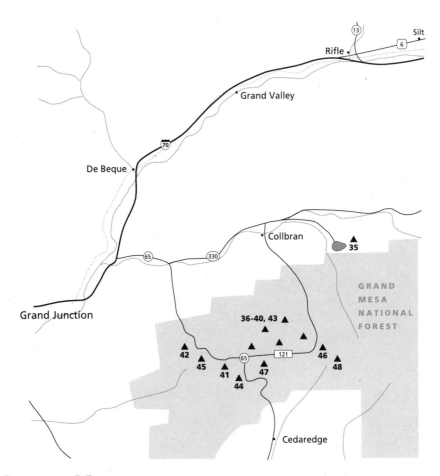

## GRAND MESA

The picturesque name says just about everything you need to know. Think "grand" in terms of height. The mesa towers over the surrounding area at more than 10,000 feet. Cross-country and downhill skiing, as well as snowmobiling are popular pastimes when the snow piles up in winter.

Think "grand" in terms of acreage. The area is so large that it encompasses its own national forest. Although this is a popular destination in the summer months, there is plenty of room to spread out. The mesa covers more than 50 square miles and is one of the largest high mesas in the country.

Think "grand" in terms of the number of campgrounds—thirteen prime national forest camps alone. With more than three hundred campsites, you should not have a difficult time finding a spot to call your own.

Think "grand" in terms of the number of lakes and the number of trout within them just waiting for you to drop your line. With the spring thaw, the water has nowhere to run on top of the mesa, so it pools in glorious blue lakes sprinkled throughout the forest.

Think "grand" in terms of beauty. The dense pine and aspen forests that cover the plateau are a pleasant surprise when you approach from the dry regions either north or south of the mesa. Lush undergrowth fills in the gaps between trees, creating a primeval setting.

And think "grand" in terms of the relaxation that you cannot help but find on Grand Mesa.

# Public

## 35 | Vega State Park

**Location:** Southeast of Collbran.
**Facilities:** Boat ramps, central water, dump station, fire rings, picnic tables, vault toilets.
**Sites:** 109.
**Fee:** $6, plus $4 daily or $40 annual vehicle pass.
**Elevation:** 8,000 feet.
**Road conditions:** Paved.
**Management:** Colorado Department of Parks and Outdoor Recreation, 970-487-3407.
**Reservations:** 800-678-CAMP, $7 fee.
**Activities:** Fishing, water sports, hiking, biking, snowmobiling.
**Season:** Year-round.
**Finding the campground:** From Interstate 70, take Exit 49 and travel south on Colorado Highway 65, then east on CO 330 through Collbran. About 6.5 miles east of town, turn south onto County Road 64.60 to the park.

**The campground:** Vega Reservoir is a welcome paradise for water-sports devotees. Water skiing is possible from June through August depending on water level. A separate fishing area is marked at the western end. The lake is well stocked and affords the longest fishing season between freezes of any lake in the Grand Valley. The campsites are divided into four campgrounds: Marmot Flats, Vega Coves, Oak Point, and Aspen Grove. Marmot Flats is on the fishing end. Access to the extensive hiking trail system in the Grand Mesa National Forest is a short drive away.

## 36 | Big Creek

**Location:** Grand Mesa Plateau.
**Facilities:** Boat ramp, fire rings, picnic tables, vault toilets, no water.
**Sites:** 26.

**Fee:** $6.
**Elevation:** 10,000 feet.
**Road conditions:** two lane, gravel; rough in places,but fairly straight.
**Management:** Grand Mesa National Forest, 970-242-8211.
**Activities:** Fishing, hiking, four-wheel driving.
**Finding the campground:** From Collbran (20 miles west of Interstate 70, Exit 49) travel south on Mesa County Road 58.50 for 1.9 miles until it turns into CR 59, which then becomes Forest Service Road 121. The turnoff to the campground is about 12 miles from Collbran.

**The campground:** Crowds on the Collbran side of the mesa seem to be slightly smaller, making Big Creek a good choice if you don't mind hauling water. The campground is lakeside and situated in a dense pine and spruce forest. As with all of the Grand Mesa campgrounds, this is a beautiful destination site.

## 37 | Carp Lake/Cobbett Lake

**Location:** Grand Mesa Plateau.
**Facilities:** Central water, fire rings, picnic tables, vault toilets.
**Sites:** 20.
**Fee:** $8.
**Elevation:** 10,300 feet.
**Road conditions:** Paved.
**Management:** Grand Mesa National Forest, 970-242-8211.
**Activities:** Fishing, hiking, four-wheel driving.
**Finding the campground:** Easiest access is from the west. From Interstate 70, Exit 49, take Colorado Highway 65 to the junction with Forest Service Road 121. The campground is the first one on the left on FSR 121, just past the visitor center.

**The campground:** Just another day in paradise. How many ways are there to say that Grand Mesa campgrounds are beautiful? Cobbett Lake itself is tiny, but the campground is no less fantastic than the others. A trail from the campground to the Cobbett Lake parking area is wheelchair-accessible.

## 38 | Cottonwood Lake

**Location:** Grand Mesa Plateau.
**Facilities:** Boat ramp, central water, fire rings, picnic tables, vault toilets.
**Sites:** 42.
**Fee:** $8.
**Elevation:** 10,000 feet.
**Road conditions:** two lane, gravel.
**Management:** Grand Mesa National Forest, 970-242-8211.
**Activities:** Fishing, hiking, four-wheel driving.
**Finding the campground:** From Collbran (20 miles west of Interstate 70, Exit 49) travel south on Mesa County Road 58.50 for 1.9 miles until it turns into CR

59, which then becomes Forest Service Road 121. Approximately 10 miles from Collbran, turn west onto FSR 257. Bear left at all forks to stay on FSR 257. The campground is about 5 miles from FSR 121.

**The campground:** This campground is a bit off the beaten path but is still accessible to trailers up to 30 feet long. Hiking and four-wheel-drive trails provide access to at least ten other lakes nearby.

## 39 | Crag Crest

**Location:** Grand Mesa Plateau.
**Facilities:** Central water, fire rings, picnic tables, vault toilets.
**Sites:** 11.
**Fee:** $6.
**Elevation:** 10,100 feet.
**Road conditions:** two lane, gravel.
**Management:** Grand Mesa National Forest, 970-242-8211.
**Activities:** Fishing, hiking, four-wheel driving, horseback riding.
**Finding the campground:** Equally accessible from the east or west. The campground is just east of the village of Grand Mesa off Forest Service Road 121.

**The campground:** Crag Crest sits above Eggleston Lake, the largest on the mesa. Because the campground is small, you may find it full, but it's worth a try anyway. Access to the lower loop portion of the Crag Crest National Recreation Trail is near the campground. This lower loop is open to hiking and horseback riding to the west. The main trail is a 10-mile loop ranging from 10,150 to 11,100 feet, providing incredible views of the mesa and the San Juan Mountains.

## 40 | Fish Hawk

**Location:** Grand Mesa Plateau.
**Facilities:** Central water, fire rings, picnic tables, vault toilets.
**Sites:** 5.
**Fee:** $5.
**Elevation:** 10,100 feet.
**Road conditions:** One-and-a-half lane, gravel.
**Management:** Grand Mesa National Forest, 970-242-8211.
**Activities:** Fishing, hiking, four-wheel driving.
**Finding the campground:** In the village of Grand Mesa, turn south onto Forest Service Road 123. The campground is about 0.25 mile on the left.

**The campground:** Want to get away from the bustle of the larger campgrounds? Then Fish Hawk is the spot to be. The sites here are shrouded in peace and quiet, which you usually can find only through backcountry camping. Both stream and lake fishing are possible nearby.

## 41 | Island Lake

**Location:** Grand Mesa Plateau.
**Facilities:** Central water, fire rings, picnic tables, vault toilets.
**Sites:** 41.
**Fee:** $8.
**Elevation:** 10,300 feet.
**Road conditions:** one lane, gravel with turnouts, some washboarding.
**Management:** Grand Mesa National Forest, 970-242-8211.
**Activities:** Fishing, hiking, four-wheel driving.
**Finding the campground:** From Colorado Highway 65, about 5 miles east of the Mesa Lakes area, turn south onto Forest Service Road 116 to the campground.

**The campground:** Island Lake is the largest campground on the mesa and perhaps the most beautiful in terms of mountain views. There are some pull-through sites, and the Forest Service claims the campground is accessible to trailers up to 41 feet long. But be aware that Forest Service Road 116 is narrow, rough, and somewhat winding. The campsites are widely spaced and densely forested. If you are looking for the site with the best view, try # 35. Island Lake also has a fishing platform that is wheelchair-accessible.

## 42 | Jumbo

**Location:** Grand Mesa Plateau.
**Facilities:** Central water, fire rings, picnic tables, vault toilets.
**Sites:** 26.
**Fee:** $10.
**Elevation:** 9,800 feet.
**Road conditions:** Paved.
**Management:** Grand Mesa National Forest, 970-242-8211.
**Activities:** Fishing, hiking, four-wheel driving.
**Finding the campground:** Easiest access is from the west. From Interstate 70, Exit 49, take Colorado Highway 65 through the town of Mesa. From there, Spruce Grove is about 12 miles away. Turn right onto the campground access road immediately after the Mesa Lakes Recreation sign. If you pass Mesa Lakes Resort, you missed the campground.

**The campground:** It is fitting that Jumbo is the first campground you encounter as you arrive on the mesa from the west. The reason is that it is one of the most beautiful. It welcomes you with widely spaced sites amid a lush pine, aspen, and spruce forest. Don't be disheartened if it's full. There are equally beautiful sites in other campgrounds. Hikers and nature watchers will enjoy the trails found around the lakes.

## 43 | Kiser Creek

**Location:** Grand Mesa Plateau.
**Facilities:** Fire rings, picnic tables, vault toilets, no water.
**Sites:** 12.
**Fee:** $8.
**Elevation:** 10,100 feet.
**Road conditions:** One-and-a-half lane, gravel.
**Management:** Grand Mesa National Forest, 970-242-8211.
**Activities:** Fishing, hiking, four-wheel driving.
**Finding the campground:** From the village of Grand Mesa, travel east on Forest Service Road 121, about 2 miles to the campground.

**The campground:** The campground is on the eastern tip of Eggleston Lake, but access to the Young's Creek reservoir is nearby, as is stream fishing. The small size and lack of water make this one of the quieter campgrounds on the mesa.

## 44 | Little Bear

**Location:** Grand Mesa Plateau.
**Facilities:** Central water, fire rings, wheelchair-accessible sites and restrooms, picnic tables, vault toilets.
**Sites:** 36.
**Fee:** $8.
**Elevation:** 10,200 feet.
**Road conditions:** one lane, gravel.
**Management:** Grand Mesa National Forest, 970-242-8211.
**Activities:** Fishing, hiking, four-wheel driving.
**Finding the campground:** From Colorado Highway 65, just past the junction with Forest Service Road 121, turn east onto FSR 116 to the campground.

**The campground:** Little Bear perches on the southeastern shore of Island Lake. It offers lake fishing and plenty of peace and quiet amid a towering spruce forest. With all its amenities, it makes an ideal family camping destination.

## 45 | Spruce Grove

**Location:** Grand Mesa Plateau.
**Facilities:** Central water, fire rings, picnic tables, vault toilets.
**Sites:** 16.
**Fee:** $8.
**Elevation:** 9,900 feet.
**Road conditions:** One-and-a-half lane, gravel.
**Management:** Grand Mesa National Forest, 970-242-8211.
**Activities:** Fishing, hiking, four-wheel driving.
**Finding the campground:** Easiest access is from the west. From Interstate 70, Exit 49, take Colorado Highway 65 through the town of Mesa. Spruce Grove is

about 13 miles east of town. It is the second campground on CO 65.

**The campground:** Spruce Grove is sometimes the last campground on the mesa to open in the summer. It is moderately sized but just as beautiful as the others. However, it does not have direct fishing access, so it may be the camp of choice for those who come here just to soak up the beauty of the mesa.

## 46 | Twin Lakes

**Location:** Grand Mesa Plateau.
**Facilities:** Fire rings, picnic tables, vault toilets; no water.
**Sites:** 13.
**Fee:** $6.
**Elevation:** 10,300 feet.
**Road conditions:** two lane, gravel.
**Management:** Grand Mesa National Forest, 970-242-8211.
**Activities:** Fishing, hiking, four-wheel driving.
**Finding the campground:** From Collbran (20 miles west of Interstate 70, Exit 49), travel south on Mesa County Road 58.50 for 1.9 miles until it turns into CR 59, which then becomes Forest Service Road 121. About 12.5 miles from Collbran, turn southeast onto FSR 126. The campground is about 1.5 miles from the turn.

**The campground:** The lack of water both here at Twin Lakes and at Weir & Johnson Campground (#48) deters many campers, but both of these campgrounds are worth the effort of hauling water from neighboring campgrounds. Twin Lakes offers both lake and stream fishing.

## 47 | Ward Lake

**Location:** Grand Mesa Plateau.
**Facilities:** Boat ramp, central water, fire rings, picnic tables, vault toilets.
**Sites:** 27.
**Fee:** $10.
**Elevation:** 10,200 feet.
**Road conditions:** Paved.
**Management:** Grand Mesa National Forest, 970-242-8211.
**Activities:** Fishing, hiking, four-wheel driving.
**Finding the campground:** Easiest access is from the west. From Interstate 70, Exit 49, take Colorado Highway 65 to the junction with Forest Service Road 121. Ward Lake is the second campground past the visitor center on FSR 121. The entrance is on the right.

**The campground:** The campgrounds on Grand Mesa are all so beautiful that choosing one may be difficult. Ward Lake is a popular choice among regulars, meaning you may find it full. The nice thing about the mesa though, is that with a total of almost three hundred improved campsites, there's usually one available for everyone.

## 48 | Weir & Johnson

**Location:** Grand Mesa Plateau.
**Facilities:** Fire rings, picnic tables, vault toilets; no water.
**Sites:** 12.
**Fee:** $6.
**Elevation:** 10,500 feet.
**Road conditions:** two lane, gravel.
**Management:** Grand Mesa National Forest, 970-242-8211.
**Activities:** Fishing, hiking, four-wheel driving.
**Finding the campground:** From Collbran (20 miles west of Interstate 70, Exit 49), travel south on Mesa County Road 58.50 for 1.9 miles until it turns into CR 59.00, which then becomes Forest Service Road 121. About 12.5 miles from Collbran, turn southeast onto FSR 126. The campground is about 2.1 miles from the turn.

**The campground:** If you can't catch your limit in the lakes surrounding Weir & Johnson, Trail 717 near the campground will take you up just about as far as you want to go in search of either fish or adventure. This is also the highest campground on the mesa, perching just 700 feet below Leon Peak.

## Additional Campgrounds in the Grand Mesa Area

|  | Type* | Contact | Location |
|---|---|---|---|
| Battlement Mesa | P (53) | 800-275-5687 | SW of Battlement Mesa on Thunderburg Trail |
| Alexander Lake Lodge | P (11) | 970-856-6700 | cabins and campground at Grand Mesa on FSR 121 |
| Trickle Park | NF | 970-487-3534 | 15 miles S of Collbran on FSR 121 |

\* See "Key to Abbreviations" p.22—(# of sites)

# Area 6: Glenwood Springs

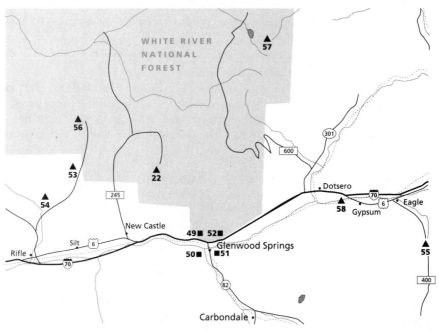

## GLENWOOD SPRINGS

Like other cities in the northwestern part of the state, Glenwood Springs offers a diversity of recreation and scenery that is difficult to believe, much less surpass. Stretching along the Colorado River, which by this point is beginning to carve its way into the soft, red earth, the town bustles with activity. Choices range from swimming in the world's largest outdoor hot-springs pool (it's more than a block long) to golfing on the side of a mesa, to dining and dancing in the clubs and restaurants downtown.

Drive west of town and you enter the rugged, high desert that struggles to hold onto this part of the state. But turn just a little north at Rifle to see the treasures of Rifle Gap and Rifle Falls state parks. Outdoor sports, such as hiking, fishing, biking, and even scuba diving, are the favored activities of visitors here, but you can also swing your golf sticks at the highly rated Rifle Creek Golf Course.

East of Glenwood Springs is Glenwood Canyon, a work of art created by the scouring river and the engineering of man. Interstate 70, which passes through the narrow canyon, has been hailed as one of the most scenic stretches of pavement in the country. The highway designers made every effort not to disturb the beauty of the canyon. One drive will convince you that they succeeded and deserved every award they collected.

To really appreciate the canyon, try rafting or biking through it. You can arrange in town to do both.

You will have a wide choice of RV parks in the area, either on the interstate or off. Public camping facilities are a bit more limited and tend to be far off the main roads, but the national forest camps to the north are pretty and quiet. Even more remote are the state parks, with Sylvan ranking as one of the prettiest in the state.

**For more information:**

Glenwood Springs Chamber Resort Association
102 Grand Ave.
Glenwood Springs, CO 81601
970-945-6589
www.glenscape.com

Glenwood Springs Golf Club
970-945-7086

Rifle Creek Golf Course
970-625-1093

Glenwood Springs Hot Springs Pool
970-945-6571

# Commercial

## 49 Ami's Acres

**Location:** Glenwood Springs.
**Affiliations:** Colorado Association of Campgrounds, Cabins, and Lodges.
**Contact:** 970-945-5340.
**Amenities:** Cabins, laundry, public phone, picnic tables, grills, showers.
**Sites:** 70, 44 full hookups.
**Price per night:** $15.75 to $18.75.
**Elevation:** 5,700 feet.
**Finding the campground:** From Exit 114 on Interstate 70, go 1 mile west on the north frontage road to the campground.

**The campground:** This is an easy-in, easy-out campground that allows full access to the attractions of the Glenwood Springs area. The golf course is nearby in the event that you have time for a round before you hit the road again.

## 50 Burning Mountain RV Park

**Location:** New Castle.
**Affiliations:** None.

**Contact:** 970-984-0331.
**Amenities:** Showers, dump station, laundry, public phone, store, picnic tables, fishing ponds, fire rings.
**Sites:** 72, no full hookups.
**Price per night:** $15.
**Elevation:** 5,500 feet.
**Season:** Year-round.
**Finding the campground:** From Exit 105 on Interstate 70, go 100 yards south and then 100 yards east on a dirt road.

**The campground:** Burning Mountain is a pleasant park from which to explore the Rifle Falls area or even farther northward into the White River National Forest. During the winter, it makes an ideal base from which to enjoy nearby ski slopes.

## 51 The Hideout Cabins & Campground

**Location:** Glenwood Springs.
**Affiliations:** AAA; Glenwood Springs Chamber of Commerce; Colorado Association of Campgrounds, Cabins, and Lodges.
**Contact:** 970-945-5621, fax 970-928-0983, e-mail hideout@rof.net.
**Amenities:** Playground, laundry, showers, public phone, cabins.
**Sites:** 53, 39 full hookups.
**Price per night:** $17 to $19.
**Season:** Year-round.
**Elevation:** 6,000 ft.
**Finding the campground:** From Exit 114 on Interstate 70, go 3.25 miles south on Midland Avenue and then 1 mile south on 27th Street/Midland Avenue.

**The campground:** What a wonderful park! It's tucked away in the tree-covered hills on the south side of town (away from the interstate). Many of the sites are streamside and screened from other sites by lush plants. A bike path that winds through town is accessible near the entrance. The Hideout is the kind of place that is truly a pleasure to come home to after a day exploring the region, and a soak in the relaxing mineral springs pool is just a short drive away.

## 52 Rock Gardens Campground & Rafting

**Location:** East of Glenwood Springs.
**Affiliations:** Colorado Association of Campgrounds, Cabins, and Lodges.
**Contact:** 970-945-6737.
**Amenities:** Cabins, dump station, public phone, store, fire rings, picnic tables, grills, showers, bike rentals.
**Sites:** 74, no full hookups.
**Price per night:** $19 to $23.
**Elevation:** 5,700 feet.
**Finding the campground:** From Exit 119 on Interstate 70, go 100 feet south on the frontage road to the park.

**The campground:** The main attraction here is that some of the sites are on the Colorado River. Fishing is allowed, and the on-site rafting operation can take you on a full- or half-day ride to remember through breathtaking Glenwood Canyon. People of all levels of experience can be accommodated. If you've never experienced whitewater rafting, this would be a perfect place to give it a try.

# Public

## 53 | Rifle Falls State Park

**Location:** North of Rifle.
**Facilities:** Central water, fire rings, picnic tables, vault toilets.
**Sites:** 18.
**Fee:** $6, plus $4 daily or $40 annual vehicle pass.
**Elevation:** 6,800 feet.
**Road conditions:** Paved.
**Management:** Colorado Department of Parks and Outdoor Recreation, 970-625-1607.
**Reservations:** 800-678-CAMP, $7 fee.
**Activities:** Fishing, hiking, biking, photography.
**Season:** Year-round.
**Finding the campground:** From Rifle, travel north on Colorado Highway 13 for 3 miles to CO 325. Continue northeast for 9.8 miles to the park.

**The campground:** Rifle Falls brings new meaning to the word oasis. The lush beauty is difficult to believe when you first see it. As you walk the trails that wind over and around the falls, it is easy to forget that you are even in Colorado. The atmosphere is almost tropical. The campsites are set in a grassy, shaded area, a short walk from the falls. Seven of the sites are walk-in tent sites along East Rifle Creek. Besides relaxing and exploring the falls area, you can take advantage of several jeep trails, a golf course, and both Harvey Gap and Rifle Gap reservoirs.

## 54 | Rifle Gap State Park

**Location:** North of Rifle.
**Facilities:** Boat ramp, central water, dump station, fire rings, picnic tables, vault toilets.
**Sites:** 46.
**Fee:** $6, plus $4 daily or $40 annual vehicle pass.
**Elevation:** 6,000 feet.
**Road conditions:** two lane, gravel.
**Management:** Colorado Department of Parks and Outdoor Recreation, 970-625-1607.
**Reservations:** 800-678-CAMP, $7 fee.

Lush waterfalls are the highlight of Rifle Falls State Park.

**Activities:** Sailing, jet skiing, scuba diving, fishing, horseback riding, biking.
**Season:** Year-round.
**Finding the campground:** From Rifle, travel north on Colorado Highway 13 for 3 miles. Turn onto CO 325 and continue about 6 miles to the park.

**The campground:** Rifle Gap is for the water-sports enthusiast. With smooth, clear, and relatively warm water (70 degrees in summer), the 359-acre reservoir draws visitors from across the western half of the state. The campsites are divided into four areas: Cedar, Cottonwood, Piñon, and Sage. All are typical lake campgrounds; access to the water is what's most important. Though they are short on amenities, all four camping areas do have incredible views of the Rocky Mountains to the south.

## 55 | Sylvan Lake State Park

**Location:** South of Eagle.
**Facilities:** Boat ramp, central water, fire rings, picnic tables, vault toilets.
**Sites:** 50.
**Fee:** $6, plus $4 daily or $40 annual vehicle pass.
**Elevation:** 8,500 feet.
**Road conditions:** two lane, gravel.
**Management:** Colorado Department of Parks and Outdoor Recreation, 970-625-1607.
**Reservations:** 800-678-CAMP, $7 fee.
**Activities:** Fishing, hiking, scenic driving.
**Season:** Year-round.
**Finding the campground:** Take Exit 147 off Interstate 70, and go through the town of Eagle on Main Street. Turn right onto Brush Creek Road and travel about 16 miles to the park entrance.

**The campground:** Sylvan Lake is a pristine mountain lake nestled in a high meadow and surrounded by towering 11,000-foot peaks. This is the Colorado people come from around the world to see. A pair of campgrounds takes full advantage of the views. Both are strategically placed in the open, on the eastern side of the lake, which then acts as a reflecting pool for the backdrop of pine-covered mountains. Gasoline-powered boats are not allowed on the lake. If you leave here without making the drive south from the lake on Forest Service Road 400, you will have missed some of the most enchanting scenery in the state. Though the red clay surface makes the road impassable when wet, it is not difficult to drive when dry.

## 56 | Rifle Mountain Park

**Location:** North of Rifle Falls.
**Facilities:** Central water, fire rings, picnic tables, vault toilets.
**Sites:** 30.
**Fee:** $10.

**Elevation:** 7,250 feet.
**Road conditions:** two lane, gravel.
**Management:** City of Rifle, 970-625-2121.
**Activities:** Hiking, four-wheel driving, rock climbing, horseback riding.
**Finding the campground:** Travel 3 miles north of Rifle on Colorado Highway 13, then northeast, 10 miles, on CO 325 to Rifle Falls State Park. Continue north 2 more miles to the campground.

**The campground:** Rifle Mountain is a city park in the country. It is situated on East Rifle Creek in a canyon that will make climbers itch to grab the gear. Jeep and pack/saddle trails climb Coulter Mesa to the west and continue through Little Box Canyon to the north. This is a good place to get lost if that's your intention.

## 57 | Deep Lake

**Location:** Northwest of Dotsero.
**Facilities:** Boat ramp, fire rings, vault toilets; no water.
**Sites:** 35.
**Fee:** $7.
**Elevation:** 10,580 feet.
**Road conditions:** One-and-a-half lane, gravel, very windy.
**Management:** White River National Forest, 970-328-6388.
**Activities:** Fishing, hiking, four-wheel driving.
**Finding the campground:** Dotsero is 17 miles east of Glenwood Springs on Interstate 70 (take Exit 133). From Dotsero travel north on County Road 301 (Colorado River Road) for 2 miles. Turn west onto Forest Service Road 600 (Deep Creek Road). Travel northwest about 27 miles to the campground.

**The campground:** High atop the White River Plateau, this scenic spot will make you feel like you are on top of the world. (The trip here feels like the journey to the top of the world, too.) You aren't likely to encounter a crowd here, but it isn't for lack of beauty or because the fish don't bite. You have your choice of several small lakes or the larger Heart Lake nearby. Trails and four-wheel-drive roads branch out in all directions, allowing you to fully appreciate the area.

## 58 | Eagle River SRMA

**Location:** West of Gypsum.
**Facilities:** Vault toilets.
**Sites:** Dispersed.
**Fee:** None.
**Elevation:** 6,300 feet.
**Road conditions:** two lane, dirt.
**Management:** Colorado Division of Wildlife, 970-248-7175.
**Activities:** Fishing, hiking, horseback riding, four-wheel driving, rockhounding.

**Finding the campground:** From Exit 140 on Interstate 70, travel south to the river access road leading to the campground.

**The campground:** If you happen to be heading west along Interstate 70 and are going to reach Glenwood Canyon after dark, then this spot is a primitive but pleasant place to stop for the night. Glenwood Canyon is a miracle of nature, and the road through it a miracle of man. You wouldn't want to miss either in the dark.

Eagle River also makes an excellent base for exploring the rugged southern half of the White River National Forest. Trails accommodating hikers, four-wheel-drivers, and horseback riders crisscross the area south of Gypsum. The camping area is peaceful, shady, and has the added benefit of being near the Eagle River, which pours into the Colorado just a few miles downriver. Before you leave, collect as souvenirs some of the delicate selenite crystals in the roadcuts along the north Interstate 70 frontage road.

# Area 7: Aspen

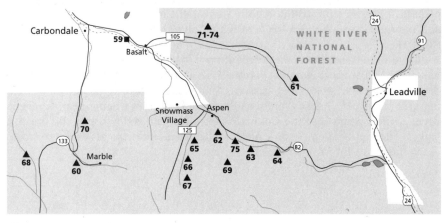

## ASPEN

Aspen is perhaps the most famous Colorado resort town. It has become a winter and summer playground for the wealthy. The airport here bears testament to that fact with its rows of private jets.

Why Aspen? In winter the answer is easy: tons of white powder, challenging runs, and a glittering nightlife draw the crowds. In summer, the answer lies in the quaint shops and eateries in town, the mountain peaks that loom beyond the red foothills, the greenest golf courses in the state, and the world-class river fishing.

Campers will be disappointed to learn that pressure from locals has forced the closure of the largest campground beneath the famous peaks known as the Maroon Bells. There are still three tiny camps open, but getting a space in one of them involves calling the reservation line months in advance. The road to Maroon Lake is closed to all motorized traffic other than buses during peak hours. That is good news for bicyclists though, who now rule the road.

Other camping choices include one RV park and some stunning national forest camps both north and south of Aspen. Fishing along the Frying Pan River is about as good as it gets anywhere, and guides can be arranged to help you catch your own trophy-sized trout.

**For More Information:**

Aspen Visitor Center
425 Rio Grande Place
Aspen, CO 81611
970-925-1940
www.aspen.com
e-mail: acra@aspeninfo.com

*This view from the east side of Independence Pass is only one of the highlights of the Aspen area.*

Basalt Area Chamber of Commerce
P.O. Box 514
Basalt, CO 81621
970-927-4031

Carbondale Chamber of Commerce
590 Highway 133
P.O. Box 1645
Carbondale, CO 81623
970-963-1890

# Commercial

## 59  Aspen-Basalt Campground

**Location:** West of Basalt.
**Affiliations:** Colorado Association of Campgrounds, Cabins, and Lodges.
**Contact:** 800-567-2773.
**Amenities:** Laundry, public phone, dump station, grills, fire rings, picnic tables, store, swimming pool, hot tub.
**Sites:** 86, 48 full hookups.
**Price per night:** $18 to $25.
**Elevation:** 6,200 feet.
**Season:** Year-round.
**Finding the campground:** Basalt is located between Aspen and Glenwood Springs on Colorado Highway 82. The campground is 2 miles northwest of Basalt on CO 82.

**The campground:** This is the only full-service RV park near Aspen. The sites are shaded and some are on the Roaring Fork River. The fact that the campground is open all year means it is the only place to camp during ski season. Ski resorts in the area include Aspen, Snowmass, Buttermilk, and Highlands. Make reservations early to ensure a spot (in any season). Summer activities include on-site river fishing and nearby hiking trails.

# Public

## 60  Bogan Flats

**Location:** South of Carbondale.
**Facilities:** Central water, fire rings, picnic tables, vault toilets.
**Sites:** 37.

**Fee:** $9.
**Elevation:** 8,800 feet.
**Road conditions:** One-and-a-half lane, gravel.
**Management:** White River National Forest, 970-963-2266.
**Reservations:** 800-280-CAMP, www.nrrc.com, $8.65 fee.
**Activities:** Fishing, hiking, horseback riding, rockhounding.
**Restrictions:** Water contains sulfur; let stand 10 minutes before drinking.
**Finding the campground:** Carbondale is south of Glenwood Springs on Colorado Highway 133. From Carbondale, travel about 20 miles south on CO 133 to Forest Service Road 314. Turn southeast and travel about 1.5 miles to the campground.

**The campground:** Bogan Flats is located on the Crystal River with nearby trails leading into the Snowmass-Maroon Bells Wilderness. The scenery is as breathtaking from the western side of these dramatic peaks as it is from the east. A bonus here is the site's proximity to the marble quarry that produced the columns for the Lincoln Memorial and the marble block for the Tomb of the Unknown Soldier. The quarry is now a national historic site, but collectors can gather small samples of the pure white stone from the surrounding areas. Be sure not to trespass on private property.

## 61 | Chapman

**Location:** East of Basalt.
**Facilities:** Central water, fire rings, wheelchair-accessible sites, picnic tables, vault toilets.
**Sites:** 84.
**Fee:** $9.
**Elevation:** 8,800 feet.
**Road conditions:** two lane, gravel.
**Management:** White River National Forest, 970-963-2266.
**Reservations:** 800-280-CAMP, www.nrrc.com, $8.65 fee.
**Activities:** Fishing, hiking, horseback riding, scenic driving, four-wheel driving.
**Restrictions:** Non-motorized boats only on Chapman Reservoir.
**Finding the campground:** Basalt is on Colorado Highway 82 between Glenwood Springs and Aspen. Travel east through the business district of Basalt on Midland Road, which becomes Frying Pan Road (Forest Service Road 105). Then travel east on FSR 105 for about 25 miles to the campground.

**The campground:** There is something for everyone at this large campground. Most sites are widely spaced, with some in open meadows, others in more shaded areas. There are a few riverside sites to choose from. Four-wheel-drive roads offer an alternative to fishing. The best is probably FSR 105 through Hagerman Pass, which ends at Turquoise Lake on the other side of the Continental Divide. Another road that is usually passable in any vehicle is FSR 400, which goes to Sylvan Lake State Park. The scenery is dramatic. There are also no less than five pack trails to choose from in the immediate vicinity. Unfortunately, there are no stock corrals near the campground.

## 62 | Difficult

**Location:** Southeast of Aspen.
**Facilities:** Central water, fire rings, picnic tables, vault toilets.
**Sites:** 47.
**Fee:** $10.
**Elevation:** 8,000 feet.
**Road conditions:** Paved.
**Management:** White River National Forest, 970-925-3445.
**Reservations:** 800-280-CAMP, www.nrrc.com, $8.65 fee.
**Activities:** Fishing, hiking, scenic driving.
**Restrictions:** Five-night maximum stay.
**Finding the campground:** From Aspen, travel about 4 miles southeast on Colorado Highway 82 (Independence Pass Road). Turn south onto Forest Service Road 108 to the campground.

**The campground:** "Difficult" depends on the direction of your approach. If you wind your way over Independence Pass to get here, you will indeed think this campground is aptly named. If you are lucky enough to approach from the west, you will find this an easily accessible campground for vehicles up to 40 feet long. The campground is lush with cottonwood, sumac, and young aspen. Wild roses fill in any remaining gaps in the foliage that divides the campsites from one another. The result is privacy but not claustrophobia. This is the largest and closest public campground from which you can enjoy the activities in Aspen, so reservations are strongly recommended.

## 63 | Lincoln Gulch

**Location:** Southeast of Aspen.
**Facilities:** Central water, fire rings, picnic tables, vault toilets.
**Sites:** 7.
**Fee:** $7.
**Elevation:** 9,700 feet.
**Road conditions:** One-and-a-half lane, dirt.
**Management:** White River National Forest, 970-925-3445.
**Activities:** Fishing, hiking, scenic driving, four-wheel driving, horseback riding.
**Finding the campground:** From Aspen, travel about 10 miles southeast on Colorado Highway 82. Turn south onto Forest Service Road 106 to the campground.

**The campground:** Lincoln Gulch is small but very pretty. From this campground, you will have easy access to the Collegiate Peaks Wilderness Area, to the south, via hiking, pack/saddle, and jeep trails. Keep in mind that all of the Independence Pass campgrounds have a short season: from July to September. Even then, it's best to call the ranger station before you go to make sure the campground is open and has water.

## 64 | Lost Man

**Location:** Southwest of Aspen.
**Facilities:** Central water, fire rings, picnic tables, vault toilets.
**Sites:** 10.
**Fee:** $7.
**Elevation:** 10,700 feet.
**Road conditions:** Paved.
**Management:** White River National Forest, 970-925-3445.
**Activities:** Fishing, hiking, scenic driving, horseback riding.
**Finding the campground:** From Aspen, travel about 14 miles southeast on Colorado Highway 82. The campground is on the south side of the highway.

**The campground:** Lost Man sits 2,000 feet below the top of Independence Pass, but it sure doesn't feel that far. This campground is a member of the elite group of roughly 20 campgrounds in the state that lie above the 10,500-foot mark. For those who like high altitudes, this is one of the best. It is small but easily accessible—something not many of the other 19 can claim. The sites are moderately spaced in a dense pine forest, which gives the camp the feel of being much farther off the road than it is. This is an ideal stopover if you are heading either direction over the pass.

## 65 | Maroon Bells Area: Silver Bar

**Location:** West of Aspen.
**Facilities:** Central water, fire rings, picnic tables, vault toilets.
**Sites:** 4.
**Fee:** $10.
**Elevation:** 8,300 feet.
**Road conditions:** Paved.
**Management:** White River National Forest, 970-925-3445.
**Reservations:** 800-280-CAMP, www.nrrc.com, $8.65 fee.
**Activities:** Fishing, hiking, biking, horseback riding.
**Restrictions:** Minimum three-day, maximum five-night stay; tents only.
**Finding the campground:** From Aspen, travel north on Colorado Highway 82 about 1.5 miles. Turn southwest onto Forest Service Road 125/County Road 13. The entrance to Maroon Bells is about 6 miles farther down this road.

**The campground:** Silver Bar is a delightful spot from which tent campers can enjoy the scenic area known as Maroon Bells. It contains four of only 14 campsites currently available in the area. Camping was once allowed at Maroon Lake farther up the road, but that campground has been removed in an effort to restore the fragile ecosystem. The road beyond the three lower campgrounds is closed to automobile traffic between 8:30 A.M. and 5:30 P.M. The only way to get to Maroon Lake from the campground during those hours is on foot or bicycle. An alternative is to return to Aspen, where bus tours depart from Rubey Park Transit Center. The cost is $5 per adult and $3 for seniors and children between the ages of six and sixteen. Information regarding the bus schedule is available at the Maroon Bells entrance.

## 66 | Maroon Bells Area: Silver Bell

**Location:** West of Aspen.
**Facilities:** Fire rings, picnic tables, vault toilets; no water.
**Sites:** 4.
**Fee:** $10.
**Elevation:** 8,400 feet.
**Road conditions:** Paved.
**Management:** White River National Forest, 970-925-3445.
**Reservations:** 800-280-CAMP, www.nrrc.com, $8.65 fee.
**Activities:** Fishing, hiking, biking, horseback riding.
**Restrictions:** Minimum three-day, maximum five-night stay required.
**Finding the campground:** From Aspen, travel north on Colorado Highway 82 about 1.5 miles. Turn southwest onto Forest Service Road 125/County Road 13. The Maroon Bells entrance is about 6 miles farther down this road.

**The campground:** Silver Bell is the middle of the three available Maroon Bells campgrounds. It is large enough to accommodate small trailers, but it has no water. The campground is quiet and scenic. It makes an ideal spot from which to enjoy hiking or biking.

## 67 | Maroon Bells Area: Silver Queen

**Location:** West of Aspen.
**Facilities:** Central water, fire rings, picnic tables, vault toilets.
**Sites:** 6.
**Fee:** $10.
**Elevation:** 9,100 feet.
**Road conditions:** Paved.
**Management:** White River National Forest, 970-925-3445.
**Reservations:** 800-280-CAMP, www.nrrc.com, $8.65 fee.
**Activities:** Fishing, hiking, biking, horseback riding.
**Restrictions:** Minimum three-day, maximum five-night stay required.
**Finding the campground:** From Aspen, travel north on Colorado Highway 82 about 1.5 miles. Turn southwest onto Forest Service Road 125/County Road 13. The Maroon Bells entrance is about 6 miles farther down this road.

**The campground:** Silver Queen is at the highest elevation you can camp with your vehicle in the Maroon Bells Recreation Area. The campground is on the river and is small and secluded in a young aspen forest. A short walk from here takes you within viewing distance of the peaks. Keep in mind as you plan your stay here that automobile traffic, even campers, is prohibited beyond your campground during daylight hours. This means that to get to Maroon Lake, you must hike, bike, drive back to Aspen to catch the bus, or rent a horse at the stables nearby.

## 68 | McClure

**Location:** South of Carbondale.
**Facilities:** Central water, fire rings, picnic tables, vault toilets.
**Sites:** 19.
**Fee:** $9.
**Elevation:** 8,200 feet.
**Road conditions:** Paved.
**Management:** Gunnison National Forest, 970-527-4131.
**Activities:** Fishing, hiking, four-wheel driving, scenic driving.
**Finding the campground:** Carbondale is 12 miles south of Glenwood Springs on Colorado Highway 82. From Carbondale, travel southwest on CO 133 about 29 miles to the campground.

**The campground:** This medium-sized campground is easily accessible from the south side of McClure Pass. Activities include stream fishing and exceptional four-wheel driving throughout this often-overlooked area.

## 69 | Portal

**Location:** Southeast of Aspen.
**Facilities:** Fire rings, picnic tables, vault toilets; no water.
**Sites:** 7.
**Fee:** $7.
**Elevation:** 10,700 feet.
**Road conditions:** Four-wheel-drive only.
**Management:** White River National Forest, 970-925-3445.
**Activities:** Fishing, hiking, four-wheel driving.
**Finding the campground:** From Aspen, travel about 10 miles southeast on Colorado Highway 82. Turn south onto Forest Service Road 106 and travel about 6.5 hard miles to the campground.

**The campground:** Very few of the campgrounds listed in this book are accessible only by four-wheel-drive. But knowing that there are a few readers who prefer to get really far away from it all, this one is included as probably the best place to do just that. Portal perches just below the Continental Divide in the Collegiate Peaks Wilderness. It offers fishing in two creeks as well as in Grizzly Reservoir. Hiking Trail 1478 will take you on a grueling hike over the divide if you are so inclined.

## 70 | Redstone

**Location:** South of Carbondale.
**Facilities:** Central water, fire rings, showers, picnic tables, flush toilets, electricity, horseshoe pits, playground.
**Sites:** 37.
**Fee:** $15 to $20.
**Elevation:** 7,200 feet.

**Road conditions:** Paved.
**Management:** White River National Forest, 970-963-2266.
**Reservations:** 800-280-CAMP, www.nrrc.com, $8.65 fee.
**Activities:** Fishing, hiking.
**Finding the campground:** Carbondale is 12 miles south of Glenwood Springs on Colorado Highway 82. From Carbondale, travel southwest on CO 133 about 13 miles to the campground.

**The campground:** The banks of the Crystal River provide an excellent site for this modernized campground. Redstone offers easy access, making it a perfect stopover between Glenwood Springs and points south. From here you can enjoy the breathtaking beauty of the Maroon Bells-Snowmass Wilderness.

## 71 | Ruedi Reservoir: Deerhamer

**Location:** East of Basalt.
**Facilities:** Central water, fire rings, picnic tables, vault toilets.
**Sites:** 13.
**Fee:** $9.
**Elevation:** 7,800 feet.
**Road conditions:** Paved.
**Management:** White River National Forest, 970-963-2266.
**Activities:** Fishing, hiking, sailboarding, sailing.
**Finding the campground:** Basalt is located on Colorado Highway 82 between Glenwood Springs and Aspen. In Basalt, travel east through the business district on Midland Road, which becomes Frying Pan Road (Forest Service Road 105). Ruedi Reservoir is about 16 miles east on FSR 105.

**The campground:** Deerhamer is located on the eastern end of Ruedi Reservoir, which draws an eclectic crowd of sailors and sportsmen from the Aspen area. The campground has its own boat ramp for easy fishing access. Some of the sites are shaded; all offer views down the length of the lake. Because of its small size, it may be a quieter choice than the western campgrounds.

## 72, 73, 74 | Ruedi Reservoir: Little Mattie, Little Maud, Mollie B

**Location:** East of Basalt.
**Facilities:** Central water, fire rings, picnic tables, vault and flush toilets.
**Sites:** 20.
**Fee:** $9.
**Elevation:** 7,800 feet.
**Road conditions:** Paved.
**Management:** White River National Forest, 970-963-2266.
**Reservations:** 800-280-CAMP, www.nrrc.com, $8.65 fee.
**Activities:** Fishing, hiking, sailboarding, sailing.
**Finding the campground:** Basalt is located on Colorado Highway 82 between Glenwood Springs and Aspen. In Basalt, travel east through the business dis-

trict on Midland Road, which becomes Frying Pan Road (Forest Service Road 105). Ruedi Reservoir is about 16 miles east on FSR 105.

**The campground:** There is little difference among any of the three campgrounds on the western end of the lake. All are beautiful and close to the water. The setting is peaceful and scenic. Some sites are completely open, while a few offer shade. All offer stunning views of this large mountain lake.

## 75 | Weller

**Location:** Southeast of Aspen.
**Facilities:** Central water, fire rings, wheelchair-accessible sites, picnic tables, vault toilets.
**Sites:** 11.
**Fee:** $7.
**Elevation:** 9,200 feet.
**Road conditions:** One-and-a-half lane, gravel.
**Management:** White River National Forest, 970-925-3445.
**Activities:** Fishing, hiking, scenic driving, horseback riding.
**Finding the campground:** From Aspen, travel southeast on Colorado Highway 82, about 11.5 miles to Forest Service Road 104. The campground is just off the highway on this road.

**The campground:** Weller is an "in-betweener" as far as campgrounds on Independence Pass go. It's not as high as Lost Man, but it's almost high enough and small enough to give you the feel of wilderness camping. The sites are moderately spaced in a lush aspen forest on the Roaring Fork River. This is a nice place to stretch out your stay along the pass road.

## Additional Campgrounds in the Aspen Area

|  | Type* | Contact | Location |
|---|---|---|---|
| BRB Crystal River Resort | P (54) | 800-963-2341 | 7 miles S of Carbondale on CO 133 |
| Meri Daes RV Park | P (15) | 970-963-1831 | Marble |
| Avalanche | NF (13) | 970-963-2266 | 13 miles SE of Carbondale on FSR 310 |
| Elk Wallow | NF (7) | 970-963-2266 | 25 miles E of Basalt on FSR 105 |
| Coke Oven | SWA DSP | 970-248-7175 | 30 miles E of Basalt on FSR 105 |

\* See "Key to Abbreviations" p.22—(# of sites)

# North Central

# Area 8: Colorado State Forest

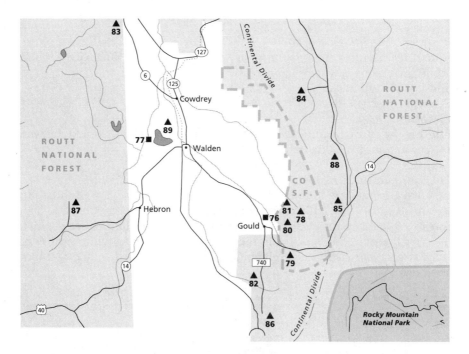

## COLORADO STATE FOREST

The beauty of the Colorado State Forest is often overlooked because of its more popular neighbor, Rocky Mountain National Park. Yet, the scenery here is almost as stunning and the wildlife almost as plentiful. The only things lacking are the bumper-to-bumper crowds you'll find at Rocky Mountain.

Activities in the forest are all of the outdoor variety: hiking, biking, fishing, four-wheel driving, climbing, and napping (campers always nap outside, don't they?).

The camping facilities in and near the state forest include a full-service RV park, several secluded national forest camps, plus four state park camping areas. Pick any one and you've picked a winner.

**For More Information:**

North Park Chamber of Commerce
P.O. Box 68
Walden, CO 80480
970-723-4600

# Commercial

## 76  North Park KOA

**Location:** West of Gould.
**Affiliations:** KOA.
**Contact:** 970-723-4310, fax 970-723-3223.
**Reservations:** 800-KOA-3240.
**Amenities:** Dump station, laundry, showers, store, public phone, playground, cabins; all buildings wheelchair-accessible.
**Sites:** 34, 16 full hookups.
**Price per night:** $16 to $22.
**Elevation:** 10,000 feet.
**Finding the campground:** From Gould, go 2 miles west on Colorado Highway 14. The entrance is on the right.

**The campground:** As in real estate, the three most important features of a great campground are location, location, location. This one has all three in a well-managed RV park. It sits right outside the entrance to the Colorado State Forest. It would be an ideal place to stay while you explore either the state forest or the rugged mountains in the surrounding area. Activities nearby include stream and lake fishing, climbing, hiking, scenic driving, and mosquito swatting.

## 77  Richard's RV Park

**Location:** Lake John.
**Affiliations:** Colorado Association of Campgrounds, Cabins, and Lodges.
**Contact:** 970-723-4407.
**Amenities:** Dump station, picnic tables.
**Sites:** 33, 13 full hookups.
**Price per night:** $9 to $11.
**Elevation:** 8,100 feet.
**Finding the campground:** From the junction of Colorado Highways 14 and 125, in Walden, go 1 mile north, then 7.5 miles west and north on County Road 12. Then drive 6 miles north on CR 7 and 4 miles on the gravel road around the lake, following the signs.

**The campground:** Richard's RV Park is a sportsman's paradise, located next to the Lake John and Richard state wildlife areas. The lake has a boat ramp at the south end, just a short drive from the RV park. All sites are open, providing a wonderful view of the surrounding mountains.

# Public

## 78 | Colorado State Forest: Bockman

**Location:** Northeast of Gould.
**Facilities:** Fire rings, picnic tables, vault toilets; no water.
**Sites:** 34.
**Fee:** $7, plus $4 daily or $40 annual vehicle pass.
**Elevation:** 9,000 feet.
**Road conditions:** One-and-a-half lane, gravel.
**Management:** Colorado Department of Parks and Outdoor Recreation, 970-723-8366.
**Reservations:** 800-678-CAMP, $7 fee.
**Activities:** Fishing, hiking, biking, four-wheel driving, horseback riding.
**Season:** Limited winter camping.
**Finding the campground:** From the North Michigan Reservoir park entrance on Colorado Highway 14 (about 2 miles north of Gould), follow County Road 41 around the reservoir to the left; then follow the signs to the campground.

**The campground:** Bockman is a semi-wild campground from which to enjoy the state forest. The lack of water might keep some away, but you can haul it from nearby North Michigan Creek Campground. Four-wheel-drive roads into the backcountry traverse the area north and south of Bockman. Fishing is possible on the North Fork Michigan River, as well as on the reservoir. This is a gorgeous place from which to explore the forest, but don't forget to bring strong insect repellent.

## 79 | Colorado State Forest: Crags

**Location:** Southeast of Gould.
**Facilities:** Central water, fire rings, picnic tables, vault toilets.
**Sites:** 26.
**Fee:** $7, plus $4 daily or $40 annual vehicle pass.
**Elevation:** 9,600 feet.
**Road conditions:** one lane, dirt, steep, winding, rocky.
**Management:** Colorado Department of Parks and Outdoor Recreation, 970-723-8366.
**Reservations:** 800-678-CAMP, $7 fee
**Activities:** Fishing, hiking, climbing, biking, four-wheel driving, horseback riding.
**Season:** Limited winter camping.
**Finding the campground:** From Gould, travel about 4.4 miles southeast on Colorado Highway 14 to the campground access road.

**The campground:** "The Crags" is an appropriate name for this campground, since it is wedged among rocky peaks at the southern end of the forest. The rough access road combines with rather small spaces to make this campground accessible only to small trailers or tenters. Those who do come are rewarded with a rugged alpine beauty unsurpassed in the state. The views are sure to stir the soul of the adventurer in almost anyone. All sites except number six are reservable, but it isn't likely that you'll need a reservation. Call the state park office if in doubt.

## 80 | Colorado State Forest: North Michigan Reservoir

**Location:** Northeast of Gould.
**Facilities:** Central water, cabins, fire rings, picnic tables, vault toilets.
**Sites:** 21.
**Fee:** $7, plus $4 daily or $40 annual vehicle pass.
**Elevation:** 9,000 feet.
**Road conditions:** One-and-a-half lane, gravel.
**Management:** Colorado Department of Parks and Outdoor Recreation, 970-723-8366.
**Reservations:** 800-678-CAMP, $7 fee.
**Activities:** Fishing, hiking, biking, four-wheel driving, horseback riding.
**Season:** Limited winter camping.
**Finding the campground:** From Gould, travel north on Colorado Highway 14 about 2 miles to County Road 41. Turn east and follow the road to the lake and the campground.

**The campground:** North Michigan provides camping near the reservoir for avid anglers. Of course, the proximity to water translates into mobs of mosquitoes. The views of the lake and surrounding mountains are magnificent. The only drawback to this camp is the relative lack of privacy. Many sites are just off County Road 41, which has considerable traffic. Only tent sites and three trailer sites are available on the south side of the lake away from the road. North Michigan is the only lake in the park that allows boating (motorized craft at wakeless speeds only).

## 81 | Colorado State Forest: Ranger Lakes

**Location:** Southeast of Gould.
**Facilities:** Central water, fire rings, picnic tables, vault toilets, dump station, amphitheater.
**Sites:** 24.
**Fee:** $7, plus $4 daily or $40 annual vehicle pass.
**Elevation:** 9,400 feet.
**Road conditions:** two lane, gravel.
**Management:** Colorado Department of Parks and Outdoor Recreation, 970-723-8366.
**Reservations:** 800-678-CAMP, $7 fee.
**Activities:** Fishing, hiking, biking, four-wheel driving, horseback riding.
**Season:** Limited winter camping.
**Finding the campground:** From Gould, travel 1.2 miles southeast on Colorado Highway 14 to the campground entrance.

**The campground:** These widely spaced sites are ideal for big rigs. The campground is heavily wooded, but nearby open areas offer excellent moose watching, which is a favored pastime anywhere in the state forest. The lakes are a short walk from the campground. Ranger Lakes are ideal for a stopover along CO 14 or for an extended stay in this prime piece of the Colorado Rockies.

## 82 | Aspen

**Location:** Southeast of Walden.
**Facilities:** Central water, fire rings, picnic tables, vault toilets.
**Sites:** 10.
**Fee:** $7.
**Elevation:** 8,900 feet.
**Road conditions:** One-and-a-half lane, gravel.
**Management:** Routt National Forest, 970-723-8204.
**Activities:** Fishing, hiking, horseback riding, four-wheel driving, scenic driving, wildlife viewing.
**Finding the campground:** From Gould, travel southwest on Forest Service Road 740 about 1 mile. Then turn west onto the campground access road.

**The campground:** Aspen is on the South Fork of the Michigan River and is only a mile from Colorado State Forest. From here you can enjoy all the beauty, but in what is likely to be a quieter setting than the state forest itself. From the road's end, a pack trail continues to follow the river to its headwaters in the Never Summer Wilderness. Jeep trails south of the campground are a great diversion, but make sure you take Forest Service maps so you can find your way back to camp.

## 83 | Big Creek Lake

**Location:** Northwest of Cowdrey.
**Facilities:** Central water, fire rings, picnic tables, vault toilets, boat ramp.
**Sites:** 54.
**Fee:** $9.
**Elevation:** 8,997 feet.
**Road conditions:** One-and-a-half lane, gravel.
**Management:** Routt National Forest, 970-723-8204.
**Reservations:** 800-280-CAMP, www.nrrc.com, $8.65 fee.
**Activities:** Fishing, hiking.
**Finding the campground:** Cowdrey is north of Walden on Colorado Highway 125. From Cowdrey, travel about 18 miles northwest on County Road 6, then about 6 miles southwest on Forest Service Road 600 to the campground.

**The campground:** With two lakes and miles of stream to choose from, you will find fishing here a real pleasure. The campground perches above the north end of the 350-acre lake, offering outstanding views. The only drawback here is the remote location. But then again, maybe that's just what you're looking for.

## 84 | Brown's Park

**Location:** North of Chambers Lake.
**Facilities:** Fire rings, picnic tables, vault toilets; no water.
**Sites:** 28.
**Fee:** $7.
**Elevation:** 8,440 feet.
**Road conditions:** One-and-a-half lane, dirt.
**Management:** Arapaho/Roosevelt National Forest, 970-498-2770.
**Activities:** Fishing, hiking, horseback riding, wildlife viewing.
**Finding the campground:** Chambers Lake is about 18 miles east of Gould, just off Colorado Highway 14. From CO 14, travel north on County Road 103, about 17 miles until it splits. Stay to the left on CR 190 (Glendevey Road) to reach the campground.

**The campground:** If you seek the sights and sounds of the wilderness, this is the place to go. The campground gets lower than average usage, but not because it isn't a delight. Some people just prefer to stay closer to civilization. At Brown's Park you are about as likely to encounter a moose as you are another human. Pack trails lead into the Rawah Wilderness on the eastern slope of the Medicine Bow Mountains. If you have the urge, the Link and McIntyre trailheads provide moderately difficult passages into the wilderness area. Both trails are open to pack/saddle animals.

## 85 | Chamber's Lake

**Location:** East of Gould.
**Facilities:** Central water, fire rings, picnic tables, vault toilets, wheelchair-accessible sites, boat ramp.
**Sites:** 52.
**Fee:** $12 to $24.
**Elevation:** 9,200 feet.
**Road conditions:** Paved.
**Management:** Arapaho/Roosevelt National Forest, 970-498-2770.
**Reservations:** 800-280-CAMP, www.nrrc.com, $8.65 fee.
**Activities:** Fishing, hiking, wildlife viewing.
**Restrictions:** No ATVs allowed.
**Finding the campground:** From Gould, travel east on Colorado Highway 14, about 18 miles to the lake turnoff on the north side of the highway.

**The campground:** It's easy to see why camping at this clear mountain lake is so popular. The campground is spacious and modern, with updated restrooms and paved roads. Sites are scattered amid a dense pine forest. Some sites are double width (double fee, also), and some have gorgeous views of the lake (try site 36). Big rigs are no problem here, so this campground works as a convenient stopover along CO 14 or for a lengthy retreat. If you plan to arrive on a weekend, you'll need a reservation.

## 86 | Pines

**Location:** Southeast of Gould.
**Facilities:** Central water, fire rings, picnic tables, vault toilets.
**Sites:** 11.
**Fee:** $7.
**Elevation:** 9,200 feet.
**Road conditions:** One-and-a-half lane, gravel, rough.
**Management:** Routt National Forest, 970-723-8204.
**Activities:** Fishing, hiking, horseback riding, four-wheel driving.
**Finding the campground:** From Gould, travel southeast on Forest Service Road 740, about 4 miles to the campground.

**The campground:** You can come here to get away from the crowds visiting Colorado State Forest, yet still enjoy the beauty of the region. (Unfortunately the crowds of mosquitoes aren't any smaller.) The road is a bit rough, and trailers longer than 20 feet aren't recommended. Jeep and pack trails crisscross the area south and west of the camp; detailed Forest Service maps are highly recommended.

## 87 | Teal Lake

**Location:** West of Hebron.
**Facilities:** Central water, fire rings, picnic tables, vault toilets.
**Sites:** 17.
**Fee:** $7.
**Elevation:** 8,812 feet.
**Road conditions:** two lane, gravel.
**Management:** Routt National Forest, 970-723-8204.
**Activities:** Fishing, hiking, four-wheel driving.
**Finding the campground:** Hebron is southwest of Walden on County Road 24. From there, travel about 11 miles west on CR 24 to Forest Service Road 615. Turn north, and travel about 2.5 miles to the lake and campground.

**The campground:** Teal Lake is typical of campgrounds that are more than a mile or two off main highways: nobody seems to know it's here. The mountain scenery is spectacular, and the campsites are often empty. Many people stop at the smaller Grizzly Creek campground at the FSR 612 turnoff, but if you plan to spend any time in the area, take advantage of Teal Lake. Four-wheel-drive enthusiasts can tackle the dramatic climb to Buffalo Pass and the Continental Divide via FSR 60.

## 88 | Tunnel

**Location:** North of Chambers Lake.
**Facilities:** Central water, fire rings, picnic tables, vault toilets.
**Sites:** 49.
**Fee:** $7.

**Elevation:** 8,600 feet.
**Road conditions:** two lane, dirt.
**Management:** Arapaho/Roosevelt National Forest, 970-498-2770.
**Activities:** Fishing, hiking, wildlife viewing.
**Finding the campground:** Chambers Lake is about 18 miles east of Gould, just off Colorado Highway 14. From CO 14, travel north on County Road 103, about 6 miles to the campground.

**The campground:** You'll want to tear out this page before showing this book to anyone else, because you'll want to keep Tunnel Campground a secret for as long as possible. It's easily accessible to trailers up to 30 feet long, it's close to both lake and stream fishing, and it's quiet. A heavy pine forest and the Laramie River combine to provide a sound barrier against the rest of the world. There isn't a bad site in this campground. The spacing is moderate to wide, providing plenty of privacy. Don't forget your camera; you never know when moose or elk will find their way into this peaceful haven.

## 89 | Diamond J State Wildlife Area

**Location:** North of Walden.
**Facilities:** Vault toilets; no water.
**Sites:** 20.
**Fee:** None.
**Elevation:** 8,100 feet.
**Road conditions:** One-and-a-half lane, dirt.
**Management:** Colorado Division of Wildlife, 970-484-2836; City of Walden, 970-723-4344.
**Activities:** Fishing, wildlife viewing.
**Finding the campground:** From Walden, travel north on Colorado Highway 125. Entrances are 1, 2, and 4 miles north of town.

**The campground:** These scattered campsites along the Michigan River provide excellent opportunities for "roughing it." Lake fishing is available just a few miles in both directions if the fish in the river are uncooperative. The open scenery can be a pleasant change from forested campgrounds, and you can view the abundance of wildlife in the area from your lawn chair in camp. Traffic noise could be a slight problem but should not be excessive.

# Additional Campgrounds in the Colorado State Forest Area

|  | Type* | Contact | Location |
|---|---|---|---|
| Grizzly Creek | NF (12) | 970-723-8204 | 25 miles SW of Walden on FSR 615 |
| Hidden Lakes | NF (9) | 970-723-8204 | 30 miles SW of Walden on FSR 20 |
| Summit Lake | NF (16) | 970-879-1870 | 16 miles NE of Steamboat Springs on FSR 60 |
| Bliss | SWA DSP | 970-484-2836 | 45 miles NW of LaPorte on CO 14 |
| Cowdrey Lake | SWA DSP | 970-484-2836 | 2 miles S of Cowdrey on CO 125 |
| Delaney Butte | SWA DSP | 970-484-2836 | miles W of Walden on CR 5 |
| Owl Mountain | SWA DSP | 970-484-2836 | 20 miles S of Walden on CR 25 |
| Seymore Lake | SWA DSP | 970-484-2836 | 18 miles SW of Walden on CR 288 |

* See "Key to Abbreviations" p.22—(# of sites)

# Area 9: Fort Collins and the Poudre River Valley

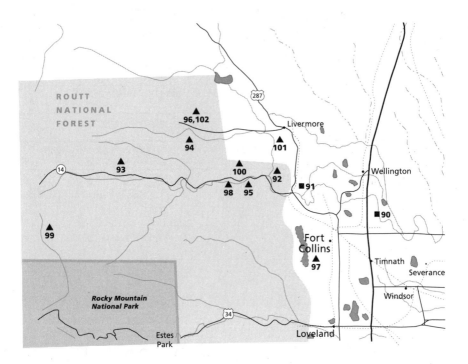

## FORT COLLINS AND THE POUDRE RIVER VALLEY

If I didn't know that *poudre* is the French word for powder, I would guess that it meant "playground." The Cache la Poudre Canyon and the gentle valley at its western end are scenic, loaded with recreational opportunities, and conveniently placed right next door to the exciting town of Fort Collins.

Activities in and around the valley include fishing, rafting, kayaking, hiking, rock climbing, horseback riding, and four-wheel driving. Or you can just stretch out in a lounge chair and watch the river flow past your camp.

In Fort Collins, there are indoor swimming, year-round ice skating, racquetball, glider flights, museums, trolley rides, and fine dining. And don't forget to tour the Anheuser Busch Brewery.

Camping facilities in the area seem limitless. Commercial RV parks are abundant along Interstate 25, as well as in Fort Collins and near the Cache la Poudre River. National forest camps stretch the length of the river for more than 60

*The Poudre River has carved a playground for campers west of Fort Collins.*

miles and encircle the Red Feather Lakes District farther north.

The crowds are slightly thinner than those a little farther south, but unless you venture off-road, don't come here looking for peace and quiet. Instead, plan on plenty of fun and excitement.

**For More Information:**

Fort Collins Visitor and Convention Bureau
420 S. Howes St. #101
P.O. Box 1998
Fort Collins, CO 80522
970-482-5821 or 800-274-FORT
www.ftcollins.com
e-mail: ftcollins@ftcollins.com

# Commercial

## 90  Fort Collins North KOA

**Location:** North of Fort Collins.
**Affiliations:** KOA.
**Contact:** 970-568-7486.
**Amenities:** Cabins, dump station, laundry, public phone, store, picnic tables, showers, fire rings, grills, playground, pool.
**Sites:** 94, 40 full hookups.
**Price per night:** $15 to $21.
**Elevation:** 5,300 feet.
**Season:** Year-round.
**Finding the campground:** From Exit 281 on Interstate 25, travel 0.25 mile east on County Road 5. The entrance is on the right.

**The campground:** This KOA campground is either your first or your last chance to spend the night in Colorado while traveling along Interstate 25. It is far enough off the interstate to reduce the all-night-traffic noise. It has all the amenities, plus a view of the Rockies. What more could you ask for, a cold beer, perhaps? The Anheuser Busch Brewery is just off Interstate 25 at Exit 271. It offers a free and informative family tour that includes a meeting with the world-famous Clydsdales. Beer samples—alcoholic and nonalcoholic—are available at the end of the tour.

## 91  Mile High/Fort Collins KOA

**Location:** Northwest of Fort Collins.
**Affiliations:** KOA.
**Contact:** 970-493-9758.
**Amenities:** Cabins, dump station, laundry, public phone, store, picnic tables, grills, showers, pool, playground, hiking trails.

**Sites:** 63, 28 full hookups.
**Price per night:** $17 to $23.
**Elevation:** 5,200 feet.
**Finding the campground:** The campground is at the northern junction of U.S. Highway 287 and Colorado Highway 14. Easiest access from Interstate 25 is at Exit 269 onto CO 14. Travel through town about 17 miles to the campground.

**The campground:** Splendid access to the Cache la Poudre River and all of its recreation possibilities is the highlight of this KOA campground. The list of things to do includes fishing, hiking, kayaking, picnicking, horseback riding, shopping, swimming, and scenic driving. Even day trips to Rocky Mountain National Park are possible from here. And when you need a break from the camp stove, a quick drive into town presents a wide array of dining choices. This campground is as close to being a perfect family destination as you are likely to find in northern Colorado.

# Public

## 92 | Ansel Watrous

**Location:** Northwest of Fort Collins.
**Facilities:** Central water, fire rings, wheelchair-accessible sites, picnic tables, vault toilets.
**Sites:** 19.
**Fee:** $9.
**Elevation:** 5,800 feet.
**Road conditions:** Paved.
**Management:** Arapaho/Roosevelt National Forest, 970-498-2770.
**Activities:** Fishing, hiking, biking, scenic driving.
**Season:** Year-round.
**Finding the campground:** From the junction of U.S. Highway 287 and Colorado Highway 14, travel west on CO 14 for about 23 miles. The campground is on the right.

**The campground:** Ansel Watrous is divided into upper, middle, and lower campgrounds. All sites are riverside and are beautiful, though tightly spaced. The middle campground has the widest spacing, with some pull-throughs. There is a limit of five people per site. As you travel west on CO 14, this is the first of several beautiful campgrounds that allows you to appreciate fully the beauty of the Cache la Poudre River. Some of the fishing along the river is subject to strict "Gold Medal" regulations, so be sure to check and adhere to posted limits. Further information on these rules, designed to protect native species, can be obtained from the Colorado Division of Wildlife in Denver, 303-297-1192. If hiking or biking is your style, the Greyrock National Recreation Trail is several miles east of the campground.

## 93 | Aspen Glen

**Location:** West of Rustic.
**Facilities:** Central water, fire rings, picnic tables, vault toilets.
**Sites:** 8.
**Fee:** $9.
**Elevation:** 9,000 feet.
**Road conditions:** Paved.
**Management:** Arapaho/Roosevelt National Forest, 970-498-2770.
**Activities:** Fishing, hiking.
**Finding the campground:** From the junction of U.S. Highway 287 and Colorado Highway 14, travel west for about 66 miles. The campground is on the right.

**The campground:** Aspen Glen is as idyllic as its name implies. This small but very pretty campground on Joe Wright Creek has widely spaced sites set in a light pine and aspen forest. The views of the surrounding mountains are incredible. Lake fishing is just a short drive down the road to either Bames Meadow Reservoir or Chambers Lake. Though pretty, Aspen Glen is best used as a brief stopover because traffic noise could get annoying during longer stays.

## 94 | Bellaire Lake

**Location:** West of Livermore.
**Facilities:** Central water, fire rings, picnic tables, vault toilets, wheelchair-accessible sites, electricity.
**Sites:** 27.
**Fee:** $10.
**Elevation:** 8,365 feet.
**Road conditions:** two lane, gravel.
**Management:** Arapaho/Roosevelt National Forest, 970-498-2770.
**Activities:** Fishing, hiking, four-wheel driving.
**Finding the campground:** Livermore is on U.S. Highway 287 north of Fort Collins. From there, travel west on County Road 74E (Red Feather Lakes Road) about 27 miles to CR 162. Turn south and travel about 3 miles to CR 163. Turn west to the lake and campground.

**The campground:** There are very few national forest campgrounds with electrical hookups, so it's a real treat when you find one like Bellaire Lake. The campground is modern and capable of accommodating trailers up to 45 feet long. Four-wheel-drive roads are the second biggest draw to this campground (fishing being number one). If the fish aren't biting at Bellaire, the Red Feather Lakes are just a short drive up the road.

## 95 | Dutch George

**Location:** West of Fort Collins.
**Facilities:** Central water, fire rings, wheelchair-accessible sites, picnic tables,

vault toilets, walking trail.
**Sites:** 20.
**Fee:** $10.
**Elevation:** 6,500 feet.
**Road conditions:** Paved.
**Management:** Arapaho/Roosevelt National Forest, 970-498-2770.
**Activities:** Fishing, hiking, scenic driving.
**Finding the campground:** From the junction of U.S. Highway 287 and Colorado Highway 14, travel west for about 31 miles. The campground is on the left.

**The campground:** Dutch George is a new campground on the Cache la Poudre River and is a fine example of the direction the Forest Service is taking with all of its Colorado campgrounds. While most of the sites are a bit more confined than those of decades past, double-wide sites are available for large families. All sites are level and widely spaced. A walking path complete with park benches connects the sites along the river, adding a nice touch to this idyllic setting. About half of the sites here are on the river and in the shade. Along with your fishing pole, be sure to bring a lounge chair. This spot will tempt you to stay awhile.

## 96 | Dowdy Lake

**Location:** West of Livermore.
**Facilities:** Central water, fire rings, picnic tables, vault toilets, boat ramp, trails.
**Sites:** 62.
**Fee:** $10.
**Elevation:** 8,365 feet.
**Road conditions:** One-and-a-half lane, gravel.
**Management:** Arapaho/Roosevelt National Forest, 970-498-2770.
**Reservations:** 800-280-CAMP, www.nrrc.com, $8.65 fee.
**Activities:** Fishing, hiking, wildlife viewing, four-wheel driving.
**Restrictions:** No ATVs allowed.
**Finding the campground:** Livermore is on U.S. Highway 287 north of Fort Collins. From there, travel west on County Road 74E (Red Feather Lakes Road) about 27 miles to CR 162. Turn north to the town of Red Feather Lakes and travel east to Dowdy Lake, 2 miles on CR 4/Forest Service Road 218.

**The campground:** The campsites at Dowdy are divided between two campgrounds, South Shore and West Shore. Both offer views of and easy access to the Red Feather Lakes. Hiking trails encircle most of the lakes, making this a prime bird-watching area in both winter and summer. After you catch your limit on the lakes, venture out onto one of the many roads that wander the Laramie Mountains. You can take a long circular route in almost any vehicle by traveling northeast on FSR 179 to CR 80C. Turn west and drive around the mountains to CR 162 (Dead Man Road), which will take you back over the mountains to Red Feather. It's not a white-knuckle drive, but it does get a bit rough in places. Be sure to take your camera because you are sure to pass deer and elk.

## 97 | Larimer County Park: Horsetooth Reservoir

**Location:** West of Fort Collins.
**Facilities:** Central water, dump station, fire rings, wheelchair-accessible sites, picnic tables, vault toilets, boat ramp, restaurant.
**Sites:** 180.
**Fee:** $6.
**Elevation:** 5,430 feet.
**Road conditions:** Paved.
**Management:** Larimer County Parks and Recreation, 970-679-4570.
**Activities:** Fishing, water sports.
**Finding the campground:** From Exit 265 on Interstate 25, travel west on Colorado Highway 68, about 6.5 miles to Taft Hill Road. Turn north and go 0.5 mile to County Road 38E. From here follow the signs to the campground.

**The campground:** Horsetooth is one of four lakes operated by Larimer County. All offer fishing and the opportunity to enjoy the fresh air and beauty of the foothills. Glimpses of the jagged peaks to the west are an added bonus. The reservoir covers roughly 1,900 acres, so there is plenty of room for water skiing. Keep in mind though, that the water temperature is a bit chilly. Three-millimeter wetsuits are standard apparel. These can be purchased at discount stores in Loveland or Fort Collins.

## 98 | Kelley Flats

**Location:** West of Fort Collins.
**Facilities:** Central water, fire rings, wheelchair-accessible sites, picnic tables, vault toilets.
**Sites:** 23.
**Fee:** $9.
**Elevation:** 6,750 feet.
**Road conditions:** Paved.
**Management:** Arapaho/Roosevelt National Forest, 970-498-2770.
**Activities:** Fishing, hiking, biking.
**Season:** Year-round.
**Finding the campground:** From the junction of U.S. Highway 287 and Colorado Highway 14, travel west for about 37 miles.

**The campground:** This airy campground features widely spaced sites amid cottonwoods and pines. There are sites on both sides of the river. There are some pull-throughs, allowing easy access for vehicles up to 40 feet long. Forest Service Road 172 heads north, nearby for those seeking an opportunity to explore the area. As at the other camps along CO 14, traffic noise could be a problem. If you plan to stay more than a night or two, try something a bit farther off the highway, such as Tunnel (see Campground 88).

## 99 | Long Draw

**Location:** South of Chambers Lake.
**Facilities:** Central water, fire rings, picnic tables, vault toilets, boat ramp, trailhead.
**Sites:** 25.
**Fee:** $9.
**Elevation:** 10,030 feet.
**Road conditions:** One-and-a-half lane, dirt, winding.
**Management:** Arapaho/Roosevelt National Forest, 970-498-2770.
**Activities:** Fishing, hiking.
**Finding the campground:** From Colorado Highway 14, about 2.25 miles southwest of the Chambers Lake turnoff, turn south onto Forest Service Road 156. Travel about 9 miles southeast to the campground.

**The campground:** For those who like high altitudes, here's the highest trailer-accessible campground in the area. As is typical of higher campgrounds, it isn't easy to reach, but the sites will accommodate trailers as long as 45 feet. The lake is blue and clear, the trout are usually hungry, and the mountains are majestic. Long Draw is the kind of place that makes you want to do a whole lot of nothing.

## 100 | Mountain Park

**Location:** West of Fort Collins.
**Facilities:** Central water, fire rings, group-use building, wheelchair-accessible sites, playground, showers, picnic tables, vault toilets, electricity, pay showers.
**Sites:** 55.
**Fee:** $10 to $15.
**Elevation:** 6,650 feet.
**Road conditions:** Paved.
**Management:** Arapaho/Roosevelt National Forest, 970-498-2770.
**Reservations:** 800-280-CAMP, www.nrrc.com, $8.65 fee.
**Activities:** Fishing, hiking, scenic driving.
**Finding the campground:** From the junction of U.S. Highway 287 and Colorado Highway 14, travel west for about 33 miles.

**The campground:** Showers at a national forest campground? You bet. This is one of only a handful of national forest campgrounds that is so equipped, so take advantage. Don't let the large size of the campground discourage you if you seek privacy. The layout is in tiered levels, with well-spaced sites. The lower loops are riverside, but trails lead from the upper loops down to the river. If you like more densely forested sites, try anything on Comanche Loop. This is a great destination spot, as well as a convenient stopover. Keep in mind that it stays full most of the summer, so reservations are recommended.

## 101 Sleeping Elephant

**Location:** West of Fort Collins.
**Facilities:** Central water, fire rings, wheelchair-accessible sites, picnic tables, vault toilets.
**Sites:** 15.
**Fee:** $7.
**Elevation:** 7,550 feet.
**Road conditions:** Paved.
**Management:** Arapaho/Roosevelt National Forest, 970-498-2770.
**Activities:** Fishing, hiking, scenic driving.
**Finding the campground:** From the junction of U.S. Highway 287 and Colorado Highway 14, travel west for about 53 miles.

**The campground:** Sleeping Elephant is one of four campgrounds on the western end of the Poudre Valley, near Joe Wright Creek. All of them are ideal stopovers with easy access to the highway. Sleeping Elephant is very pretty with small, widely spaced sites. The sites will not accommodate trailers longer than 20 feet, making it perfect for pop-ups and tents. Access to the river is across the road.

## 102 West Lake

**Location:** West of Livermore.
**Facilities:** Central water, fire rings, picnic tables, vault toilets, boat ramp, trails.
**Sites:** 29.
**Fee:** $9.
**Elevation:** 8,365 feet.
**Road conditions:** One-and-a-half lane, gravel.
**Management:** Arapaho/Roosevelt National Forest, 970-498-2770.
**Activities:** Fishing, hiking, wildlife viewing, four-wheel driving.
**Finding the campground:** Livermore is on U.S. Highway 287 north of Fort Collins. From there, travel west on County Road 74E (Red Feather Lakes Road), about 26 miles to the campground.

**The campground:** West Lake is another of the beautiful destinations at Red Feather Lakes. The fishing is said to be excellent, and the scenery is supreme. This area makes a wonderful getaway for fishing or just enjoying the peace and quiet of northern Colorado.

# Additional Campgrounds in the Fort Collins and Poudre Canyon Area

| | Type* | Contact | Location |
|---|---|---|---|
| Glen Echo Resort | P (80) | 970-881-2208 | CO 14 in Rustic |
| Home Moraine Trailer Park | P (52) | 970-881-2356 | 6.5 miles W of Rustic on CO 14 |
| Poudre River Resort | P (6) | 970-881-2139 | CO 14 near milepost 89 |
| Sportsman's Lodge & Store | P (10) | 970-881-2272 | CO 14 between mileposts 78 & 79 |
| Lory State Park | SP (6) | 970-493-1623 | W of Fort Collins on Lodgepole Drive (tents only) |
| Big Bend | NF (6) | 970-498-2770 | 10 miles W of Rustic on CO 14 |
| Big South | NF (4) | 970-498-2770 | 65 miles W of Laporte on CO 14 |
| Grandview | NF (8) | 970-498-2770 | 15 miles SE of Chambers Lake on FSR 156 (tents only) |
| Jack's Gulch | NF (12) | 970-498-2770 | 41 miles W of LaPorte on CR 131 |
| Narrows | NF (12) | 970-498-2770 | 11 miles E of Rustic on CO 14 |
| North Fork Poudre | NF (9) | 970-498-2770 | 8 miles S of Red Feather on CR 162 |
| Stove Prairie Landing | NF (9) | 970-498-2770 | 12 miles E of Rustic on CO 14 |
| Cherokee Park | SWA DSP | 970-484-2836 | 28 miles NW of Fort Collins on CR 80C |
| Watson Lake | SWA DSP | 970-484-2836 | 8 miles NW of Fort Collins on Rist Canyon Road |
| Wellington Reservoir and Smith Lake | SWA DSP | 970-484-2836 | 7 miles NW of Wellington on CR 66 |

* See "Key to Abbreviations" p.22—(# of sites)

# Area 10: Granby and Grand Lakes

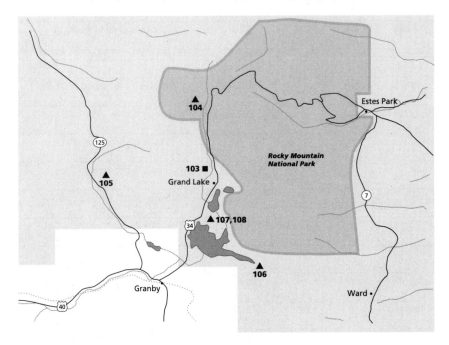

## GRANBY AND GRAND LAKES

Busy and popular are the best words to describe this area on the western edge of Rocky Mountain National Park—and for good reason. The list of recreational activities available here is long and includes sailing, bicycling, golfing, rafting, windsurfing, tennis, and, of course, fishing.

Add to all that a string of gemstone lakes surrounded by camping sites, tucked away in the pines, and you've got a wonderful family destination.

Oh, and there's always Rocky Mountain National Park if you get tired of the lakes.

**For More Information:**

Grand Lake Chamber of Commerce
P.O. Box 57
Grand Lake, CO 80447
970-627-3402 or 970-627-3372
www.grandlakecolorado.com

*Views like this are just around the bend from Grand Lake in Rocky Mountain National Park.*

# Commercial

## 103 Elk Creek Campground

**Location:** North of Grand Lake.
**Affiliations:** Colorado Association of Campgrounds, Cabins, and Lodges.
**Contact:** 970-627-8502, fax 970-627-3076, e-mail elkcreek@rkymtnhi.com.
**Reservations:** 800-355-2733.
**Amenities:** Dump station, laundry, showers, store, public phone, playground, cabins, fishing pond, grills, picnic tables, fire rings.
**Sites:** 66.
**Price per night:** $15 to $19.
**Elevation:** 8,500 feet.
**Season:** Year-round.
**Finding the campground:** From Grand Lake, travel north on U.S. Highway 34, about 0.75 mile. Turn west on Golf Course Road. The campground is on the right.

**The campground:** Elk Creek is a pleasant place to stay to enjoy both the grandeur of Rocky Mountain National Park and the Arapaho National Recreation Area. In addition to fishing at the large lakes in the area, you can try your luck at a stocked trout pond on site. An eighteen-hole championship golf course is located just a mile away, and horseback riding is right down the road. The campground is shady, and sites are not too tightly spaced.

# Public

## 104 Rocky Mountain National Park: Timber Creek

**Location:** Western side of the park.
**Facilities:** Central water, fire rings, public phone, picnic tables, flush toilets, dump station.
**Sites:** 100.
**Fee:** $12, plus $10 per vehicle park entrance fee.
**Elevation:** 8,900 feet.
**Road conditions:** Paved.
**Management:** National Park Service, 970-586-1399.
**Reservations:** None.
**Activities:** Hiking, campfire ranger programs, scenic driving, wildlife viewing, fishing.
**Restrictions:** Seven-night maximum stay.
**Finding the campground:** From the Grand Lake entrance station on U.S. Highway 34, travel about 10 miles north to the campground.

**The campground:** Aptly named, Timber Creek sits in a dense pine forest surrounded by the open meadows through which the North Fork of the Colorado

River meanders. Wildlife viewing right from your campsite is possible if you are lucky enough to snag a site on the outer edge of the campground, facing the meadow. If not, try hiking across the river to see the Never Summer Ranch south of the campground off US 34. The meadow will likely be so full of elk that you can't count them all.

The sites in camp are tightly spaced but can accommodate even large RVs. Keep in mind that access to the eastside campgrounds is best accomplished via Estes Park. Towing over the 12,000-foot-high Trail Ridge Road (US 34) is possible but not recommended. The road is steep, narrow, and bumper to bumper with sightseers. When you drive the road (and you must if you really want to appreciate the park), allow plenty of time for the 50-mile trip each way. Three hours will probably give you enough time to stop at the overlooks and view the majestic peaks.

## 105 Denver Creek

**Location:** Northwest of Granby.
**Facilities:** Central water, fire rings, picnic tables, vault toilets.
**Sites:** 25.
**Fee:** $8.
**Elevation:** 8,600 feet.
**Road conditions:** Paved.
**Management:** Arapaho/Roosevelt National Forest, 970-887-3331.
**Activities:** Fishing, hiking.
**Finding the campground:** From Granby, travel west on U.S. Highway 40 about 3 miles. Turn north onto Colorado Highway 125 and travel about 12 miles to the campground.

**The campground:** Denver Creek Campground is a good place to get away from the crowds found at the large lakes in and around the national park. Even though it is a roadside camp, you likely will not find it full. Sites on the west side of the road are on Willow Creek, allowing easy fishing access and adding the lullaby of the stream to the attractiveness of the camp. Nearby trails run east and west, crisscrossing the mountains and open park areas.

## 106 Lake Granby: Arapaho Bay

**Location:** Northeast of Granby.
**Facilities:** Central water, boat ramp, fire rings, wheelchair-accessible sites, picnic tables, vault toilets.
**Sites:** 84.
**Fee:** $10.
**Elevation:** 8,400 feet.
**Road conditions:** One-and-a-half lane, gravel.
**Management:** Arapaho/Roosevelt National Forest, 970-887-3331.
**Reservations:** 800-280-CAMP, www.nrrc.com, $8.65 fee.

**Activities:** Fishing, hiking, scenic driving.
**Restrictions:** Fee for second vehicle.
**Finding the campground:** From Granby, travel north about 6.5 miles to County Road 6. Turn east and travel about 9 miles to the campground.

**The campground:** Located on the scenic southeastern tip of Lake Granby, Arapaho Bay is a popular destination. Though the campground is often crowded, it seems aloof from the busy world. The fishing here is said to be extraordinary. Trails lead to two smaller lakes to the south, Strawberry and Monarch. Serious hikers may wish to continue past Monarch Lake on Arapaho Pass Trail, which climbs to almost 12,000 feet, following Arapaho Creek to its source at Caribou Lake. From there, the trail traverses Arapaho Pass near the Fourth of July Mine. Be sure to check with rangers about trail conditions before setting out.

## 107 Lake Granby: Stillwater

**Location:** South of Grand Lake.
**Facilities:** Amphitheater, central water, dump station, boat ramp, wheelchair-accessible sites, fire rings, picnic tables, vault and flush toilets.
**Sites:** 148.
**Fee:** $12 to $24.
**Elevation:** 8,400 feet.
**Road conditions:** Paved.
**Management:** Arapaho/Roosevelt National Forest, 970-887-3331.
**Reservations:** 800-280-CAMP, www.nrrc.com, $8.65 fee.
**Activities:** Fishing, hiking, scenic driving.
**Restrictions:** Fee for second vehicle.
**Finding the campground:** From Grand Lake, travel south on U.S. Highway 34, about 6.5 miles to the campground entrance.

**The campground:** Stillwater is the most popular destination on Lake Granby. It is a pretty but crowded fishing camp. If the fish aren't biting, or after you've caught your limit, the opportunities for hiking and scenic driving are almost limitless in Rocky Mountain National Park next door.

## 108 Shadow Mountain Reservoir: Green Ridge

**Location:** South of Grand Lake.
**Facilities:** Boat ramp, central water, dump station, fire rings, picnic tables, flush toilets.
**Sites:** 81.
**Fee:** $10 to $30.
**Elevation:** 8,400 feet.
**Road conditions:** two lane, gravel.
**Management:** Arapaho/Roosevelt National Forest, 970-887-3331.
**Reservations:** 800-280-CAMP, www.nrrc.com, $8.65 fee.

**Activities:** Fishing, hiking.

**Restrictions:** Fee for second vehicle.

**Finding the campground:** From Grand Lake, travel south on U.S. Highway 34, about 3 miles to County Road 66. Turn southwest and go about 1 mile to the campground.

**The campground:** Situated on the southern tip of Shadow Mountain Reservoir, this beautiful campground attracts a crowd throughout the summer. The fishing is good, the setting is serene, and the proximity to Rocky Mountain National Park draws campers in droves. The campsites are moderately spaced amid the tall pines, but to really get away from the crowds, try hiking Shadow Mountain Trail, which parallels the eastern shore of the lake. Reservations are recommended for this campground throughout the summer season.

## Additional Campgrounds in the Granby and Grand Lakes Area

| | Type* | Contact | Location |
|---|---|---|---|
| Lake Shore Marina | P (10) | 970-887-2295 | 250 CR 640 |
| Shadow Mountain Marina RV Park & Camping | P (51) | 970-627-9970 | 2 miles S of Grand Lake on US 34 |
| Western Hills Cottages & RV Park | P (8) | 970-627-3632 | 12082 US 34 |
| Winding River Resort | P (155) | 970-627-3215 | 1.5 miles N of Grand Lake on CR 491 |
| Williams Fork Reservoir | CP (42) | 303-628-6526 | 4 miles S of Parshall |
| Sawmill Gulch | NF (5) | 970-887-3331 | 13 miles NW of Granby on CO 125 |
| Willow Creek | NF (35) | 970-887-3331 | 7 miles NE of Granby on CO 125 |
| Hot Sulphur Springs | SWA DSP | 970-484-2836 | 3 miles W of Hot Sulphur Springs on US 40 |

* See "Key to Abbreviations" p.22—(# of sites)

# Area 11: Estes Park

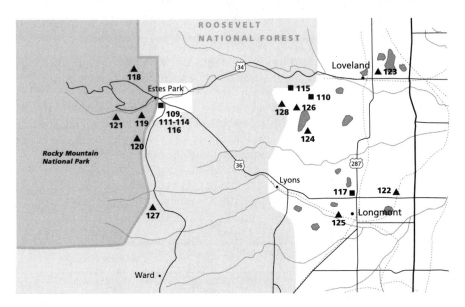

## ESTES PARK

The town of Estes Park and its backyard playground, Rocky Mountain National Park, draw hundreds of thousands of travelers each year. Fortunately, the facilities are equipped to handle the crowds. The beauty of the area is hypnotic. Seventy-eight 12,000-foot peaks tower over lush pine forests and meandering, meadow rivers.

A drive through the park on Colorado Highway 34 (Trail Ridge Road) is a must. There are sights to see here that you will not find anywhere else in the state. Huge herds of elk graze in the meadows. Near the highest point on the road, pull off and play in the snow (even in August) at a spot designated just for that purpose.

In town, the activities include an eclectic mix of miniature golf, shopping for art, and fine dining. The quaint community has an indoor/outdoor swimming pool, a country-music dinner theater, two golf courses, and an aerial tramway. You can arrange guided llama tours, mountain-climbing lessons, and breakfast hayrides. The fun never ends.

Campers here must make a difficult choice between the fun-filled RV parks in and around town and the crowded but beautiful campgrounds in the national park. Those who want to enjoy the area but get a little farther away from the crowds might want to try the national forest camps southwest of town.

**For More Information:**

Estes Park Chamber of Commerce and Information Center
500 Big Thompson Avenue
Estes Park, CO 80517
970-586-4431 or 800-443-7837
www.estesnet.com

# Commercial

## 109 Blue Arrow RV Park

**Location:** West of Estes Park.
**Affiliations:** Good Sam, AAA.
**Contact:** 970-586-5342, fax 970-586-5013.
**Reservations:** 800-582-5342.
**Amenities:** Dump station, playground, laundry, showers, store, public phone, restaurant.
**Sites:** 170, 83 full hookups.
**Price per night:** $18 to $25.
**Elevation:** 8,200 feet.
**Finding the campground:** From the junction of U.S. Highway 36W and Colorado Highway 66, go 0.25 mile southwest on CO 66.

**The campground:** Blue Arrow is not only the largest RV park in the Estes Park area, but it has beautiful views of the mountains and comes complete with an intriguing history. Ask camp employees about the lodge and the recreation hall, both of which you may have seen in movies. The park is on 30 acres adjacent to Rocky Mountain National Park. Pets are welcome. Group events such as rallies, reunions, and weddings are not a problem here.

## 110 Carter Valley Campground

**Location:** West of Loveland.
**Affiliations:** AAA.
**Contact:** 970-663-3131, fax 970-663-3737.
**Amenities:** Dump station, laundry, showers, store, public phone, playground.
**Sites:** 57, 48 full hookups.
**Price per night:** $12 to $16.
**Elevation:** 5,200 feet.
**Restrictions:** 40-foot trailer maximum.
**Season:** Year-round.
**Finding the campground:** From Loveland, travel west on U.S. Highway 34, about 7 miles to Carter Lake Road (County Road 29). Turn south and travel about 0.5 mile.

**The campground:** This quiet park is far enough away from the rush of the crowd to make it a pleasant place to stay, yet close enough to allow you to see the sights of the area. Horseback riding and hayrides are available nearby for the young at heart, and the fish are just a few miles down the road. This makes a good base camp for the entire region.

## 111 Estes Park Campground

**Location:** West of Estes Park.
**Affiliations:** Colorado Association of Campgrounds, Cabins, and Lodges.
**Contact:** 970-586-4188.
**Amenities:** Fire rings, playground, picnic tables, hiking trails, public phone, laundry, showers.
**Sites:** 65, no full hookups.
**Price per night:** $17.26 per family.
**Elevation:** 8,200 feet.
**Finding the campground:** From the junction of U.S. Highway 36W and Colorado Highway 66, travel southwest to the end of the road.

**The campground:** Catering to pop-up and tent campers who wish to experience the grandeur of the Rockies, with a few more amenities and a few less people than they would find inside the national park, is the goal at this quiet park. It's a short drive from here, either into town or into the park, so convenience is added to the list of attractive qualities. And the price is hard to beat in this area.

## 112 Estes Park KOA

**Location:** East of Estes Park.
**Affiliations:** KOA.
**Contact:** 970-586-2888, fax 970-586-1828, e-mail jhalstvedt@compuserve.com.
**Reservations:** 800-562-1887.
**Amenities:** Dump station, laundry, showers, store, public phone, playground, cabins, restaurant, tepees, miniature golf.
**Sites:** 115, 28 full hookups.
**Price per night:** $20 to $26.
**Elevation:** 8,200 feet.
**Finding the campground:** From Estes Park, travel 1 mile east on U.S. Highway 34 to the campground.

**The campground:** There's no better way to spend a family vacation than right in the heart of Estes Park at this KOA. Nearby activities besides the national park include golf, shopping, horseback riding, go-carts, and bicycling. This is a good base camp for active people who want to do it all while still enjoying the camping experience.

## 113 Mary's Lake Campground

**Location:** West of Estes Park.
**Affiliations:** Colorado Association of Campgrounds, Cabins, and Lodges.
**Contact:** 970-586-4411, fax 970-586-4493.
**Reservations:** 800-45-6279.
**Amenities:** Dump station, laundry, showers, store, pool, public phone, playground, picnic tables, fire rings.
**Sites:** 90, 40 full hookups.
**Price per night:** $18.50 to $23.
**Elevation:** 8,200 feet.
**Restrictions:** 45-foot trailer maximum.
**Finding the campground:** From the junction of U.S. Highways 34 and 36, go 0.5 mile southeast on US 36, then 1.5 miles southwest on Colorado Highway 7 to Peak View Drive. Turn west and go about 1.5 miles to the campground.

**The campground:** Mary's Lake is a wonderful place to come home to after spending the day exploring the area. If you have any energy left, you can catch your dinner in the lake, then go for an after-dinner walk along one of the hiking trails. Be sure to take your camera to capture that elk you might pass along the way.

## 114 National Park Resort Campground & Cabins

**Location:** West of Estes Park.
**Affiliations:** Colorado Association of Campgrounds, Cabins, and Lodges.
**Contact:** 970-586-4563.
**Amenities:** Dump station, laundry, showers, store, public phone, cabins
**Sites:** 100, 22 full hookups.
**Price per night:** $19 to $21.
**Elevation:** 8,200 feet.
**Finding the campground:** From Estes Park, travel west on U.S. Highway 34 for about 4 miles.

**The campground:** You can't camp much closer to the national park and still have hot showers. The sites at the resort are set among the pines and aspen and are moderately spaced. The park welcomes all types of campers, from those with tents to those with 32-foot trailers. A livery stable is on site. If you choose to forego camping for a night, or if you visit in the winter when the campground is closed, the full-service cabins and motel rooms here are attractive and reasonably priced.

## 115 Riverview RV Park & Campground

**Location:** West of Loveland.
**Affiliations:** Good Sam, Colorado Association of Campgrounds, Cabins, and Lodges.

**Contact:** 970-667-9910.
**Amenities:** Dump station, laundry, showers, store, public phone, playground, cabin, picnic tables, grills.
**Sites:** 173, 128 full hookups.
**Price per night:** $15 to $22.
**Elevation:** 5,100 feet.
**Season:** Year-round.
**Finding the campground:** From Exit 257 on Interstate 25, travel about 10 miles west on U.S. Highway 34.

**The campground:** At this campground, you can forget about the roar of the crowds and listen to the roar of the river. Most of the sites are shaded; some are a stone's throw from the Big Thompson River, where fishing is permitted. The location is ideal for making day trips into Estes Park or Rocky Mountain National Park, as well as into Loveland, Fort Collins, or even Denver.

## 116 Spruce Lake RV Park

**Location:** West of Estes Park.
**Affiliations:** Colorado Association of Campgrounds, Cabins, and Lodges.
**Contact:** 970-586-2889.
**Amenities:** Dump station, laundry, showers, store, pool, public phone, playground, miniature golf, hiking trails, lake/river fishing, tables.
**Sites:** 110, 87 full hookups.
**Price per night:** $16 to $26.25.
**Elevation:** 7,600 feet.
**Season:** Year-round.
**Restrictions:** No tents.
**Finding the campground:** From the junction of U.S. Highways 34 and 36 in Estes Park, travel west through town on Elkhorn Avenue about 0.25 mile. Then turn southwest on Moraine Avenue and travel about 1.5 miles to Mary's Lake Road. Turn left. The campground is on the left.

**The campground:** Spruce Lake is an attractive campground that is a mere 1.5 miles from an entrance of Rocky Mountain National Park. It is one of the few campgrounds in the area with a heated pool. Besides the swimming, there are plenty of activities to allow the kids to burn off all that surplus energy, including free miniature golf and fishing in either the stocked lake or the Big Thompson River.

## 117 Westwood Inn Motel & Campground

**Location:** Longmont.
**Affiliations:** None.
**Contact:** 303-776-2185.
**Amenities:** Laundry, showers, public phone, cabins.
**Sites:** 17, all full hookups.

**Price per night:** $19.
**Elevation:** 5,047 feet.
**Season:** Year-round.
**Restrictions:** No tents.
**Finding the campground:** Located at the intersection of Highway 287 and Main Street in Longmont.

**The campground:** Here is an ideal RV park for extended visits to the Boulder/ Longmont area. Day trips to Estes Park and Rocky Mountain National Park are easily accomplished. Weekly rates are available, as are motel rooms.

# Public

## 118 Rocky Mountain National Park: Aspenglen

**Location:** Fall River entrance.
**Facilities:** Central water, fire rings, picnic tables, flush toilets, public phone nearby.
**Sites:** 54.
**Fee:** $12, plus $10 per vehicle entrance fee.
**Elevation:** 8,230 feet.
**Road conditions:** Paved.
**Management:** National Park Service, 970-586-1399.
**Activities:** Hiking, campfire ranger programs, scenic driving, wildlife viewing, fishing.
**Restrictions:** Seven-night maximum stay.
**Finding the campground:** From Estes Park, travel west on U.S. Highway 34, following the signs to the Fall River entrance. The campground is just beyond the entrance station.

**The campground:** Aspenglen is a beautiful place to stay. The sites are a bit close together, but the serenity of the towering trees settles over the place like a soft quilt. Like all of the campgrounds in the park, Aspenglen fills quickly, but if you arrive near the noon checkout time on a weekday, you should secure a spot. If you arrive on a weekend, a reserved site at either Moraine (Campground 121) or Glacier Basin (Campground 119) would be a safer choice. The Fall River Road is one lane and gravel, making it a real white-knuckle drive, but one of astonishing beauty. Trailheads abound in and near the campground, so this a great home base for day hikes.

## 119 Rocky Mountain National Park: Glacier Basin

**Location:** Bear Lake Road.
**Facilities:** Central water, dump station, fire rings, public phone, picnic tables, flush toilets.

**Sites:** 150.
**Fee:** $14, plus $10 per vehicle entrance fee.
**Elevation:** 8,600 feet.
**Road conditions:** Paved.
**Management:** National Park Service, 970-586-1399.
**Reservations:** 800-365-CAMP.
**Activities:** Hiking, campfire ranger programs, scenic driving, wildlife viewing, fishing, horseback riding.
**Restrictions:** Seven-night maximum stay.
**Finding the campground:** Enter the park on U.S. Highway 36, traveling west to the Beaver Meadows Entrance Station. Turn left just past the station, stay left on Bear Lake Road, and follow the signs about 3 miles to the campground.

**The campground:** Glacier Basin offers perhaps the best views of the mountains out of all the campgrounds in the park. It is also located amid a huge cluster of hiking trails, making exploration on foot easy. Bear Lake shuttle buses pick up and drop off at the campground. Livery stables are a short distance up the road at Sprague Lake. As with the other campgrounds in the park, the sites are a bit closely spaced, but spending time in the park is well worth that small aggravation. It may not seem like it upon arrival, but there are places in the park where you can get away from the crowds. They usually involve hiking, so ask a ranger for help finding trails suitable to your skill level.

## 120 Rocky Mountain National Park: Long's Peak

**Location:** Southeastern edge of the park.
**Facilities:** Central water, fire rings, public phone, picnic tables, flush toilets.
**Sites:** 26.
**Fee:** $12, plus $10 per vehicle entrance fee.
**Elevation:** 9,400 feet.
**Road conditions:** Paved.
**Management:** National Park Service, 970-586-1399.
**Reservations:** None.
**Activities:** Hiking, climbing, wildlife viewing.
**Restrictions:** Three-night maximum stay; tents only.
**Finding the campground:** From Estes Park, travel south on Colorado Highway 7, about 8 miles to reach the campground turnoff.

**The campground:** Long's Peak is a wonderful campground, which offers tent campers an opportunity to experience a less crowded region of the park. Views are incredible, and the challenging Long's Peak Trail begins here. Though by no means an easy hike, the trail, known as the Keyhole, allows non-technical climbers to reach the 14,255 summit of Long's Peak. Check with rangers for more information and trail conditions. Advanced climbers with proper equipment can take on the north and east faces of the highest point in the park.

## 121 Rocky Mountain National Park: Moraine Park

**Location:** Eastern side of the park.
**Facilities:** Central water, dump station, fire rings, public phone, tables, flush toilets.
**Sites:** 247.
**Fee:** $14, plus $10 per vehicle entrance fee.
**Elevation:** 8,150 feet.
**Road conditions:** Paved.
**Management:** National Park Service, 970-586-1399.
**Reservations:** 800-365-CAMP (summer only).
**Activities:** Hiking, campfire ranger programs, scenic driving, wildlife viewing, fishing, horseback riding.
**Season:** Year-round.
**Restrictions:** Seven-night maximum stay.
**Finding the campground:** Enter the park via U.S. Highway 36 at the Beaver Meadows Entrance Station. Go left just past the station and turn right into the campground.

**The campground:** Moraine Park is pretty, but about as crowded as you would expect. You cannot reserve specific sites, but when you check in, ask for a site along the outer edges of the campground. These offer a bit wider spacing, but the real advantage is the meadow view. The best places to see the abundance of wildlife in the park are open meadows, particularly those with a water source. Several trails branch out from the campground, including one to the livery stables. Shuttle buses travel to several destinations from the campground.

## 122 Barbour Ponds State Park

**Location:** East of Longmont.
**Facilities:** Central water, fire rings, picnic tables, vault toilets, dump stations.
**Sites:** 60.
**Fee:** $6, plus $4 daily or $40 annual vehicle pass.
**Elevation:** 4,830 feet.
**Road conditions:** Paved.
**Management:** Colorado Department of Parks and Outdoor Recreation, 970-226-6641.
**Reservations:** 800-678-CAMP, $7 fee.
**Activities:** Fishing.
**Season:** Year-round.
**Finding the campground:** From Exit 240 on Interstate 25, travel west on Colorado Highway 119 about 1 mile. Turn north onto County Road 7 and follow it to the campground.

**The campground:** Though lacking in scenic beauty, the campground at Barbour Ponds allows direct access to some of the best warm-water fishing in the state. The ponds, which originated as gravel pits, are frequently stocked through the fall. Ice fishing and ice skating are popular winter activities here.

## 123 Boyd Lake State Park

**Location:** Northeast of Loveland.
**Facilities:** Central water, fire rings, grills, showers, swim beach, bath house, boat ramp, marina, concrete walking path, playground, picnic tables, vault toilets.
**Sites:** 148.
**Fee:** $7, plus $4 daily or $40 annual vehicle pass.
**Elevation:** 5,000 feet.
**Road conditions:** Paved.
**Management:** Colorado Department of Parks and Outdoor Recreation, 970-669-1739.
**Reservations:** 800-678-CAMP, $7 fee.
**Activities:** Fishing, walking, swimming, water sports, biking.
**Finding the campground:** From Exit 257 on Interstate 25, travel west on U.S. Highway 34, about 3.5 miles to Madison Avenue. Turn north and follow the signs to the park.

**The campground:** Boyd Lake is a haven for water-sports enthusiasts. The grassy campsites are tightly packed in loops just off the lakeshore. There is little shade, but most campers spend their days in or on the water anyway. The lake is divided in half, with one end reserved for fishing and the other for water sports. The campground is located on the sport's end.

So why would you want to stay here if you don't water ski? There are plenty of reasons, sheer beauty being at the top of the list. A concrete path along the western shore affords the opportunity to enjoy the water and an incredible view of the Rockies. Sunsets here are breathtaking. The park makes an ideal midweek stopover; the crowds are smaller and the park is quieter.

## 124 Larimer County Park: Carter Lake

**Location:** West of Loveland.
**Facilities:** Central water, dump station, fire rings, wheelchair-accessible sites, picnic tables, vault toilets, boat ramp, restaurant, boat rentals.
**Sites:** 190.
**Fee:** $6.
**Elevation:** 5,760 feet.
**Road conditions:** One-and-a-half lane, dirt.
**Management:** Larimer County, 970-679-4570.
**Activities:** Fishing, water sports.
**Finding the campground:** From Exit 250 on Interstate 25, travel west on Colorado Highway 56, about 9 miles to County Road 23. Turn north and go 0.5 mile to CR 8E. Turn west and travel about 3.75 miles to CR 31, which circles the lake.

**The campground:** Carter Lake is the largest of the three Larimer County lakes close to Loveland, and the only one where water-skiing is possible. Even with the abundance of sites for skiing in the Loveland area, Carter can get crowded on weekends. The cold water isn't a deterrent to water enthusiasts of northern

Colorado. None of the Larimer County parks has a reservation system, so you always take a chance of finding the park full.

## 125 Boulder County Park: Fairgrounds

**Location:** Longmont.
**Facilities:** Central water, grills, wheelchair-accessible sites, picnic tables, flush toilets.
**Sites:** 52.
**Fee:** $6.
**Elevation:** 5,000 feet.
**Road conditions:** Paved.
**Management:** Boulder County Parks, 303-441-3408.
**Activities:** Shopping, sightseeing, scenic driving.
**Season:** Year-round.
**Finding the campground:** From Exit 240 on Interstate 25, travel west on Colorado Highway 119, about 8 miles (take Business 119 through town) to Hover Street. Turn south and travel about 2.5 miles to the Boulder County Fairgrounds, where the campground is located.

**The campground:** This campground is included as a pleasant stopover in the town of Longmont. It makes a good low-elevation base camp from which to explore the entire region, including Rocky Mountain National Park and the Denver area. A delightful scenic drive from here would be to connect with Colorado Highway 66 (take Hover Street north 3.5 miles) and travel west to Lyons. In Lyons, turn southwest on CO 7 and travel to Peaceful Valley and the junction with CO 72. Travel south on CO 72 to Nederland. There, take CO 119 back to Longmont via Boulder. The drive takes you to the edge of the national park and through historic mining communities.

## 126 Larimer County Park: Flatiron Reservoir

**Location:** West of Loveland.
**Facilities:** Central water, fire rings, wheelchair-accessible sites, picnic tables, vault toilets.
**Sites:** 42.
**Fee:** $6.
**Elevation:** 5,470 feet.
**Road conditions:** Paved.
**Management:** Larimer County, 970-679-4570.
**Activities:** Fishing, hiking, biking.
**Finding the campground:** From Exit 250 on Interstate 25, travel west on Colorado Highway 56, about 9 miles to County Road 23. Turn north and go 0.5 mile to CR 8E. Turn west and travel about 3.75 miles to CR 31, which circles Carter Lake. Turn north and go about 4.5 miles to CR 18E. Turn west and follow the signs to the reservoir.

The campground: Flatiron is the smallest of the lakes in Larimer County that offers camping. No boating is allowed, but plenty of campsites means plenty of fishing possibilities from shore. Hiking and biking trails head south from the lake through the foothills. In early summer, be sure to bring the insect repellent, because the mosquitoes thrive here in the land of runoff lakes.

## 127 Olive Ridge

**Location:** South of Estes Park.
**Facilities:** Central water, fire rings, playground, picnic tables, vault toilets, amphitheater.
**Sites:** 56.
**Fee:** $12.
**Elevation:** 8,350 feet.
**Road conditions:** Paved.
**Management:** Arapaho/Roosevelt National Forest, 303-444-6600.
**Reservations:** 800-282-CAMP, www.nrrc.com, $8.65 fee.
**Activities:** Hiking, fishing, horseback riding.
**Finding the campground:** From Estes Park, travel south on Colorado Highway 7, about 15 miles to the campground.

The campground: Olive Ridge Campground is set in a pine forest with widely spaced sites. The views of Long's Peak to the north are enough to bring most people here, but the hiking trails are another great attraction. Trails from the campground connect with others leading to Wild Basin in Rocky Mountain National Park. The campground makes a good impromptu stopover during the week, but reservations are recommended on weekends.

## 128 Larimer County Park: Pinewood Lake

**Location:** West of Loveland.
**Facilities:** Central water, fire rings, wheelchair-accessible sites, picnic tables, vault toilets, boat ramp.
**Sites:** 16.
**Fee:** $6.
**Elevation:** 6,580 feet.
**Road conditions:** Paved.
**Management:** Larimer County, 970-679-4570.
**Activities:** Fishing, hiking, biking.
**Finding the campground:** From Exit 250 on Interstate 25, travel west on Colorado Highway 56, about 9 miles to County Road 23. Turn north and go 0.5 mile to CR 8E. Turn west and travel about 3.75 miles to CR 31, which circles Carter Lake. Turn north and go about 4.5 miles to CR 18E. Turn west and travel about 4 miles to Pinewood Lake.

The campground: Pinewood offers a bit more seclusion than the other three Larimer County parks. With only 16 places to camp, the crowd is limited. Wakeless boating is allowed on this 100-acre lake, which boasts some of the best trout fishing in the area.

## Additional Campgrounds in the Estes Park Area

|  | Type* | Contact | Location |
|---|---|---|---|
| 7 Pines Campground & Cabins | P (23) | 970-586-3809 | 7 miles E of Estes Park on US 34 |
| Fireside RV Park & Cabins | P (42) | 970-667-2903 | 9.5 miles W of I-25 on US 34, Loveland |
| Greely Campground & RV Park | P (80) | 970-353-6476 | On US 34 in Greely |
| Johnson's Corner Campground | P (143) | 800-322-5416 | 3618 SE Frontage Road, Loveland |
| Loveland RV Village | P (194) | 970-667-1204 | 4421 E US 34, Loveland |
| Manor RV Park & Motel | P (110) | 800-344-3256 | 815 E Riverside Drive, Estes Park |
| Paradise RV Park | P (171) | 970-586-5513 | CO 66 in Estes Park |
| Park Place Camping Resort & Campground | P (110) | 970-586-4230 | 5495 US 36, Estes Park |
| Riverview RV Park & | P (171) | 800-447-9910 | 7806 W US 34, Loveland |
| Lon Hagler | SWA DSP | 970-484-2836 | 5 miles W of Champion on CR 21 |

* See "Key to Abbreviations" p.22—(# of sites)

# Area 12: Frisco, Dillon, and Kremmling

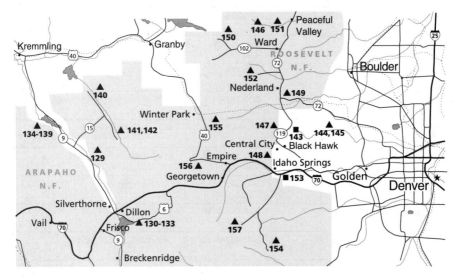

## FRISCO, DILLON, AND KREMMLING

Want to fish a high-mountain lake, bike to Vail, and shop factory outlets all in the same trip without ever leaving the pavement? Dillon Reservoir is the place.

The lake is beautiful and clear, reflecting the glorious peaks that surround it. You can rent a boat or take a guided tour on the water. The national forest campgrounds surrounding the lake are first class, with paved sites set amid lush pine forests.

Farther to the north, lovers of wide-open spaces will find Green Mountain Reservoir. East of the reservoir, in a forgotten section of national forest, are two specialized campgrounds worth investigating. Southfork is for horse lovers, with trailer parking and a corral right in camp. Sugarloaf is for nature lovers for whom typical trails create access problems. A 1,600-foot boardwalk eliminates all the barriers.

Whatever your camping or recreation choice, this area is a wonderful place to stop for a night or the whole summer.

**For More Information:**

Summit County Chamber of Commerce
970-668-5800

# Public

## 129 Blue River

**Location:** North of Dillon.
**Facilities:** Central water, fire rings, picnic tables, vault toilets.
**Sites:** 21.
**Fee:** $9.
**Elevation:** 8,420 feet.
**Road conditions:** two lane, dirt,
**Management:** White River National Forest, 970-468-5400.
**Activities:** Fishing, rafting, kayaking,
**Finding the campground:** From Exit 205 on Interstate 70, travel north on Colorado Highway 9, about 8.5 miles to the campground entrance.

**The campground:** Easy accessibility to the highway makes this an ideal stop-over campground. It is moderately wooded, and some spaces have river access. Rafters and kayakers can use this as a base camp while in the area. The only drawback here is the possibility of road noise, but if you're lucky enough to get a riverside site, all you'll hear is the rush of water. Keep in mind that during spring runoff the Blue River can reach dramatic levels, forcing closure of the campground, so have an alternate plan—Dillon Reservoir perhaps?

## 130 Dillon Reservoir: Heaton Bay

**Location:** Dillon.
**Facilities:** Central water, fire rings, picnic tables, vault toilets, recreation trail.
**Sites:** 72.
**Fee:** $11, plus $4.25 for second vehicle.
**Elevation:** 9,000 feet.
**Road conditions:** Paved.
**Management:** White River National Forest, 970-468-5400.
**Reservations:** 800-280-CAMP, www.nrrc.com, $8.65 fee.
**Activities:** Fishing, biking, shopping, boating, sailing.
**Restrictions:** No water contact sports allowed due to water temperature; wind surfing allowed with full wetsuits; no jet skiing allowed.
**Finding the campground:** From Exit 205 on Interstate 70, go under the interstate to the southeast on Colorado Highway 9. About 1 mile from the interstate, the road splits. CO 9 goes right; U.S. Highway 6 goes left. Take CO 9 along the dam to the campground on the other side.

**The campground:** There's a reason you won't find privately owned RV parks in Dillon: they couldn't compete with the campgrounds on the reservoir. Heaton Bay is beautiful and offers perhaps the best views of the lake and surrounding mountains. Sites are widely set amid massive lodgepole pines. The road and most sites are paved. Heaton Bay also offers access to the Summit County Recreational Trail, which connects Dillon, Frisco, Keystone, Breckenridge, Copper

Mountain, and Vail. This 50-mile, paved trail is open to all forms of non-motorized recreational transportation, but the primary users are bicyclists.

## 131 Dillon Reservoir: Peak One

**Location:** Frisco.
**Facilities:** Central water, fire rings, picnic tables, flush toilets, recreation trail.
**Sites:** 79.
**Fee:** $11, plus $4.25 for second vehicle.
**Elevation:** 9,000 feet.
**Road conditions:** Paved.
**Management:** White River National Forest, 970-468-5400.
**Reservations:** 800-280-CAMP, www.nrrc.com, $8.65 fee.
**Activities:** Fishing, biking, shopping, boating.
**Restrictions:** No water contact sports allowed due to water temperature; wind surfing allowed with full wetsuits; no jet skiing allowed.
**Finding the campground:** From Exit 203 on Interstate 70, travel through Frisco on Colorado Highway 9, about 2.5 miles to the campground turnoff. The turn is clearly marked on the left. Peak One is the first campground on the left.

**The campground:** Peak One has the same sparkling air found in Heaton Bay, but not all the sites have views of the lake. The campground is a short drive from the marina, where canoe rentals and tours can be arranged. Fishing on the reservoir is said to be best in spring. The lake is stocked with trout and small kokanee salmon. Some sites at all of the campgrounds are available first-come, first-served, but they fill quickly, so reservations are a good idea.

## 132 Dillon Reservoir: Pine Cove

**Location:** Frisco.
**Facilities:** Central water, fire rings, picnic tables, vault toilets, recreation trail.
**Sites:** 55.
**Fee:** $10.
**Elevation:** 9,000 feet.
**Road conditions:** Paved.
**Management:** White River National Forest, 970-468-5400.
**Activities:** Fishing, biking, shopping, boating.
**Restrictions:** No water contact sports allowed due to water temperature; wind surfing allowed with full wetsuits; no jet skiing allowed.
**Finding the campground:** From Exit 203 on Interstate 70, travel through Frisco on Colorado Highway 9, about 2.5 miles to the campground turnoff. Pass the turnoff for Peak One Campground and continue north to the clearly marked turnoff to Pine Cove.

**The campground:** Pine Cove has the closest access to a boat ramp of all the campgrounds on the reservoir. The campground itself is just as beautiful and well maintained as the other three. The cities of Dillon and Frisco have a top-notch image to uphold and aren't likely to allow these campgrounds ever to fall into a state of disrepair, even though they are not directly responsible for the management. In the unlikely event that you tire of the lake, don't forget the outlet shopping malls across the highway in Silverthorne.

## 133 Dillon Reservoir: Prospector

**Location:** Near Keystone.
**Facilities:** Central water, fire rings, picnic tables, vault toilets, recreation trail.
**Sites:** 107.
**Fee:** $10, plus $4.25 for second vehicle.
**Elevation:** 9,000 feet.
**Road conditions:** Paved.
**Management:** White River National Forest, 970-468-5400.
**Reservations:** 800-280-CAMP, www.nrrc.com, $8.65 fee.
**Activities:** Fishing, biking, boating.
**Restrictions:** No water contact sports allowed due to water temperature; wind surfing allowed with full wetsuits; no jet skiing allowed.
**Finding the campground:** From Exit 205 on Interstate 70, go under the interstate to the southeast on Colorado Highway 9. About 1 mile from the interstate, the road splits. CO 9 goes right; U.S. Highway 6 goes left. Take US 6 through Dillon toward Keystone. After about 4.25 miles, turn southwest toward the lake and campground.

**The campground:** Prospector is the largest of the four campgrounds on the reservoir. Its distance from the interstate tends to make it the last to fill. If you love to mix golfing with your camping and fishing, this is the campground for you. The Keystone Ranch Golf Club has an 18-hole course designed by Robert Trent Jones, Jr. For more information, call the club at 303-468-4250.

## 134 Green Mountain Reservoir: Cow Creek

**Location:** North of Silverthorne.
**Facilities:** Fire rings, swim beach, vault toilets; no water.
**Sites:** Dispersed.
**Fee:** $3.
**Elevation:** 8,000 feet.
**Road conditions:** two lane, gravel.
**Management:** White River National Forest, 970-468-5400.
**Activities:** Fishing, swimming, boating, sailing, hiking, four-wheel driving.
**Finding the campground:** From Exit 205 on Interstate 70 in Silverthorne, travel north on Colorado Highway 9, about 20 miles to the lake access road.

**The campground:** Cow Creek is the least developed camping area on the reservoir, and it offers unimpeded views of the rugged Gore Mountains. Swimming is allowed off the sandy swim beach, but the water is cold.

## 135 Green Mountain Reservoir: Davis Spring

**Location:** North of Silverthorne.
**Facilities:** Fire rings, vault toilets; no water.
**Sites:** 7.
**Fee:** $5.
**Elevation:** 8,000 feet.
**Road conditions:** two lane, gravel.
**Management:** White River National Forest, 970-468-5400.
**Activities:** Fishing, boating, sailing, hiking, four-wheel driving.
**Finding the campground:** From Exit 205 on Interstate 70 in Silverthorne, travel north on Colorado Highway 9, about 18 miles to the southern access road leading to Prairie Point, Davis Springs, and McDonald Flats campgrounds.

**The campground:** Davis Spring is located on the narrow southern tip of the reservoir. The Gore Range Trailhead is just south of the campground turnoff. This trail traverses the eastern slope of the mountains, meeting up with trails that lead into the Eagle's Nest Wilderness, one of the most rugged wilderness areas in the state. Advanced hikers will find more than 100 miles of challenging trails.

## 136 Green Mountain Reservoir: Elliot Creek

**Location:** North of Silverthorne.
**Facilities:** Central water, fire rings, picnic tables, vault toilets.
**Sites:** 64.
**Fee:** $7.
**Elevation:** 8,000 feet.
**Road conditions:** two lane, gravel.
**Management:** White River National Forest, 970-468-5400.
**Activities:** Fishing, boating, sailing, hiking, four-wheel driving.
**Finding the campground:** From Exit 205 on Interstate 70 in Silverthorne, travel north on Colorado Highway 9, about 27 miles to the northern access road that leads to Willows and Elliot Creek campgrounds.

**The campground:** Elliot Creek is probably the best campground in the vicinity if you plan to fish from a boat or engage in any other water sport. The boat ramp is just down the road in Heeney, as are any forgotten supplies. The views across the lake at the serene Williams Fork Mountains are other reasons to stay here.

## 137 Green Mountain Reservoir: McDonald Flats

**Location:** North of Silverthorne.
**Facilities:** Central water, fire rings, picnic tables, vault toilets.
**Sites:** 13.
**Fee:** $9.
**Elevation:** 8,000 feet.

**Road conditions:** two lane, gravel.
**Management:** White River National Forest, 970-468-5400.
**Activities:** Fishing, boating, sailing, hiking, four-wheel driving.
**Finding the campground:** From Exit 205 on Interstate 70 in Silverthorne, travel north on Colorado Highway 9, about 18 miles to the southern access road leading to Prairie Point, Davis Springs, and McDonald Flats campgrounds.

**The campground:** If you prefer wooded campgrounds, Green Mountain Reservoir isn't likely to attract you. Aptly named, McDonald Flats is situated on the flat shoreline of the southern tip of the lake. All of the campgrounds here allow incredible views of the mountains east and west of this wide valley. The contrast between the two mountain ranges is the very thing that appeals to many who come here. To the west is the jagged, snowcapped Gore Range; to the east are the softly rounded, lush green Williams Fork Mountains. While fishing at Williams Fork, you'll have a good view to the east.

## 138 Green Mountain Reservoir: Prairie Point

**Location:** North of Silverthorne.
**Facilities:** Central water, fire rings, picnic tables, vault toilets.
**Sites:** 24.
**Fee:** $9.
**Elevation:** 8,000 feet.
**Road conditions:** two lane, gravel.
**Management:** White River National Forest, 970-468-5400.
**Activities:** Fishing, boating, sailing, hiking, four-wheel driving.
**Finding the campground:** From Exit 205 on Interstate 70 in Silverthorne, travel north on Colorado Highway 9, about 18 miles to the southern access road leading to Prairie Point, Davis Springs, and McDonald Flats campgrounds.

**The campground:** Prairie Point is one of the two developed campgrounds on the lake. Again, keep in mind that by definition, prairie means flat. This is not your typical mountain camping, but if you come for the fishing and the views, you'll love Green Mountain Reservoir.

## 139 Green Mountain Reservoir: Willows

**Location:** North of Silverthorne.
**Facilities:** Fire rings, vault toilets; no water.
**Sites:** 35.
**Fee:** $7.
**Elevation:** 8,000 feet.
**Road conditions:** two lane, gravel.
**Management:** White River National Forest, 970-468-5400.
**Activities:** Fishing, boating, sailing, hiking, four-wheel driving.
**Finding the campground:** From Exit 205 on Interstate 70 in Silverthorne,

travel north on Colorado Highway 9, about 27 miles to the northern access road that leads to Willows and Elliot Creek campgrounds.

**The campground:** Green Mountain Reservoir is best known for yielding the largest kokanee salmon in the state. Catches are typically 2 pounds and up. Be sure to check posted regulations on both salmon and trout fishing. Willows is a nice campground from which to fish the lake. A boat ramp is available just around the tip of the lake at Heeney. Four-wheel-drive roads into the Gore Mountains also head out from there.

## 140 Horseshoe

**Location:** North of Silverthorne.
**Facilities:** Central water, fire rings, picnic tables, vault toilets.
**Sites:** 7.
**Fee:** $7.
**Elevation:** 8,700 feet.
**Road conditions:** two lane, gravel.
**Management:** Arapaho/Roosevelt National Forest, 970-887-3331.
**Activities:** Hiking, horseback riding, fishing, dirt biking, four-wheel driving.
**Finding the campground:** From Exit 205 on Interstate 70 in Silverthorne, travel northwest on Colorado Highway 9, about 16 miles. Turn east onto County Road 15/Forest Service Road 132. Travel about 10 miles to FSR 138. Turn north and go about 4 miles to the campground entrance.

**The campground:** Horseshoe is small and not well maintained, but it is pretty enough to warrant a visit, especially if dirt bikes and ATVs are your passion. The sites are scattered among a pine and aspen forest on the Williams Fork River. For playing in the dirt, try Forest Service Road 140, which branches off from FSR 139 just north of camp. FSR 253 is another choice. Non-bikers should be aware that dirt lovers frequent this camp. If you're looking for peace and quiet, you might want to move down the road to South Fork or Sugar Loaf.

## 141 South Fork

**Location:** North of Silverthorne.
**Facilities:** Central water, fire rings, picnic tables, vault toilets.
**Sites:** 21.
**Fee:** $7.
**Elevation:** 8,940 feet.
**Road conditions:** two lane, gravel.
**Management:** Arapaho/Roosevelt National Forest, 970-887-3331.
**Activities:** Hiking, horseback riding, fishing, dirt biking, four-wheel driving.
**Finding the campground:** From Exit 205 on Interstate 70 in Silverthorne, travel northwest on Colorado Highway 9, about 16 miles. Turn east onto County Road 15/Forest Service Road 132. Travel about 10 miles to FSR 138. Turn southeast and go about 4 miles to the campground entrance.

**The campground:** Equestrians take note: this campground ranks as one of the best in the state for horseback riders. Some of the spaces have extra parking for trailers, there are two corrals in good condition, and there is an eye-popping trail that brushes the Continental Divide at close to 12,000 feet before returning to camp. The campground feels isolated amid the dense pines. Recent maintenance has involved installation of modernized toilets and new tables and fire rings at many sites. The Williams Fork River is close, providing fishing access as well.

## 142 | Sugarloaf

**Location:** North of Silverthorne.
**Facilities:** Central water, fire rings, picnic tables, wheelchair-accessible sites, vault toilets.
**Sites:** 11.
**Fee:** $7.
**Elevation:** 9,000 feet.
**Road conditions:** two lane, gravel.
**Management:** Routt National Forest, 970-724-9004.
**Activities:** Hiking, horseback riding, fishing, dirt biking, four-wheel driving.
**Finding the campground:** From Exit 205 on Interstate 70 in Silverthorne, travel northwest on Colorado Highway 9, about 16 miles. Turn east onto County Road 15/Forest Service Road 132. Travel about 10 miles to FSR 138. Turn southeast and go about 4 miles to the campground entrance.

**The campground:** Sugarloaf is across the road from South Fork. The two campgrounds share the same dense, isolated atmosphere. The added attractions here are the wheelchair-accessible sites and the Williams Fork Boardwalk, a 1,600-foot-long trail that can be maneuvered by wheelchair.

## Additional Campgrounds in the Frisco/Dillon/Kremmling Areas

| | Type* | Contact | Location |
|---|---|---|---|
| Alpine RV Park | P (19) | 970-724-9655 | 115 W Central, Kremmling |
| Kremmling RV Park | P (43) | 970-724-6593 | 1.5 miles E of Kremmling on CR 22 |
| Wolford Mountain Reservoir | Water Dist. (48) | 970-724-9590 | 5 miles N of Kremmling on US 40 |
| Cataract Creek | NF (4) | 970-468-5400 | 2 miles SW of Green Mountain Reservoir on CR 1725 |
| Pumphouse | BLM (14) | 970-824-4441 | 16 miles SW of Kremmling on Trough Road (CR 1) |
| Radium | BLM (2) | 970-824-4441 | 25 miles S of Kremmling on Trough Road (CR 1) |
| Radium | SWA DSP | 970-248-7175 | 16 miles S of Kremmling on Trough Road (CR 1) |

* See "Key to Abbreviations" p.22—(# of sites)

# Area 13: Black Hawk, Central City, and Boulder

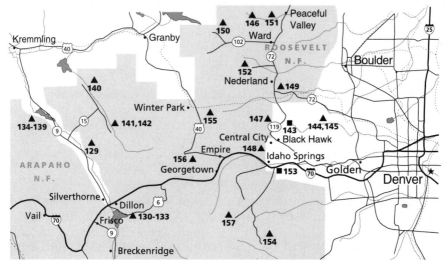

## BLACK HAWK, CENTRAL CITY, AND BOULDER

Step back in time as you pan for gold in this area. These days, the prime search for gold, in the sister cities of Black Hawk and Central City, takes place at the slot machines. Gambling, including blackjack, is a highlight of a visit here, but history buffs may want to spend time walking the towns that once formed the population center of the state. The restored buildings in both communities stand as testament to the riches once found here. They drip with opulence and ornamentation.

Graveyards west of town tell the story of the hard lives lived and lost here as prospectors scraped the earth for the precious metal. Serving as either the sheriff or the preacher here must have seemed like a lost cause as men fought over the gold. Besides the gambling, other area activities include hiking, fishing, four-wheel driving, and even opera.

Camping accommodations are varied, but RV parks are scarce. Golden Gate State Park has some of the best tent camping in the state, but trailer campers will probably be most interested in the national forest camps.

**For More Information:**

Central City
117 Eureka Street; P.O. Box 249

Central City, CO 80427
303-582-5251

Boulder Chamber of Commerce
2440 Pearl Street
Boulder, CO 80302
303-442-1044
www.chamber.boulder.co.us

# Commercial

## 143 Dory Hill/Central City/Black Hawk KOA

**Location:** North of Black Hawk.
**Affiliations:** KOA.
**Contact:** 303-582-9979.
**Reservations:** 800-KOA-1620.
**Amenities:** Dump station, laundry, showers, store, pool, public phone, playground, cabins.
**Sites:** 26, no full hookups.
**Price per night:** $18 to $25.
**Elevation:** 9,230 feet.
**Season:** Year-round.
**Finding the campground:** From Exit 244 on Interstate 70, go north on Colorado Highway 119. Travel about 5 miles beyond Blackhawk to CO 46. Turn right and travel about 0.5 mile to the campground entrance.

**The campground:** Situated in an area rich in scenery, history, and recreation, this small KOA perches on a pine-covered hill. It is the closest privately owned RV park to the casinos of Black Hawk and Central City, plus it's only a short drive from here to attractions in Golden and Denver. This would make a great base camp from which to explore much of north-central Colorado.

# Public

## 144 Golden Gate State Park: Aspen Meadow

**Location:** Northeast of Blackhawk.
**Facilities:** Central water, fire rings, picnic tables, vault toilets.
**Sites:** 35.
**Fee:** $7, plus $4 daily or $40 annual vehicle pass.
**Elevation:** 9,200 feet.
**Road conditions:** Paved.
**Management:** Colorado Department of Parks and Outdoor Recreation, 303-

791-1957.
**Reservations:** 800-678-CAMP, $7 fee.
**Activities:** Hiking, biking, horseback riding.
**Restrictions:** Tents only.
**Season:** Year-round.
**Finding the campground:** From Blackhawk, travel north on Colorado Highway 119 to CO 46. Turn right and continue about 5 miles to the park. The campground is north, on Mountain Base Road, then east on Gap Road.

**The campground:** Golden Gate is a park designed to be enjoyed by outdoor enthusiasts. It has almost as many campsites for tents as it does for trailers. But Aspen Meadow has no trailer sites. Rimrock Loop has sites and parking designed for horseback riders. This beautiful park is best experienced by traveling along one of 12 trails that range from easy to difficult. Mountain biking is allowed on trails only in the portion of the park that lies in Jefferson County. Park rangers can supply maps of all trails at the information centers.

## 145 | Golden Gate State Park: Reverend's Ridge

**Location:** Northeast of Blackhawk.
**Facilities:** Central water, fire rings, picnic tables, flush toilets, showers, dump station, laundry, public phone.
**Sites:** 106.
**Fee:** $10, plus $4 daily or $40 annual vehicle pass.
**Elevation:** 9,200 feet.
**Road conditions:** Paved.
**Management:** Colorado Department of Parks and Outdoor Recreation, 303-791-1957.
**Reservations:** 800-678-CAMP, $7 fee.
**Activities:** Hiking, biking, scenic driving.
**Season:** Year-round.
**Finding the campground:** From Black Hawk, travel north on Colorado Highway 119 to CO 46. Turn right and continue about 5 miles to the park. The campground is north, on Mountain Base Road.

**The campground:** Reverend's Ridge offers the only trailer camping in the park. It is large but tightly spaced. If you're looking to get away from the crowd, this probably isn't the best choice unless it's mid-week. The park sees heavy use by city residents. (Golden is just 13 miles to the south.) However, if you're just looking for a place to sleep after a long day of hiking or biking, Reverend's Ridge has what you need. For a change of pace, you might want to try backcountry camping. The park has twenty-three backcountry tent sites, as well as four three-sided shelters that sleep six people each.

## 146 Camp Dick

**Location:** South of Estes Park.
**Facilities:** Central water, fire rings, picnic tables, vault toilets.
**Sites:** 34.
**Fee:** $12.
**Elevation:** 8,600 feet.
**Road conditions:** two lane, gravel.
**Management:** Arapaho/Roosevelt National Forest, 303-444-6001.
**Reservations:** 800-280-CAMP, www.nrrc.com, $8.65 fee.
**Activities:** Fishing, hiking, four-wheel driving.
**Finding the campground:** From the town of Peaceful Valley on Colorado Highway 72, travel west on County Road 92 for about 1 mile.

**The campground:** This is a campground for those who enjoy an open view of their surroundings. Very few of the sites are wooded, but all are pretty. Trail 910 from the campground connects with the Saint Vrain Glacier Trail near the Indian Peaks Wilderness. This day hike is moderately difficult. The sights along the trail are spectacular, including the glaciers themselves, which are remnants of the great Ice Age. A short trail also leads south to Beaver Reservoir. You can make reservations at Camp Dick and probably should most of the season due to its close proximity to Rocky Mountain National Park.

## 147 Cold Springs

**Location:** North of Black Hawk.
**Facilities:** Central water, fire rings, picnic tables, vault toilets, playground.
**Sites:** 38.
**Fee:** $9, plus $5 for second vehicle.
**Elevation:** 9,200 feet.
**Road conditions:** Paved.
**Management:** Arapaho/Roosevelt National Forest, 303-567-2901.
**Reservations:** 800-280-CAMP, www.nrrc.com, $8.65 fee.
**Activities:** Hiking, scenic driving.
**Finding the campground:** From Black Hawk, travel north on Colorado Highway 119, about 5 miles to the campground.

**The campground:** The sites here are scattered among the aspens atop a hill. The sites have been leveled and upgraded recently. Colorado Highway 119 has been designated a scenic byway; the drive from Black Hawk and beyond the campground to Nederland is a pleasant way to pass the time. Cold Springs is a good place from which to enjoy the activities in the region. These range from panning for gold to hiking the backcountry.

## 148 Columbine

**Location:** Northwest of Central City.
**Facilities:** Central water, fire rings, picnic tables, vault toilets.
**Sites:** 47.
**Fee:** $9.
**Elevation:** 9,020 feet.
**Road conditions:** two lane, dirt, rough.
**Management:** Arapaho/Roosevelt National Forest, 303-567-2901.
**Reservations:** 800-280-CAMP, www.nrrc.com, $8.65 fee.
**Activities:** Hiking, four-wheel driving.
**Finding the campground:** Travel through Black Hawk and Central City to the west. The main road becomes County Road 279 at the edge of Central City. The campground is about 3 miles northwest of town.

**The campground:** Nobody seems to know this campground is here, but it is the ideal place to come home to after a few hours spent trying to claim your share of the "gold" in the casinos. When you're not playing in town, you may want to explore this historic mining region by jeep. You can also grab a pan and try taking home the gold the old-fashioned way.

## 149 Kelly Dahl

**Location:** South of Nederland.
**Facilities:** Central water, fire rings, playground, picnic tables, vault toilets.
**Sites:** 46.
**Fee:** $12.
**Elevation:** 8,600 feet.
**Road conditions:** Paved.
**Management:** Arapaho/Roosevelt National Forest 303-444-6600.
**Reservations:** 800-280-CAMP, www.nrrc.com, $8.65 fee.
**Activities:** Hiking.
**Finding the campground:** From Nederland, travel south on Colorado Highway 119, about 3 miles to the campground.

**The campground:** This is another of the roadside campgrounds that allow you to fully explore the incredibly diverse region along the scenic Peak to Peak Highway. The history of the area, as well as the wide range of activities, make this a wonderful family vacation spot. If you are just passing through on Colorado Highway 119, Kelly Dahl is the best choice for a night's stopover.

## 150 Pawnee

**Location:** West of Ward.
**Facilities:** Central water, fire rings, picnic tables, vault toilets.
**Sites:** 55.
**Fee:** $12.

**Elevation:** 10,350 feet.
**Road conditions:** One-and-a-half lane, gravel.
**Management:** Arapaho/Roosevelt National Forest, 303-444-6600.
**Reservations:** 800-280-CAMP, www.nrrc.com, $8.65 fee.
**Activities:** Fishing, hiking.
**Finding the campground:** From the town of Ward on Colorado Highway 72, travel west on County Road 102, which splits into Forest Service Road 112 and FSR 232. Stay to the right on FSR 112 to the campground. Total distance from CO 72 is about 5 miles.

**The campground:** Pawnee is a high-altitude camp worth considering. The weather will be cool, but the scenery is worth bundling up for. Hiking trails head west from here into the Indian Peaks Wilderness, which gets the heaviest use of any wilderness area in the state. Most of the trails are short and rather steep from this point. Talk to a ranger about one suited to your abilities before setting out. Fishing on Brainard Lake is a short hike from camp, and Long Lake is just a bit farther.

## 151 Peaceful Valley

**Location:** South of Estes Park.
**Facilities:** Central water, fire rings, wheelchair-accessible sites, picnic tables, vault toilets.
**Sites:** 15.
**Fee:** $12.
**Elevation:** 8,500 feet.
**Road conditions:** Paved.
**Management:** Arapaho/Roosevelt National Forest, 303-444-6001.
**Reservations:** 800-280-CAMP, www.nrrc.com, $8.65 fee.
**Activities:** Fishing, hiking, four-wheel driving.
**Finding the campground:** From the town of Peaceful Valley on Colorado Highway 72, travel west on Forest Service Road 92 for about 0.25 mile.

**The campground:** Peaceful Valley has been recently remodeled. All sites are accessible by wheelchair. The road is paved and the sites are graveled. The campground is set in an open meadow, with some sites backing up to the trees and Middle Saint Vrain Creek. Pack trails in the area make this a popular destination for wheelchair-bound people who enjoy horseback riding. Rent horses near town.

## 152 Rainbow Lakes

**Location:** Northwest of Nederland.
**Facilities:** Fire rings, tables, vault toilets; no water.
**Sites:** 16.
**Fee:** $7.
**Elevation:** 10,000 feet.

**Road conditions:** two lane, dirt, rough, and very rocky,
**Management:** Arapaho/Roosevelt National Forest, 303-444-6600.
**Activities:** Fishing, hiking, four-wheel driving.
**Restrictions:** 18-foot maximum trailer length.
**Finding the campground:** From Nederland, travel north on Colorado Highway 72, about 6.5 miles to County Road 116. Turn west and travel about 5 miles to the campground.

**The campground:** Whoever said, "If the road ain't bumpy, the campground's no good," must have been to Rainbow Lakes. This hard-to-reach campground is a real delight for those willing to brave the rough and rocky access road. The sites are widely spaced in a dense forest of pine and spruce. The best news is that you aren't likely to have much company besides the deer. The lakes are a short hike from camp. Come prepared for the cold temperatures that prevail at this elevation. You will likely see snow in the shade almost any time of year.

## Additional Campgrounds in the Black Hawk, Central City, and Boulder Area

| | Type* | Contact | Location |
|---|---|---|---|
| Boulder Mountain Lodge | P (25) | 303-444-0882 | 4 miles W of Boulder on CO 119 |
| Buckingham | CP (10) | 303-441-3408 | 10 miles NW of Nederland on CR 111 |

* See "Key to Abbreviations" p.22—(# of sites)

# Area 14: Idaho Springs and Winter Park

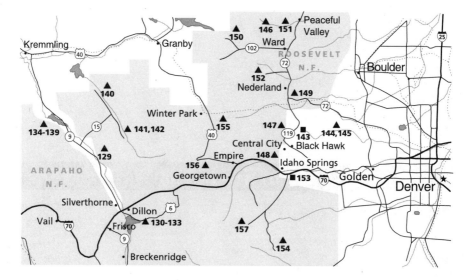

## IDAHO SPRINGS AND WINTER PARK

Though most people familiar with Colorado have heard of Winter Park, the mention of Idaho Springs often brings puzzled looks. Nestled among the mountains along Interstate 70, west of Denver, Idaho Springs is rich in history, bustling with activity, and surrounded by eye-popping scenery.

You can shop here for antiques, sip a beer at a microbrewery, or lunch at an outdoor café. After all that, you can soak your tired body in a mineral bath at Indian Springs Resort before returning to your camp.

You can drive south of town on Colorado Highway 103 to get away from the noise and rush of the interstate. The highway eventually takes you to the 14,264-foot summit of Mount Evans, making it the highest road in the country. Halfway up, you'll find a beautiful lake, a campground, and a café and gift shop.

Probably the best part about vacationing near Idaho Springs is the ability to take day trips into Denver to see the sites, while still enjoying the slower pace of this historical mining community.

But what about Winter Park? The pace here never slows, in any season. From the luge-like Alpine Slide to the 700 miles of mountain-biking trails, there is something for everyone who has a yearning for the outdoors and a sense of adventure.

A drawback to this area is the limited number of camping facilities. (But then, that also can be an advantage, too.) There are a few RV parks worth considering and several national forest camps, but the total number of campsites is just over two hundred. Make reservations where you can, or plan for a mid-week arrival to ensure a spot.

**For More Information:**

Idaho Springs Visitor Center
2200 Miner Street
P.O. Box 97
Idaho Springs, CO 80452
303-547-4382

Winter Park/Fraser Valley Chamber of Commerce
P.O. Box 3236
Winter Park, CO 80482
800-722-4118

# Commercial

## 153 Indian Springs Resort

**Location:** Idaho Springs.
**Affiliations:** None.
**Contact:** 303-989-6666.
**Amenities:** Dump station, picnic tables, public phone, mineral baths, vapor caves, pool.
**Sites:** 32, no full hookups.
**Price per night:** $15.25.
**Elevation:** 8,000 feet.
**Season:** Year-round.
**Finding the campground:** From Exit 240 on Interstate 70, travel about 100 yards north on Colorado Highway 103, 0.5 mile east on Miner Street, and then about 100 yards on Soda Creek Road.

**The campground:** The campground here is nothing but a parking lot, but if you want to enjoy the mineral baths, this is the closest place. The resort offers private tubs, both indoor and out, as well as geothermal caves and an indoor mineral swimming pool. The seventh night in the campground is free if you pay for the full week upon arrival. Just think of how good you'll feel after a whole week of soaking in the mineral water. If you only plan to treat yourself to a one-time soak, the outdoor whirlpools are a wonderful way to relax. Each tub is tucked away in its own fenced enclosure, complete with shower and a view of the mountainside.

# Public

## 154 Echo Lake

**Location:** Southwest of Idaho Springs.
**Facilities:** Central water, fire rings, picnic tables, vault toilets.
**Sites:** 17.
**Fee:** $9, plus $4 for second vehicle.
**Elevation:** 10,600 feet.
**Road conditions:** Paved.
**Management:** Arapaho/Roosevelt National Forest, 303-567-2901.
**Reservations:** 800-280-CAMP, www.nrrc.com, $8.65 fee.
**Activities:** Biking, fishing, scenic driving, horseback riding.
**Finding the campground:** From Exit 240 on Interstate 70, travel southwest on Colorado Highway 103, about 13 miles to the campground.

**The campground:** Echo Lake is one of the few campgrounds over 10,000-feet in elevation that you could easily drive to in the dark if it were necessary. The road is a little windy but plenty wide. The campground is not on the lake itself, but rather across the road from it. Sites are set in a pine forest, most with enough space to afford some privacy. The camp has a beautiful tent area separate from the main camp. Driving the Mount Evans Highway to the 14,264-foot summit is the main attraction here. It isn't the highest peak in the state, but it is the highest paved highway. Hiking is the other reason people come here. Trails from camp lead into the Mount Evans State Wildlife Area and the Mount Evans Wilderness, including one trail that almost reaches the top of Mount Evans itself.

## 155 Idlewild

**Location:** South of Winter Park.
**Facilities:** Central water, fire rings, picnic tables, vault toilets, bike path.
**Sites:** 26.
**Fee:** $9.
**Elevation:** 9,000 feet.
**Road conditions:** Paved.
**Management:** Arapaho/Roosevelt National Forest, 970-887-3331.
**Activities:** Hiking, biking, fishing, horseback riding, four-wheel driving, Alpine Slide, tennis, golf.
**More information:** Winter Park/Fraser Valley Chamber of Commerce 303-726-4118.
**Finding the campground:** From Winter Park, travel about 1 mile south on U.S. Highway 40 to the campground entrance.

**The campground:** Winter Park may be best known for its winter sports, but campers will find a wide range of activities to enjoy during the summer as well. Idlewild is the perfect place from which to do it all. The Winter Park Trail, a paved recreation trail, cuts right through the campground, making bicycling an ideal form of recreation. There are also hundreds of miles of mountain biking trails throughout the area. The campground itself is very pretty, with widely spaced and heavily wooded sites. The only potential problem is the traffic noise, but if you really want to "do" Winter Park, this is the closest place to camp.

## 156 Mizpah

**Location:** West of Empire.
**Facilities:** Central water, fire rings, picnic tables, vault toilets.
**Sites:** 10.
**Fee:** $9.
**Elevation:** 9,600 feet.
**Road conditions:** Paved.
**Management:** Arapaho/Roosevelt National Forest, 303-567-2901.
**Activities:** Fishing, scenic driving.
**Finding the campground:** From Exit 232/233 on Interstate 70, travel northwest on U.S. Highway 40 through Empire. The campground is about 7 miles from Empire. The entrance is on the left.

**The campground:** Mizpah is a traveler's dream. It has access to two major highways that make it a good base for exploring the whole Interstate 70 area between Denver and Dillon. Besides that, there's a good Italian restaurant just down the road. The sites are widely spaced in a terraced fashion, up the side of a hill. At first glance it would seem that the higher sites would be choicest, but the lower ones have the advantage of the rushing creek to drown out the considerable traffic noise from US 40. That noise and the lack of reservations are the only drawbacks here.

## 157 West Chicago Creek

**Location:** Southwest of Idaho Springs.
**Facilities:** Central water, fire rings, picnic tables, vault toilets.
**Sites:** 16.
**Fee:** $7.55, plus $4 for second vehicle.
**Elevation:** 9,600 feet.
**Road conditions:** One-and-a-half lane, gravel, somewhat rough.
**Management:** Arapaho/Roosevelt National Forest, 303-567-2901.
**Reservations:** 800-280-CAMP, www.nrrc.com, $8.65 fee.
**Activities:** Fishing, hiking, horseback riding, scenic driving.
**Finding the campground:** From Exit 240 on Interstate 70, travel southwest on Colorado Highway 103, about 6 miles to Forest Service Road 188. Turn southwest and go about 4 miles to the campground.

**The campground:** Leave the interstate behind and get away from the crowds at this pretty campground. Sites are set amid a light pine and aspen forest. They have recently been improved and leveled. Fishing at Lake Edith is a short hike from camp. Clear Lake is a second option, but it requires a lengthy hike. A pack/saddle trail heads south from Lake Edith up the side of Gray Wolf Mountain. If you need a change from the peace of the forest, the drive to the top of Mount Evans is incredible.

## Additional Campgrounds in the Idaho Springs and Winter Park Area

| | Type* | Contact | Location |
|---|---|---|---|
| Cottonwood RV Campground | P (20) | 303-567-2617 | 1.5 miles S of Idaho Springs on CO 103 |
| Mountian Meadow Camp | P (50) | 303-569-2424 | 3 miles W of I-70 on US 40 |
| Snow Mountain YMCA of the Rockies | P (35) | 970-725-4628 | Milepost 219 on US 40 between Winter Park and Granby |
| Byers Creek | NF (6) | 970-887-3331 | 7 miles SW of Fraser on FSR 160 |
| Clear Lake | NF (8) | 970-567-2901 | 4 miles S of Georgetown on FSR 118 |
| Guanella Pass | NF (18) | 303-567-2901 | 8 miles S of Georgetown on FSR 118 |
| St. Louis Creek | NF (18) | 970-887-3331 | 3 miles S of Fraser on FSR 160 |

* See "Key to Abbreviations" p.22—(# of sites)

# Area 15: Denver Metro

## DENVER METRO

Denver is Colorado's crown-jewel capital. Known as the "Mile-High City," it sprawls among the foothills just east of the Rockies, and like any city its size, it is prone to air pollution and traffic jams. But those are about the only drawbacks to vacationing in the Denver area. Except in the winter, the weather is near perfect, with sunny days and cool nights.

The list of things to do here is long and includes golfing on twenty public courses, tennis at most city parks, and five amusement parks, including a water park. The Colorado State Capitol and the U.S. Mint are high on the list of popular tours. Want museums? There's the Colorado History Museum, the Children's Museum, the Denver Art Museum, the Denver Museum of Natural History, and the Museum of Western Art, just to name a few. And don't forget the fabulous zoo.

As for nightlife, there's everything from theater to comedy. Dining choices range from gourmet to fast food, and the entire city is a shopper's paradise. From Southwest art to designer clothing, if you can't find it in Denver, it probably isn't available anywhere.

Where do you camp to enjoy all of this? There are dozens of commercial choices, many just a short drive from all the fun. But if you're looking for some green space and a wide range of outdoor activities to mix with your metro vacation, the best places to camp are at the two state parks on the southern edge of the city.

Chatfield and Cherry Creek are two of Colorado's most popular family camping destinations. They deftly blend wildlife habitat with outdoor recreation. Make your reservations early.

**For More Information:**

Denver Metro Visitor and Convention Bureau
303-892-1112 or 800-645-3446
www.denver.org

# Commercial

## 158 Chief Hosa Campground

**Location:** West of Denver.
**Affiliations:** Colorado Association of Campgrounds, Cabins, and Lodges.
**Contact:** 303-526-7329, fax 303-526-5330.
**Amenities:** Dump station, laundry, showers, pool, public phone, playground, picnic tables, hiking trails.
**Sites:** 198, 3 full hookups.
**Price per night:** $16 to $21.
**Elevation:** 7,700 feet.
**Finding the campground:** Take Exit 253 off Interstate 70.

**The campground:** Chief Hosa is easily accessible from the interstate, but it offers more than parking-lot camping. Situated on 55 wooded acres, the park has hiking trails and beautiful views of the Continental Divide. You can explore attractions both in Denver and the surrounding area from here, making it an ideal family destination camp.

## 159 Dakota Ridge RV Park

**Location:** South of Golden.
**Affiliations:** Good Sam; Colorado Association of Campgrounds, Cabins, and Lodges.
**Contact:** 303-279-1625, fax 303-279-5027.
**Reservations:** 800-398-1625.
**Amenities:** Dump station, laundry, showers, store, public phone, playground, picnic tables, grills.
**Sites:** 141, all full hookups.
**Price per night:** $27.
**Elevation:** 5,300 feet.
**Restrictions:** No tents.

**Season:** Year-round.

**Finding the campground:** From Exit 262 on Interstate 70, travel west on Colfax Avenue about 2 miles to the campground.

**The campground:** This grassy RV park makes a good base camp for exploring the Denver area and points west. A short drive into Golden takes you to shopping, delightful restaurants, and of course, the Coors Brewery. Tours of the brewery last about half an hour and end in the tasting room. Call 303-277-BEER for more information.

## 160 Denver Meadows RV Park

**Location:** Aurora.
**Affiliations:** Colorado Association of Campgrounds, Cabins, and Lodges.
**Contact:** 303-364-9483.
**Amenities:** Cabins, laundry, showers, public phone, picnic tables, grills, playground, whirlpool, swimming pool.
**Sites:** 287, all full hookups.
**Price per night:** $22.
**Elevation:** 5,280 feet.
**Season:** Year-round.
**Finding the campground:** From the intersection of Interstates 70 and 225, at Exit 282, go 2 miles south on I-225 to Exit 10, then 1 block south on Colfax Avenue, and then 0.25 mile north on Potomac.

**The campground:** Denver Meadows offers about what you would expect from an RV park with 287 sites: tight spacing and limited shade. Its advantage is its proximity to many of Denver's family attractions. From here you can easily take in a tour at the U.S. Mint, select from the array of museums downtown, and visit the first-rate zoo. The wonderful thing about the zoo here is that it isn't spread over thousands of acres. It's compact but still spectacular. After a day of touring with the kids, what parent wouldn't appreciate a soak in the whirlpool back at camp?

## 161 Denver North Campground & RV Park

**Location:** Broomfield.
**Affiliations:** Colorado Association of Campgrounds, Cabins, and Lodges.
**Contact:** 303-452-4150.
**Amenities:** Laundry, showers, public phone, cabins, store, picnic tables, grills, playground, swimming pool.
**Sites:** 150, 80 full hookups.
**Price per night:** $15 to $23.50.
**Elevation:** 5,300 feet.
**Season:** Year-round.
**Finding the campground:** From Exit 229 on Interstate 25, go about 100 yards east on Colorado Highway 7 to the park.

**The campground:** This shady campground gets you out of the hustle and bustle of the city but keeps you close enough to make day trips to Denver and Boulder. It's also a perfect stopover along I-25.

# Public

## 162 Chatfield State Park

**Location:** Southwest Denver.
**Facilities:** Water, electricity, laundry, flush toilets, dump station, showers, swim beach, bath house, snack bar, boat ramps, marina, boat rentals, personal-water-craft rentals, hiking trails, bike trails, horseback trails, horse rental, wheelchair-accessible trails, water-fowl preserve.
**Sites:** 153.
**Fee:** $7 to $10, plus $4 daily or $40 annual vehicle pass.
**Elevation:** 5,432 feet.
**Road conditions:** Paved.
**Management:** Colorado Department of Parks and Outdoor Recreation 303-791-1957.
**Reservations:** 800-678-CAMP, $7 fee.
**Activities:** Fishing, water sports, biking, hiking, horseback riding, birding.
**Finding the campground:** From Colorado Highway 470, travel south on U.S. Highway 85 about 4 miles. Turn west onto Titan Road, then right onto Roxborough Road. Travel about 1 mile to the park. The campground is just beyond the entrance gate.

**The campground:** As you can see from the list of facilities, this is a park with something for everyone, but it isn't the kind of place you visit to relax and take in the scenery. The campground on the shore of Chatfield Lake is a busy place. If you don't want to be awakened by boaters at dawn, try another place to camp. However, if you love to cram as much into one vacation as possible, you have found your spot, because if you run out of things to do at Chatfield, there's all of Denver waiting just over your shoulder. Reservations are a must throughout the summer.

## 163 Cherry Creek State Park

**Location:** Southeast Denver.
**Facilities:** Water, electricity, dump station, laundry, showers, swim beach, bath house, snack bar, boat ramps, marina, boat rentals, sailboard rentals, personal-watercraft rentals, hiking trails, biking trails, horseback trails, horse rentals, nature trails.
**Sites:** 102.

**Fee:** $7 to $10, plus $4 daily or $40 annual vehicle pass.

**Elevation:** 5,550 feet.

**Road conditions:** Paved.

**Management:** Colorado Department of Parks and Outdoor Recreation, 303-791-1957.

**Reservations:** 800-678-CAMP, $7 fee.

**Activities:** Swimming, hiking, biking, horseback riding, water sports.

**Finding the campground:** From downtown Denver, drive southeast on Colorado Highway 83. The park entrance is 1 mile south of Interstate 225 on Parker Road. The campground is north of this entrance.

**The campground:** Like Chatfield, Cherry Creek is a place oriented to the recreation junkie and families with active kids. The difference between the two parks is the ratio of water to land. The lake takes up almost half of the total park area at Chatfield, whereas less than one-fourth of Cherry Creek State Park is water. That means a greater abundance of green space here and larger areas in which to find a moment or two of peace.

## Additional Campgrounds in the Denver Metro Area

| | Type* | Contact | Location |
|---|---|---|---|
| Barr Lake RV Park | P (98) | 800-654-7988 | 17189 E 136 Avenue, Brighton |
| Delux RV park | P (29) | 303-433-0452 | 5520 N Federal, Denver |
| Elms Mobile Home Park | P (20) | 303-341-1820 | 15680 E Colfax, Aurora |
| Flying Saucer RV Park | P (120) | 303-789-1707 | 2500 W Hampton, Englewood |
| Golden's Scenic Rock Park | P (141) | 303-279-1625 | 17700 E Colfax, Golden |
| Northeast Denver/Pepperpod KOA | P (75) | 303-536-4673 | I-76, exit 31, Hudson |
| Prospector RV Park | P (70) | 800-344-5702 | I-70, exit 266, Wheatridge |
| Stagestop Campground | P (15) | 303-697-4901 | 8884S US 285, Morrison |
| Westwood Campground | P (16) | 303-776-2185 | 1550 N Main, Longmont |
| Bear Creek Lake Park | MP (52) | 303-697-6159 | Morrison Road and CR 470 |
| Golden Clear Creek RV Park | MP (38) | 303-278-1437 | 10th Street, Golden |
| Bergen Peak | SWA DSP | 303-297-1192 | 3 miles NW of Evergreen on Stagecoach Boulevard |
| Mount Evans | SWA | 303-297-1192 | 10 miles W of Evergreen off CO 74 |

* See "Key to Abbreviations" p.22—(# of sites)

# Area 16: Vail and Leadville

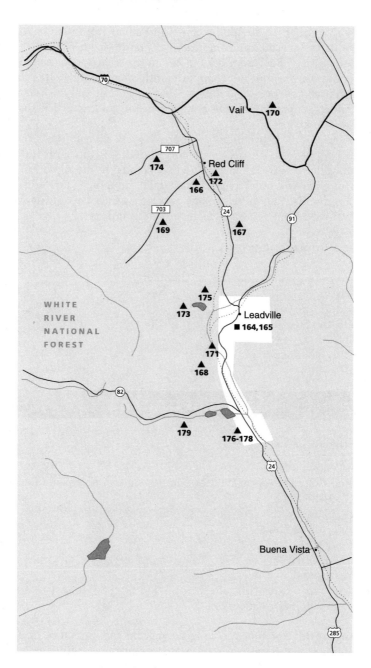

# VAIL AND LEADVILLE

Vail and Leadville are only 34 miles apart, but they are polar opposites in a socioeconomic sense. Vail is home to the rich and super rich. Million-dollar homes line lush green golf courses that are woven among the ski runs. Leadville is a once-bustling gold-mining town now occupied by quaint shops in restored buildings and frequented by middle-class Coloradans from rustic homes.

The mountains surrounding these two communities are what draw most people to the area. They are works of art in emerald green, slate gray, and alabaster snow. Throughout the summer months, snowmelt creates enchanting waterfalls that will surprise and delight. Besides golf in Vail, visitors can hike, bike, raft, ride the chair lifts, ride horses, pan for gold, and fish some of the prettiest lakes in all of Colorado.

History buffs will enjoy hiking or four-wheel driving to the remote ghost town of Holy Cross City. An easier historical outing is to Camp Hale on U.S. Highway 24, where soldiers once trained for combat in the Alps.

Except for a handful of RV parks in Leadville, camping is limited to national forest campgrounds. But these include some easy-in, easy-out highway stop-overs and off-road camps that are secluded and primitive.

**For More Information:**

Leadville/Lake County Chamber of Commerce
809 Harrison
P.O. Box 861
Leadville, CO 80461
719-486-3900
www.leadvilleusa.com

## Commercial

### 164  Leadville RV Corral

**Location:** Leadville.
**Affiliations:** Colorado Association of Campgrounds, Cabins, and Lodges.
**Contact:** 719-486-3111.
**Amenities:** Laundry, showers, public phone, picnic tables, grills, dump station.
**Sites:** 33, all full hookups.
**Price per night:** $16.
**Elevation:** 9,600 feet.
**Season:** Year-round.
**Finding the campground:** From the junction of U.S. Highway 24 and West 2nd Street, go 300 feet west on 2nd St.

**The campground:** For those looking to soak up the ambiance of a restored mining community, this campground in the center of Leadville is the solution.

The mountain views from Leadville are some of the best in the state. Flatlanders from all over make Leadville their second home, just so they can enjoy the views. Activities in the area include antique shopping, golf, hiking, four-wheel driving, river rafting, and horseback riding.

## 165 Sugar Loafin' Campground

**Location:** West of Leadville.
**Affiliations:** Colorado Association of Campgrounds, Cabins, and Lodges.
**Contact:** 719-486-1031.
**Amenities:** Dump station, laundry, public phone, store, picnic tables, grills, fire rings, playground, bike rentals, river fishing, tours.
**Sites:** 98, 38 full hookups.
**Price per night:** $19.05 to $22.12.
**Elevation:** 9,696 feet.
**Finding the campground:** From milepost 177 on U.S. Highway 24, turn northwest onto County Road 4. Go 3.5 miles to the campground

**The campground:** A spark of the gold fever that once ruled the region comes with this campground. You can pan for gold right from camp. They have all the supplies you need in the store. When you've made your fortune you can either kick back in your lawn chair and enjoy a beautiful skyline that includes Colorado's two highest peaks,or head out to blow your gold on the many activities offered in the area—everything from jeep tours to rafting trips.

# Public

## 166 Blodgett

**Location:** South of Red Cliff.
**Facilities:** Central water, fire rings, picnic tables, vault toilets.
**Sites:** 6.
**Fee:** $7.
**Elevation:** 8,900 feet.
**Road conditions:** One-and-a-half lane, gravel.
**Management:** White River National Forest, 970-827-5715.
**Activities:** Fishing.
**Finding the campground:** Red Cliff is south of Vail on U.S. Highway 24. From Red Cliff, travel south on US 24 about 3 miles. Turn west onto Forest Service Road 703. The campground is about 0.5 mile down this road.

**The campground:** This tiny campground is included here because it is a quiet stopover with incredible views. The open meadow surrounding the camp is the perfect place to await the evening arrival of wildlife. Deer and elk water frequently at Homestake Creek. If you choose to stay a day, fishing is possible here and upstream at Homestake Reservoir.

## 167 Camp Hale

**Location:** North of Leadville.
**Facilities:** Central water, fire rings, picnic tables, vault toilets.
**Sites:** 21.
**Fee:** $8.
**Elevation:** 9,200 feet.
**Road conditions:** two lane, gravel.
**Management:** White River National Forest, 970-827-5715.
**Reservations:** 800-280-CAMP, www.nrrc.com, $8.65 fee.
**Activities:** Fishing, hiking.
**Finding the campground:** From Leadville, travel north on U.S. Highway 24, about 17 miles. Turn east onto Forest Service Road 716 to the campground.

**The campground:** Camp Hale is situated on the former training grounds of the 10th Mountain Division. More than 11,000 soldiers trained here for Alpine battle during World War I. All that remains of the training camp are the building foundations, but it only takes a bit of imagination to see the valley and surrounding mountains bustling with uniforms.

The mountain meadow campground has views of this historical site against a backdrop of the stunning Sawatch Range. The campsites are lightly forested and moderately spaced. Fishing is possible in Eagle River and Resolution Creek, both just a short walk from camp. Access to the Colorado Trail is south of camp.

## 168 Elbert Creek

**Location:** Southwest of Leadville.
**Facilities:** Central water, fire rings, picnic tables, vault toilets.
**Sites:** 17.
**Fee:** $9.
**Elevation:** 10,000 feet.
**Road conditions:** One-and-a-half lane, gravel.
**Management:** San Isabel National Forest, 719-486-0749.
**Activities:** Fishing, hiking, four-wheel driving.
**Finding the campground:** From Leadville, travel southwest on U.S. Highway 24, about 3 miles to County Road 300. Go 0.75 mile west to Forest Service Road 110, and then go about 6 miles to the campground.

**The campground:** For those who aren't satisfied just looking at the mountains from a distance, this high-country campground is the place to camp. From here you have access to both the Colorado Trail and the Mount Massive Wilderness. Forest Service Road 110 continues beyond the camp, eventually turning into a jeep road that makes it most of the way to the top of Casco Peak. It passes an abandoned mine along the way. Fishing is possible in Halfmoon Creek where it flows past the campground.

## 169 Gold Park

**Location:** Southwest of Red Cliff.
**Facilities:** Central water, fire rings, picnic tables, vault toilets.
**Sites:** 11.
**Fee:** $7.
**Elevation:** 9,300 feet.
**Road conditions:** One-and-a-half lane, gravel.
**Management:** White River National Forest, 970-827-5715.
**Activities:** Fishing, four-wheel driving, horseback riding.
**Finding the campground:** Red Cliff is south of Vail on U.S. Highway 24. From Red Cliff travel south on US 24 about 3 miles. Turn west onto Forest Service Road 703. The campground is about 9 miles down this road.

**The campground:** Gold Park affords one of the best opportunities to get close to the Holy Cross Wilderness. Hiking, jeep, and pack/saddle trails will take you the rest of the way into the wilderness. Fishing opportunities from this quiet campground include Homestake Creek and several small tributaries, as well as Homestake Reservoir. If it's solitude you seek, break out your lawn chair because this is the place for you.

## 170 Gore Creek

**Location:** East of Vail.
**Facilities:** Central water, fire rings, picnic tables, vault toilets.
**Sites:** 25.
**Fee:** $9.
**Elevation:** 8,700 feet.
**Road conditions:** Paved.
**Management:** White River National Forest, 970-827-5715.
**Activities:** Fishing, hiking, biking, sightseeing, golf.
**Finding the campground:** From Exit 180 on Interstate 70, turn left under the underpass, then left again onto Bighorn Road. Travel east about 2.5 miles to the campground.

**The campground:** Gore Creek is the closest campground to Vail, public or private. It is set in a dense aspen, pine, and spruce forest. Most of the sites are widely spaced, with some pull-throughs. The one drawback is the traffic noise from I-75. Fishing in nearby Gore Creek is subject to "Gold Medal" restrictions designed to protect native trout. So check posted information. Bicycle paths traverse the city, making bikes the preferred mode of transportation in this congested community of the wealthy. Golf is the predominate summer pastime, while skiing reigns in winter. Unfortunately, the campground closes in early

September, creating a complete lack of camping accommodations in the immediate area during ski season.

## 171 Halfmoon

**Location:** Southwest of Leadville.
**Facilities:** Central water, fire rings, picnic tables, vault toilets.
**Sites:** 24.
**Fee:** $9.
**Elevation:** 9,900 feet.
**Road conditions:** One-and-a-half lane, gravel.
**Management:** San Isabel National Forest, 719-486-0749.
**Activities:** Fishing, hiking, four-wheel driving.
**Finding the campground:** From Leadville, travel southwest on U.S. Highway 24, about 3 miles to County Road 300. Go 0.75 mile west to Forest Service Road 110, and then go about 5.5 miles to the campground.

**The campground:** Halfmoon is a beautiful campground set amid the pines. The sites are moderately spaced. Access to the Colorado Trail is just up the road beyond Elbert Creek Campground (Campground 168). From Halfmoon you can enjoy everything the area has to offer: rafting trips, gold panning, shopping, golfing, or just kicking back and doing absolutely nothing.

## 172 Horn Silver

**Location:** South of Red Cliff.
**Facilities:** Central water, fire rings, picnic tables, vault toilets.
**Sites:** 12.
**Fee:** $8.
**Elevation:** 8,800 feet.
**Road conditions:** Paved.
**Management:** White River National Forest, 970-827-5715.
**Activities:** Fishing, hiking.
**Finding the campground:** Red Cliff is south of Vail on U.S. Highway 24. From Red Cliff, travel 2.5 miles south on US 24 to the campground.

**The campground:** Horn Silver makes a nice place to stop for the night. The scenery in both directions on US 24 is too spectacular to miss because of darkness. If you happen to get here and find the campground full, Blodgett (Campground 166) is just 0.5 mile south. Horn Silver is pretty and offers fishing access to Homestake Creek. The trailhead into the Holy Cross Wilderness is near the camp. You might consider this as a destination campground if you want to be close to the action in Vail (like the golf), but be prepared for the constant coming and going of others who are just passing through.

## 173 | Parry Peak

**Location:** West of Twin Lakes.
**Facilities:** Central water, fire rings, wheelchair-accessible sites, picnic tables, vault toilets.
**Sites:** 26.
**Fee:** $9.
**Elevation:** 9,500 feet.
**Road conditions:** Paved.
**Management:** San Isabel National Forest, 719-486-0749.
**Activities:** Fishing, hiking, scenic driving.
**Finding the campground:** From Twin Lakes, travel 2.7 miles west on County Road 82 to the campground.

**The campground:** This lightly forested campground on Lake Creek is a wonderful stopover or fishing destination. It has recently been rejuvenated, including some reforestation of young pines. It has modernized toilets, new level parking, and tent pads. The sites are a bit close together, but the campground is not usually busy. It is ideal for those who like a mix of lake and stream fishing.

## 174 | Tigiwon

**Location:** Southwest of Vail.
**Facilities:** Fire rings, tables, vault toilets, lodge; no water.
**Sites:** 9.
**Fee:** $7.
**Elevation:** 9,900 feet.
**Road conditions:** one lane, dirt, winding.
**Management:** White River National Forest, 970-827-5715.
**Activities:** Hiking, horseback riding.
**Finding the campground:** From Exit 171 on Interstate 70, travel south on U.S. Highway 24 about 5 miles. Turn southwest onto Forest Service Road 707 and travel about 6 miles to the campground.

**The campground:** For most vehicle campers, Tigiwon is about as close to backcountry camping as you can get. The quiet surrounds you here, broken only by the call of the wild. The views along Tigiwon Road (Forest Service Road 707) are fabulous as you near the Holy Cross Wilderness. Hiking and pack/saddle trails will take you all the way to the remote ghost town known as Holy Cross City. There is a lodge near Tigiwon available to groups of up to 150.

## 175 | Turquoise Lake

**Location:** West of Leadville.
**Facilities:** Central water, fire rings, wheelchair-accessible sites, picnic tables, vault toilets.
**Sites:** 243.

**Fee:** $10 to $11, plus fee for second vehicle.
**Elevation:** 9,900 feet.
**Road conditions:** two lane, gravel.
**Management:** San Isabel National Forest, 719-486-0749.
**Reservations:** 800-280-CAMP, www.nrrc.com, $8.65 fee.
**Activities:** Fishing, hiking, four-wheel driving, horseback riding, golf.
**Finding the campground:** From Leadville, travel west on Forest Service Road 105 (Sixth Street), about 6 miles to FSR 104. Turn north to reach all of the campgrounds except May Queen, which is accessed from the west end of the lake.

**The campground:** Seven campgrounds line the shores of Turquoise Lake: Baby Doe, Belle of Colorado, Father Dyer, May Queen, Molly Brown, Silver Dollar, and Tabor. The 243 available campsites attest to the popularity of this recreational mecca. Tell anyone familiar with Colorado that you are going to Leadville and they will likely ask, "To Turquoise Lake?" The fishing is top-notch and the mountain views beautiful, but don't come here looking to get away from the crowds, because they will be here waiting for you all summer.

## 176 Twin Lakes: Dexter

**Location:** South of Leadville.
**Facilities:** Central water, fire rings, picnic tables, vault toilets, boat ramp.
**Sites:** 26.
**Fee:** $9.
**Elevation:** 9,300 feet.
**Road conditions:** two lane, gravel.
**Management:** San Isabel National Forest, 719-486-0749.
**Activities:** Fishing, hiking, scenic driving.
**Finding the campground:** From Leadville, travel south on U.S. Highway 24 to Colorado Highway 82. Turn west and travel to the lakes. The campground access is on the left.

**The campground:** The Twin Lakes area between Buena Vista and Leadville is a very popular fishing destination. There are three campgrounds from which to choose. If you love camping right on the shore, Dexter is your choice. There are no trees to impede your view of the lake or the surrounding mountains. The Colorado Trail passes the camp as it circles the lakes, so hiking is the second most popular activity here after fishing.

## 177 Twin Lakes: Lakeview

**Location:** South of Leadville.
**Facilities:** Central water, fire rings, picnic tables, vault toilets.
**Sites:** 59.
**Fee:** $9.
**Elevation:** 9,500 feet.

**Road conditions:** two lane, gravel.
**Management:** San Isabel National Forest, 719-486-0749.
**Reservations:** 800-280-CAMP, www.nrrc.com, $8.65 fee.
**Activities:** Fishing, hiking, scenic driving.
**Finding the campground:** From Leadville, travel south on U.S. Highway 24 to Colorado Highway 82. Turn west toward the lakes. The access road to Lakeview is on the right.

**The campground:** Besides the fishing, Twin Lakes also offers a nice place to stay on the east side of Independence Pass. Lakeview is the largest campground at the lakes. It perches on a cliff above the lake with no direct fishing access, but it does have some nice views. The campground is very thinly forested and the sites are somewhat close together, but if you're here to enjoy the fishing and the scenery you probably won't mind.

## 178 Twin Lakes: Whitestar

**Location:** South of Leadville.
**Facilities:** Central water, fire rings, picnic tables, vault toilets, boat ramp.
**Sites:** 64.
**Fee:** $10, plus fee for second vehicle.
**Elevation:** 9,500 feet.
**Road conditions:** two lane, gravel.
**Management:** San Isabel National Forest, 719-486-0749.
**Reservations:** 800-280-CAMP, www.nrrc.com, $8.65 fee.
**Activities:** Fishing, hiking.
**Finding the campground:** From Leadville, travel south on U.S. Highway 24 to Colorado Highway 82. Turn west to the lakes. Whitestar is the third campground; access is on the left.

**The campground:** Whitestar is lightly forested (pine) and sits on the shore of the western lake. Sites are a bit close together here, as they are in all of the Twin Lakes campgrounds, but this campground sees slightly lower usage than the others. If you prefer more trees, try Twin Peaks (Campground 179) farther west on County Road 82. You can always drive back to fish. Hiking trails to Parry Peak are across the road from the camp.

## 179 Twin Peaks

**Location:** West of Twin Lakes.
**Facilities:** Central water, fire rings, picnic tables, vault toilets.
**Sites:** 37.
**Fee:** $9.
**Elevation:** 9,600 feet.
**Road conditions:** Paved.
**Management:** San Isabel National Forest, 719-486-0749.
**Activities:** Fishing, hiking, scenic driving.

**Finding the campground:** From Twin Lakes, travel west on County Road 82, about 3 miles to the campground.

**The campground:** Twin Peaks is a bit prettier than Parry Peak (Campground 173). It is set among older pines, and sites are spaced farther apart. In fact, many of the sites are so far apart that you can't see one from another. The sites are strung along the banks of the creek, providing direct fishing access from most. This is your last chance to camp on the east side of Independence Pass, so if the sun is on its way down, you probably should stop here.

# Area 17: Fairplay

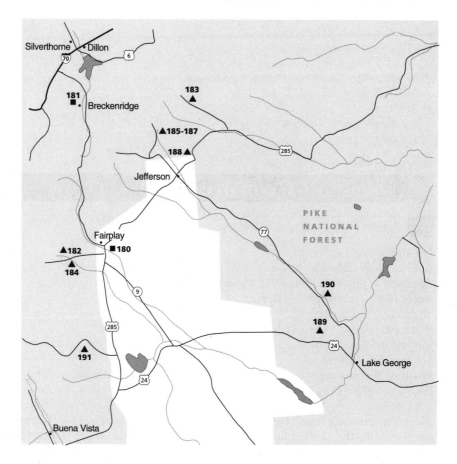

## FAIRPLAY

Huddled beneath the 13,000- to 14,000-foot Mosquito Range at the edge of a vast parkland, the town of Fairplay stands in contrast to many other former mining towns in the state: it is quiet and understated, as are the attractions that surround it. Most people find their way here looking for a place to hide from the roaring crowds on the other side of the mountains.

Camping is limited to national forest camps and a trio of commercial campgrounds, one of which is near the bright and busy town of Breckenridge. Keep in mind that the quietest campgrounds are close to Fairplay. The farther east and north you travel, the closer you are to the bustle of civilization.

**For More Information:**

Park County Regional Tourism Office
P.O. Box 701
Fairplay, CO 80440
719-836-2771, ext. 203

Breckenridge Chamber Resort Association
555 S. Columbine
Box 1909
Breckenridge, CO 80424
303-453-6018

# Commercial

## 180 South Park Lodge & RV Park

**Location:** Fairplay.
**Affiliations:** Colorado Association of Campgrounds, Cabins, and Lodges.
**Contact:** 719-836-3278, fax 719-836-0155.
**Amenities:** Dump station, showers.
**Sites:** 37, 7 full hookups.
**Price per night:** $14 to $20.
**Elevation:** 9,900 feet.
**Season:** Year-round.
**Finding the campground:** At the junction of Colorado Highway 9 and U.S. Highway 285 in Fairplay.

**The campground:** South Park Lodge is a no-frills place designed for RVers who come to enjoy the historic mining town. The park is within walking distance of shops, restaurants, and the local museum. Activities in the area include gold panning, four-wheel driving, and fishing.

## 181 Tiger Run RV Resort

**Location:** North of Breckenridge.
**Affiliations:** Colorado Association of Campgrounds, Cabins, and Lodges.
**Contact:** 970-453-9690.
**Amenities:** Cabins, laundry, showers, public phone, store, picnic tables, grills, church services, indoor pool, whirlpool, playground, horse rentals, tours, bike rentals, group activities.
**Sites:** 300, 125 full hookups.
**Price per night:** $25 to $35.
**Elevation:** 9,200 feet.
**Restrictions:** No tents or tent trailers.
**Finding the campground:** From Exit 203 on Interstate 70, travel about 6.5 miles south on Colorado Highway 9.

**The campground:** As you can see by the list of amenities, Tiger Run is a full-service RV park. It offers just about anything you could want in terms of recreation in this area. The park is landscaped, bisected by a river, and surrounded by gorgeous mountain scenery. Its one drawback is the rule prohibiting tents and even tent trailers.

| Public |
|:---:|

## 182 Four Mile

**Location:** Southwest of Fairplay.
**Facilities:** Central water, fire rings, picnic tables, vault toilets.
**Sites:** 14.
**Fee:** $7.
**Elevation:** 10,800 feet.
**Road conditions:** two lane, gravel, rough.
**Management:** Pike National Forest, 719-836-2031.
**Activities:** Fishing, hiking, four-wheel driving.
**Finding the campground:** From Fairplay, travel 1.4 miles south on U.S. Highway 285 to Forest Service Road 421. Turn west and go 6.9 miles to the campground.

**The campground:** This is another one of those campgrounds that very few people seem to use. It is a beautiful retreat into a heavily wooded area. The sites are well spaced. Four Mile Creek is right across the road, and Forest Service Road 421 continues into the mountains, allowing four-wheel-drive enthusiasts a chance to test their skills and rattle their brains.

## 183 Geneva Park

**Location:** Northwest of Grant.
**Facilities:** Central water, fire rings, picnic tables, vault toilets.
**Sites:** 26.
**Fee:** $9.
**Elevation:** 9,800 feet.
**Road conditions:** two lane, gravel.
**Management:** Pike National Forest, 303-275-5610.
**Activities:** Fishing, hiking, four-wheel driving, horseback riding.
**Finding the campground:** Grant is located on U.S. Highway 285, northeast of Fairplay. From Grant, travel northwest on County Road 62 for about 7 miles to Forest Service Road 119. Continue northwest about 0.5 mile to the campground.

**The campground:** Geneva Park is a gloriously hidden campground below Guanella Pass between Grant and Georgetown. It sits barely 1 mile from the

Mount Evans Wilderness Area. From here you can enjoy the best of both worlds: the gentle rolling hills to the south and the rugged mining country to the north. The road over Guanella Pass is difficult but passable even in a two-wheel-drive vehicle. Fishing Geneva Creek is possible from camp, and Duck Creek is nearby. Pack/saddle trails lead into the wilderness.

## 184  Horseshoe

**Location:** Southwest of Fairplay.
**Facilities:** Central water, fire rings, picnic tables, vault toilets.
**Sites:** 19.
**Fee:** $7.
**Elevation:** 10,600 feet.
**Road conditions:** two lane, gravel, rough.
**Management:** Pike National Forest, 719-836-2031.
**Activities:** Fishing, hiking.
**Finding the campground:** From Fairplay, travel 1.4 miles south on U.S. Highway 285 to Forest Service Road 421. Turn west and go about 6 miles to the campground.

**The campground:** Horseshoe is the nicer of the two camps on this road. It gets low usage and is heavily forested. Forest Service Road 423 leads off to the east from camp into the Thompson Park area, which is an ideal spot to watch for elk. Fishing is possible in Four Mile Creek above and below camp. It seems incredible that a campground this pretty gets so few visitors. If you don't mind the rough access road, you'll find this a near-perfect hideaway.

## 185  Jefferson Creek Recreation Area: Aspen

**Location:** Northwest of Jefferson.
**Facilities:** Central water, fire rings, picnic tables, vault toilets.
**Sites:** 12.
**Fee:** $9.
**Elevation:** 9,900 feet.
**Road conditions:** One-and-a-half lane, gravel.
**Management:** Pike National Forest, 719-836-2031.
**Reservations:** 800-280-CAMP, www.nrrc.com, $8.65 fee.
**Activities:** Fishing, hiking.
**Finding the campground:** From Jefferson, travel northwest on County Road 35 about 2 miles, then 1 mile north on CR 37. Turn northwest onto Forest Service Road 401. The campground is 1.8 miles to the north.

**The campground:** The Jefferson Creek Recreation Area is a wonderful retreat with three campgrounds situated below Jefferson Lake. Aspen is the middle campground. As its name implies, it hides among the aspens. Spaces are somewhat close together in many cases, but the scenery is lovely. Fishing access to

Jefferson Creek is a short walk away and the lake a short drive. (You can walk, but it's close to 2 miles, uphill.) Reservations are recommended for weekends.

## 186 Jefferson Creek Recreation Area: Jefferson Creek

**Location:** Northwest of Jefferson.
**Facilities:** Central water, fire rings, picnic tables, vault toilets.
**Sites:** 17.
**Fee:** $9.
**Elevation:** 10,100 feet.
**Road conditions:** One-and-a-half lane, gravel.
**Management:** Pike National Forest, 719-836-2031.
**Reservations:** 800-280-CAMP, www.nrrc.com, $8.65 fee.
**Activities:** Fishing, hiking.
**Finding the campground:** From Jefferson, travel northwest on County Road 35 about 2 miles, then 1 mile north on CR 37. Turn northwest onto Forest Service Road 401. The campground is 2.9 miles to the north.

**The campground:** Jefferson Creek is the highest of the three campgrounds in the recreation area, making it the closest to Jefferson Lake. The lake is the kind of high mountain lake that people come to Colorado from all over the world to see. The snowcapped peaks to the north reflect off the surface of the water in a postcard-perfect setting, so be sure to take your camera with you when you go.

## 187 Jefferson Creek Recreation Area: Lodgepole/Pike

**Location:** Northwest of Jefferson.
**Facilities:** Central water, fire rings, picnic tables, vault toilets.
**Sites:** 35.
**Fee:** $9.
**Elevation:** 9,900 feet.
**Road conditions:** One-and-a-half lane, gravel.
**Management:** Pike National Forest, 719-836-2031.
**Reservations:** 800-280-CAMP, www.nrrc.com, $8.65 fee.
**Activities:** Fishing, hiking.
**Finding the campground:** From Jefferson, travel northwest on County Road 35 about 2 miles, then 1 mile north on CR 37. Turn northwest onto Forest Service Road 401. The campground is 1.4 miles to the north.

**The campground:** Lodgepole/Pike is the first of the three campgrounds in Jefferson Creek Recreation Area. It is also the largest, making it the one most likely to have available sites. Though it is farthest from Jefferson Lake, it is still quite pretty. Access to Jefferson Creek is nearby. Sites are closely spaced in a pine forest. Hikers will appreciate its proximity to the Colorado Trail, which passes near the campground on its way to the Kenosha Pass Trailhead.

## 188 Kenosha Pass

**Location:** Northeast of Jefferson.
**Facilities:** Central water, fire rings, picnic tables, vault toilets.
**Sites:** 25.
**Fee:** $9.
**Elevation:** 10,000 feet.
**Road conditions:** Paved.
**Management:** Pike National Forest, 303-275-5610.
**Activities:** Hiking, four-wheel driving.
**Finding the campground:** From Jefferson, travel 4.2 miles northeast on U.S. Highway 285 to the campground.

**The campground:** This campground serves two main purposes: it's a good drop-off or pick-up point along the Colorado Trail, and it's an ideal stopover along US 285 before or after visiting Denver. If you can stay awhile, you might want to explore two short jeep roads, Forest Service Road 124 and FSR 126.

## 189 Round Mountain

**Location:** Northwest of Lake George.
**Facilities:** Central water, fire rings, picnic tables, vault toilets.
**Sites:** 16.
**Fee:** $9.
**Elevation:** 8,500 feet.
**Road conditions:** Paved.
**Management:** Pike National Forest, 719-836-2031.
**Activities:** Four-wheel driving, rockhounding.
**Finding the campground:** From Lake George, travel 5.5 miles northwest on U.S. Highway 24 to the campground.

**The campground:** Crass as it may sound, Round Mountain is good for a one-night stand and not much else. Still, it's important to know where to find this type of spot, because sooner or later you're bound to need a place to lay your head at midnight. Many people traveling east or west across the state opt to avoid the tangle of traffic in Denver by using U.S. Highway 24. This is a good way to avoid Vail Pass and the Eisenhower Tunnel Pass as well. If the campground is full when you arrive, there are plenty of other options in both directions.

There are several good sites for rockhounding along US 24 between Lake George and Buena Vista. For more information, see pages 100–106 of the FalconGuide *Rockhounding Colorado*.

## 190 Spruce Grove

**Location:** Northwest of Lake George.
**Facilities:** Central water, fire rings, picnic tables, vault toilets.

**Sites:** 26.
**Fee:** $9.
**Elevation:** 8,600 feet.
**Road conditions:** Paved.
**Management:** Pike National Forest, 719-836-2031.
**Activities:** Fishing, hiking, wildlife viewing.
**Finding the campground:** From Lake George, travel 1.2 miles northwest on U.S. Highway 24 to County Road 77. Turn north and travel 12.2 miles to the campground.

**The campground:** The area along the Tarryall River is a bit more arid than much of the state, so it has the feel of a desert wilderness. If you're looking for tall trees and scenic peaks, this isn't the place for you. However, if you want to get away from the crowds seeking those trees and peaks, you might give Spruce Grove a try. Fishing is good on the river and at Tarryall Reservoir just up the road. Trails from camp are abundant and provide an excellent opportunity to watch for wildlife, particularly bighorn sheep, which are plentiful here.

## 191 Weston Pass

**Location:** Southwest of Fairplay.
**Facilities:** Central water, fire rings, picnic tables, vault toilets.
**Sites:** 15.
**Fee:** $9.
**Elevation:** 10,200 feet.
**Road conditions:** two lane, gravel.
**Management:** Pike National Forest, 719-836-2031.
**Activities:** Fishing, hiking, four-wheel driving, wildlife viewing.
**Finding the campground:** From Fairplay, travel southwest on U.S. Highway 285, about 5 miles to Forest Service Road 425. Turn west and travel about 11 miles to the campground.

**The campground:** This is a very nice campground in which to get away from nearly every other soul on the planet. If you're lucky, you might end up with these 15 sites all to yourself. Fishing on the South Fork of the Platte River is limited since, at this elevation, it's merely a small stream. Weston Pass Road is passable by most vehicles up to the summit. Maintenance ends at that point, and the road thereafter is recommended for four-wheel-drive vehicles only. The road comes out at Mount Massive Lakes, south of Leadville. The journey is interesting if you have the vehicle for it.

# Additional Campgrounds in the Fairplay Area

| | Type* | Contact | Location |
|---|---|---|---|
| Travel Port Campground & Mini Storage | P (38) | 719-748-8191 | 1 mile E of Lake George |
| Western Inn Motel & RV Park | P (14) | 719-836-2026 | US 285, Fairplay |
| Beaver Creek | NF (3) | 719-836-2031 | 5 miles N of Fairplay on FSR 413 |
| Burning Bear | NF (13) | 303-275-5610 | 5.2 miles NW of Grant on CR 62 |
| Deer Creek | NF (13) | 303-275-5610 | 10 miles NW of Bailey on FSR 100 |
| Hall Valley | NF (9) | 303-275-5610 | 7 miles NW of Grant on FSR 120 |
| Hand Cart | NF (10) | 303-275-5610 | 8 miles NW of Grant on FSR 120 |
| Happy Meadows | NF (7) | 719-836-2031 | 3 miles n of Lake George on FSR 207 |
| Kite Lake | NF (7) | 719-836-2031 | 6 miles NW of Alma on FSR 416 |
| Lost Park | NF (10) | 719-836-2031 | 20 miles SE of Jefferson on FSR 127 |
| Meridian | NF (18) | 303-275-5610 | 10 miles NW on Bailey on FSR 102 |
| Michigan Creek | NF (13) | 719-835-2031 | 6 miles NW of Jefferson on FSR 400113 |
| Selkirk | NF (15) | 719-836-2031 | 7 miles NW of Como on FSR 120 |
| Twin Eagles Trailhead | NF (9) | 719-836-2031 | 16 miles NW of Lake George on CR 77 |
| Whiteside | NF (5) | 303-275-5610 | 2.2 miles NW of Gratn on CR 62 |
| Alma | SWA DSP | 719-473-2945 | 1.5 miles N of ALma on CO 9 |
| Tarryall Reservoir | SWA DSP | 719-473-2945 | 15 miles SE of Jefferson on CR 77 |

* See "Key to Abbreviations" p.22—(# of sites)

# Area 18: Castle Rock

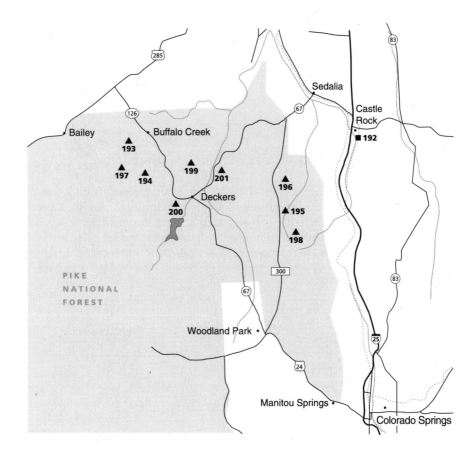

## CASTLE ROCK

Castle Rock is really a southern suburb of Denver, but the area merits its own section in the book because it offers such a diversity of camping choices, most of which are not easily accessible from the city.

Named for its fortress-like rock formation, the town of Castle Rock is famous for factory outlet shopping. You can buy everything from perfume to dishcloths, from children's clothing to chocolate, all presumably at prices below retail.

If you are here just to shop, stay at the KOA. It puts you close to the action as none of the other campgrounds in the area can.

Beyond the shops lies a recreational mecca known as the Pike National Forest. Here, you can ride your dirt bike along miles of forest trails or fish waters so popular that people fight for camping spots. The 470-mile Colorado Trail also grazes the area on its diagonal journey across the state.

The remaining camping choices (besides the KOA) are all national forest campgrounds, with a total of just over two hundred sites, all in high demand.

# Commercial

## 192 Castle Rock KOA

**Location:** South of Castle Rock.
**Affiliations:** KOA.
**Contact:** 303-681-3169.
**Amenities:** Dump station, laundry, showers, public phones, store, picnic tables, grills, pool, playground, cabins.
**Sites:** 92, 24 full hookups.
**Price per night:** $15.95 to $21.
**Elevation:** 6,200 feet.
**Finding the campground:** Take Exit 174 off Interstate 25.

**The campground:** This is a typical KOA campground: clean, friendly, and no surprises. It makes a good base from which to shop in the Castle Rock Factory Stores (one of the largest outlet centers in the state). Campsites are scattered across a lightly wooded hillside. The trees help block the traffic noise from I-25. The central location also allows you to explore both Denver and Colorado Springs.

# Public

## 193 Baldy, Tramway, & Top of the World

**Location:** Southwest of Buffalo Creek.
**Management:** Pike National Forest, 303-275-5610.

**The campground:** These three small campgrounds were permanently closed in 1997 after the area was ravaged by fire and flood. For more information, contact the South Platte Ranger District at the number listed above.

## 194 Buffalo

**Location:** Southwest of Buffalo Creek.
**Facilities:** Central water, fire rings, picnic tables, vault toilets.
**Sites:** 41.
**Fee:** $9.
**Elevation:** 7,400 feet.
**Road conditions:** Call Pike National Forest.
**Management:** Pike National Forest, 303-275-5610.
**Reservations:** 800-280-CAMP, www.nrrc.com, $8.65 fee.
**Activities:** Hiking, fishing, biking.
**Finding the campground:** From Buffalo Creek, travel southeast about 4 miles to Forest Service Road 550. Turn west and go about 5 miles to FSR 543. Turn

south and go about 1 mile to the campground.

**The campground:** The ultimate fate of this campground is still up in the air following the restoration of the entire Buffalo Creek area, which was ravaged first by fire, then by floods. It is best to call the Pike National Forest district office regarding campground and road conditions before setting out for any campground in this area.

## 195 Devil's Head

**Location:** Southwest of Sedalia.
**Facilities:** Central water, fire rings, picnic tables, vault toilets.
**Sites:** 21.
**Fee:** $9.
**Elevation:** 8,800 feet.
**Road conditions:** two lane, gravel.
**Management:** Pike National Forest, 303-275-5610.
**Activities:** Hiking, rock climbing, dirt biking.
**Finding the campground:** From Sedalia, travel southwest on Colorado Highway 67, about 10 miles to Forest Service Road 300. Turn south and go 9.1 miles to Devil's Head Road. The campground is 0.4 mile to the southeast.

**The campground:** If you don't ride dirt bikes, stay clear of this pretty campground, especially on weekends. The Devil's Head National Recreation Trail is the mountain home of motorcyclists from across the state and beyond. But if you love to play in the dirt, this is your chance to do so in the woods.

## 196 Flat Rocks

**Location:** Southwest of Sedalia.
**Facilities:** Central water, fire rings, picnic tables, vault toilets.
**Sites:** 19.
**Fee:** $9.
**Elevation:** 8,200 feet.
**Road conditions:** two lane, gravel.
**Management:** Pike National Forest, 303-275-5610.
**Activities:** Dirt biking.
**Finding the campground:** From Sedalia, travel southwest on Colorado Highway 67, about 10 miles to Forest Service Road 300. Turn south and go about 8 miles to the campground.

**The campground:** This is another motorcycle base camp along the Devil's Head Recreation Trail. It is pretty, as is the entire area. If you plan a weekend visit here, it would be wise to call the ranger station at the above number before setting out to see if there are any large groups scheduled to use the trail.

## 197 | Green Mountain

**Location:** Southwest of Buffalo Creek.
**Facilities:** Fire rings, picnic tables, vault toilets; no water.
**Sites:** 6.
**Fee:** $7.
**Elevation:** 7,600 feet.
**Road conditions:** Call Pike National Forest.
**Management:** Pike National Forest, 303-275-5610.
**Activities:** Fishing, hiking, biking.
**Finding the campground:** From Buffalo Creek, travel southeast about 4 miles to Forest Service Road 550. Turn west and go about 5 miles to FSR 543. Turn south and go about 1 mile to the campground.

**The campground:** As with Buffalo (Campground 194), the fate of Green Mountain is still up in the air following the restoration of the entire Buffalo Creek area, which was ravaged recently by fire and flood. It is best to call the Forest Service at the number listed above before setting out for any campground in the area.

## 198 | Jackson Creek

**Location:** Southwest of Sedalia.
**Facilities:** Central water, fire rings, picnic tables, vault toilets.
**Sites:** 9.
**Fee:** $7.
**Elevation:** 8,100 feet.
**Road conditions:** one lane, dirt.
**Management:** Pike National Forest, 303-275-5610.
**Activities:** Hiking, dirt biking.
**Restrictions:** 16-foot maximum trailer length.
**Finding the campground:** From Sedalia, travel southwest on Colorado Highway 67, about 10 miles to Forest Service Road 300. Turn south and go 13.9 miles to FSR 502. Turn north and go 1.5 miles to the campground.

**The campground:** Jackson Creek presents an opportunity to get away from most of the motorcycle crowd, but you can count on some of them finding this pretty little valley. The campsites are small and there's not much turn-around space, so trailer length is limited to 16 feet. Access to the Devil's Head Recreation Trail is just around the bend.

## 199 | Kelsey

**Location:** South of Buffalo Creek.
**Facilities:** Central water, fire rings, picnic tables, vault toilets.
**Sites:** 17.
**Fee:** $9.

**Elevation:** 8,000 feet.
**Road conditions:** Paved.
**Management:** Pike National Forest, 303-275-5610.
**Reservations:** 800-280-CAMP, www.nrrc.com, $8.65 fee.
**Activities:** Hiking, biking.
**Finding the campground:** From Buffalo Creek, travel 7.9 miles south on County Road 126 to the campground.

**The campground:** Kelsey is a safe bet if you're looking for camping accommodations in the Buffalo Springs area. The sites are moderately spaced, and some facilities have been updated. Access to the Colorado Trail is nearby.

## 200 Lone Rock

**Location:** West of Deckers.
**Facilities:** Central water, fire rings, picnic tables, vault toilets.
**Sites:** 19.
**Fee:** $9.
**Elevation:** 6,400 feet.
**Road conditions:** Paved.
**Management:** Pike National Forest, 303-275-5610.
**Reservations:** 800-280-CAMP, www.nrrc.com, $8.65 fee.
**Activities:** Fishing, hiking.
**Finding the campground:** From Deckers, travel west on County Road 126, 0.5 mile to the campground.

**The campground:** Lone Rock is a fishing camp and nothing more. Trees are scarce, sites are cramped, and reservations are mandatory. Still, people wait in line to get these sites and a chance at the fish swimming in the South Platte River. There are fishing restrictions, so pay attention to posted information.

## 201 Platte River

**Location:** Northwest of Deckers.
**Facilities:** Central water, fire rings, picnic tables, vault toilets.
**Sites:** 10.
**Fee:** $7.
**Elevation:** 6,300 feet.
**Road conditions:** two lane, gravel.
**Management:** Pike National Forest, 303-275-5610.
**Activities:** Fishing.
**Finding the campground:** From Deckers travel 3.5 miles northwest on County Road 67 to the campground.

**The campground:** This camp is much like Lone Rock (Campground 200): small, crowded, and not terribly attractive. But it offers a second chance at catching those South Platte River fish.

## Additional Campgrounds in the Castle Rock Area

|  | Type* | Contact | Location |
|---|---|---|---|
| Goose Creek | NF (10) | 303-275-5610 | 13 miles SW of Dallas on FSR 211 |
| Indian Creek | NF (11) | 303-275-5610 | 10 miles W of Sedalia on CR 67 |
| Molly Gulch | NF (15) | 303-275-5610 | 9 miles SW of Deckers on FSR 211 |
| Ouzel | NF (13) | 303-275-5610 | 5 miles N of Deckers |
| Wigwam | NF | 303-275-5610 | 3 miles S of Deckers on CO 126 |

* See "Key to Abbreviations" p.22.

# Southwest

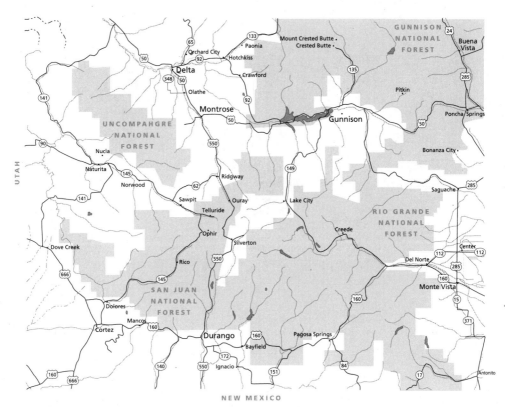

# Area 19: Montrose

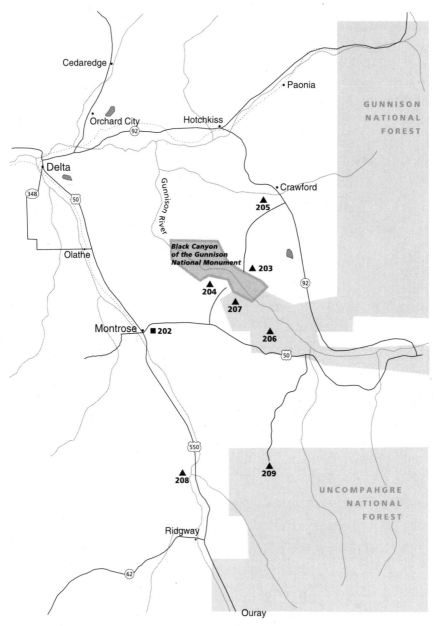

## MONTROSE

In the area around Montrose, you never quite know what to expect beyond the next bend in the road. It could be the yawning crevice of the Black Canyon or the rich green of the Uncompahgre National Forest. This is a land of wild rivers, huge trout, and golden sunsets reflected off red rock mesas. It is a land that lets your imagination soar as you picture Ute Indians camped along the upper stretches of the Gunnison River or cowboys driving meager herds of raw-boned cattle to the river to drink.

The recreational opportunities are what you would expect: fishing, hiking, four-wheel driving, river rafting (if you dare), and more fishing and hiking. But there are a few surprises in this lonely place. One is something called "Thunder Mountain Lives Tonight." It's an outdoor historical performance near Delta that is fun and entertaining for the whole family. Another diversion is the Hotchkiss National Fish Hatchery near Lazear. Tours are entertaining and free.

Camping choices are another pleasant surprise. There are 14 commercial campgrounds in the area, plus a handful of national forest camps and three state parks. The total number of campsites is close to a thousand, many of which are open year-round. Bring your family and friends; the welcome mat is definitely out here.

### For More Information:

Delta Chamber of Commerce
301 Main Street
Delta, CO 81416
970-874-8616
e-mail: chamber@deltacolorado.com

Hotchkiss Chamber of Commerce
P.O. Box 158
Hotchkiss, CO 81419
970-872-3226
e-mail: hotchkiss@aol.com

Montrose Chamber of Commerce
1519 E. Main
Montrose, CO 81401
970-249-5000
www.rmi.net/mntrscoc
e-mail: mntrscoc@rmii.com

Paonia Chamber of Commerce
P.O. Box 366
Paonia, CO 81428
970-527-3886

Hotchkiss National Fish Hatchery
970-872-3170

# Commercial

## 202 Mountain View RV Park

**Location:** Montrose.
**Affiliations:** Colorado Association of Campgrounds, Cabins, and Lodges.
**Contact:** 970-249-3884.
**Amenities:** Dump station, laundry, showers, public phone, picnic tables, patios, grills.
**Sites:** 49, 26 full hookups.
**Price per night:** $12.50 to $16.
**Elevation:** 5,800 feet.
**Season:** Year-round.
**Finding the campground:** From the junction of U.S. Highways 50 and 550, travel 1.25 miles east on US 50, go 1 block south on Hillcrest, and west on Alley Way to the campground.

**The campground:** For either a stopover or a lengthy stay in the Montrose area, this shady park situated along Cedar Creek is a nice choice. The Black Canyon of the Gunnison National Monument is a short drive away, as is fishing along the Gunnison River.

# Public

## 203 Black Canyon of the Gunnison National Monument: North Rim

**Location:** Northwest of Montrose.
**Facilities:** Central water, fire rings, picnic tables, vault toilets.
**Sites:** 13.
**Fee:** $7, plus $10 per vehicle entrance fee.
**Elevation:** 8,000 feet.
**Road conditions:** two lane, gravel.
**Management:** National Park Service, 970-249-7036.
**Activities:** Hiking, scenic driving, limited fishing, wildlife viewing.
**Finding the campground:** From Montrose, travel north on U.S. Highway 50 to Delta, then southeast to Hotchkiss on Colorado Highway 92. From Hotchkiss continue south on CO 92 for about 13 miles to Crawford Reservoir. Turn right and follow the signs to the campground.

**The campground:** The Black Canyon of the Gunnison is one of the most stunning geologic sites in the world. It's worth a trip out of your way to see it, even if you don't stay the night. The North Rim campground is more difficult to reach than South Rim (Campground 204), but if you prefer to soak in the mystic atmosphere of the canyon in relative solitude, this is the option for you. The views are nothing short of magnificent.

## 204 Black Canyon of the Gunnison National Monument: South Rim

**Location:** Northeast of Montrose.
**Facilities:** Central water, fire rings, picnic tables, vault toilets.
**Sites:** 102.
**Fee:** $5, plus $10 per vehicle entrance fee.
**Elevation:** 8,400 feet.
**Road conditions:** two lane, gravel.
**Management:** National Park Service, 970-249-7036.
**Activities:** Hiking, scenic driving, limited fishing.
**Finding the campground:** From Montrose, travel east on U.S. Highway 50, about 6 miles to Colorado Highway 347. Follow the signs to the entrance.

**The campground:** This is the most popular and easily accessed side of the canyon, hence the large campground. The sites are closely spaced, and vegetation is sparse in this arid region of the state. But the views are nothing short of incredible. Trails lead down to the river, but they are poorly marked and very hazardous. Proceed with caution. Fishing is limited by your ability to make it down to the river, but the few who do are usually not disappointed.

## 205 Crawford Reservoir State Park

**Location:** Southeast of Hotchkiss.
**Facilities:** Dump station, swim beach, boat ramps, trails, grills, central water, picnic tables.
**Sites:** 55.
**Fee:** $6, plus $4 daily or $40 annual vehicle pass.
**Elevation:** 6,600 feet.
**Road conditions:** two lane, gravel.
**Management:** Colorado Department of Parks and Outdoor Recreation, 970-921-5721.
**Reservations:** 800-678-CAMP, $7 fee.
**Activities:** Fishing, hiking, water sports.
**Season:** Year-round.
**Finding the campground:** From Hotchkiss, travel southeast on Colorado Highway 92, about 10 miles to Crawford, then another 1 mile to the park entrance.

**The campground:** Camping at Crawford Reservoir is split among three campgrounds along the eastern shore, adding to the sense of isolation you get from this lake cradled in the rolling hills. Vegetation is low-growing, but that allows you to enjoy spectacular sunsets and sunrises. Fishing is mixed: trout, bass, and perch. Unfortunately, there are not separate areas designated for fishing and water sports. There is a short hiking trail at the park, and additional trails branch off from Colorado Highway 92 south of the park.

## 206 | Curecanti National Recreation Area: Cimarron

**Location:** East of Montrose.
**Facilities:** Central water, fire rings, picnic tables, flush toilets, dump.
**Sites:** 22.
**Fee:** $6.
**Elevation:** 6,906 feet.
**Road conditions:** two lane, dirt.
**Management:** National Park Service, 970-641-2337.
**Activities:** Fishing, hiking, horseback riding, four-wheel driving.
**Finding the campground:** From Montrose, travel east on U.S. Highway 50, about 17 miles to County Road Q83. Turn north and go about 1 mile to the campground.

**The campground:** Curecanti is not your typical Colorado destination. The area is rugged, the landscape harsh, and the climate arid. In the midst of the red-cliff desert are the manmade reservoirs along the Gunnison that make up the recreation area. Fishing is the prime attraction; hiking is number two. Everyone else seems to come simply to enjoy the cool water. Cimarron is one of the more secluded camps at Curecanti. It offers access to the Gunnison River but not to the lakes.

## 207 | Curecanti National Recreation Area: East Portal

**Location:** Northeast of Montrose.
**Facilities:** Central water, fire rings, picnic tables, flush toilets.
**Sites:** 15.
**Fee:** $6.
**Elevation:** 7,519 feet.
**Road conditions:** one lane, dirt.
**Management:** National Park Service, 970-641-2337.
**Activities:** Fishing, hiking, river sports, four-wheel driving.
**Restrictions:** Not accessible to trailers or RVs.
**Finding the campground:** From Montrose, travel east on U.S. Highway 50, about 6 miles to Colorado Highway 347. Turn north and go about 6 miles to East Portal Road. Turn southeast and go about 5 miles to the campground.

**The campground:** East Portal presents an opportunity to enjoy a bit of the Black Canyon—from the bottom. The road down is steep and narrow, but if you can make it, fishing in the Gunnison is superb. Kayakers often use this camp as a put-in point when water levels are suitable.

## 208 | Ridgeway State Park

**Location:** South of Montrose.
**Facilities:** Dump station, electricity, laundry, showers, swim beach, bath house, snack bar, boat ramp, marina, boat rental, trails, picnic tables, fire rings, central

water, playground.
**Sites:** 283.
**Fee:** $7 to $12, plus $4 daily or $40 annual vehicle pass.
**Elevation:** 6,870 feet.
**Road conditions:** two lane, gravel.
**Management:** Colorado Department of Parks and Outdoor Recreation, 970-626-5822.
**Reservations:** 800-678-CAMP, $7 fee.
**Activities:** Fishing, water sports, hiking, biking.
**Season:** Year-round.
**Finding the campground:** From Montrose, travel south on U.S. Highway 550, about 20 miles to the park.

**The campground:** Ridgeway is a diverse state park offering recreation on Ridgeway Reservoir and along the Uncompahgre River as it enters and leaves the park. Campsites are divided between two areas: one on the river, and one on the lake. Most have views of the snowcapped San Juan Mountains. The Pa-Co-Chu-Puk Recreation Site is along the river and has trout ponds for fishing. On the reservoir itself, camping is in an area called Dutch Charlie, which is further divided into campgrounds: Elk Ridge, which perches on a bluff above the water, and Dakota Terraces, which is a short walk from the swim beach. The park has roughly 17 miles of hiking trails circling the lake, some of which allow mountain biking as well.

## 209 | Silver Jack

**Location:** Southeast of Montrose.
**Facilities:** Central water, fire rings, picnic tables, vault toilets.
**Sites:** 60.
**Fee:** $9.
**Elevation:** 8,900 feet.
**Road conditions:** two lane, gravel.
**Management:** Uncompahgre National Forest, 970-249-3711.
**Activities:** Fishing, hiking, horseback riding.
**Finding the campground:** From Montrose, travel east on U.S. Highway 50, about 20 miles to Cimarron Road. Turn south and go about 22 miles to the campground.

**The campground:** This large camp takes advantage of a beautiful setting below Cimarron Ridge. Silver Jack Reservoir is the centerpiece, but other activities include hiking the many trails that head in all directions. Forest Service Roads 858 and 863 eventually dwindle to pack/saddle trails that parallel the ridge into the Big Blue Wilderness Area. Campsite choices are varied, and you will usually have your pick here.

# Additional Campgrounds in the Montrose Area

| | Type* | Contact | Location |
|---|---|---|---|
| Alexander Lake Lodge, Cabins, & Campground | P (11) | 970-856-6700 | 2121 AA 50 road in Cedaredge |
| Aspen Trails Campground | P (30) | 970-856-6321 | N of Cedaredge on CO 65 |
| Beckly Trailer Park | P (19) | 970-856-3509 | S of Cedaredge on CR 2300 |
| Black Canyon RV Park & | P (43) | 970-249-1147 | E of Cimarron on US 50 |
| Delta/Grand Mesa KOA | P (50) | 800-562-3351 | CR 1675 in Delta |
| Flying A Motel & RV Park | P (35) | 970-874-9659 | US 50 in Delta |
| The Hangin' Tree | P (25) | 970-249-9966 | S of Montrose on US 550 |
| Montrose KOA | P (39) | 970-249-9177 | Cedar Avenue in Montrose |
| Pleasant Valley Campground Cabins, & Campground | P (13) | 970-249-8330 | US 50 in Cimarron |
| Riverwood Motel & RV Park | P (39) | 970-874-5787 | US 50 in Delta |
| RV Camperland | P (24) | 970-249-8314 | US 50 in Montrose |
| Shady Creek RV Park | P | 970-856-7522 | CO 65 in Cedaredge |
| Weber's RV Park | P (30) | 970-626-5383 | US 550 in Ridgeway |
| Paonia State Park | SP (16) | 970-921-5721 | S of Carbondale on CO 133 |
| Beaver Lake | NF (11) | 970-249-3711 | SW of Montrose on CR 69 |
| Big Blue | NF (11) | 970-249-3711 | SW of Gunnison on FSR 868 |
| Big Cimarron | NF (10) | 970-249-3711 | SE of Montrose on CR 69 |
| Divide Fork | NF (11) | 970-242-8211 | S of Grand Junction on FSR 402 |
| Big Dominguez | BLM (9) | 970-945-2341 | S of Grand Junction on FSR 402 |
| Chukar Trailhead | BLM (4) | 970-249-6047 | N of Montrose off Holly Road |
| Ute Trailhead | BLM (2) | 970-249-6047 | NEof Olathe off Peach Valley Road |
| Escalante | SWA | 970-242-8211 | NW of Delta off Escalante Road |

* See "Key to Abbreviations" p.22—(# of sites)

# Area 20: Gunnison

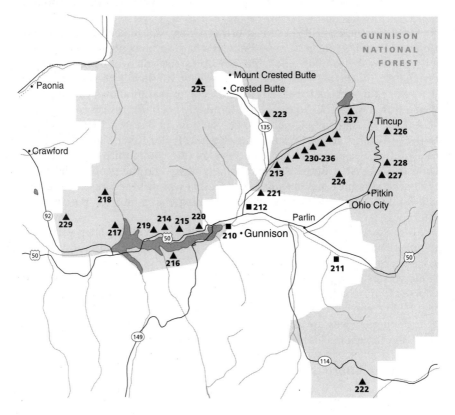

Montrose •

## GUNNISON

Like neighboring Montrose, Gunnison is not quite what most people expect, but it has something for everyone. Sandwiched between the harsh red cliffs at Curecanti and the fantastic mountain peaks surrounding Crested Butte, the town itself it almost anticlimactic. It seems to exist simply as a place to stop for gas and groceries or maybe a quick bite of pizza. But go beyond the edges of town for a taste of what Colorado is all about.

To the west lies the Curecanti National Recreation Area, which draws watersports enthusiasts like a magnet. Surrounded by rugged, barren cliffs, the blue waters of the Gunnison River form reservoirs that are the heart of the recreation area.

To the north are three rivers for which the area is famous: the East, the Gunnison, and the Taylor. Fly fishing is excellent here, as are such river sports as rafting and kayaking.

Farther north is the town of Crested Butte and the resort community of Mount

Crested Butte. Once a step away from being a ghost town, Crested Butte is now a lively collection of sidewalk cafes, antique shops, and clothing stores. A ski resort perches near the top of the mountain with its own entourage of shops and villas.

A ride on the chairlift here is a breathtaking way to see the southwestern slopes of Aspen's famed Maroon Bells. It's hard to imagine that they could be any more lovely from the other side. The lift carries you over fields of wildflowers that so fill the air with their perfume that you'll still be smelling it once you're back inside the lodge. A trail at the top of the lift allows you to prove to yourself that this is one of the most stunningly beautiful resorts in the state.

As if all of that isn't enough to keep you busy in the area, there's still more. Between Gunnison and Crested Butte lies the Taylor River Valley, which leads to a shining reservoir and on to another mining community, Tincup. In sharp contrast to Crested Butte, Tincup is barely alive, and the people who make it their second home seem to want to keep it that way. It's the kind of place where you're likely to see people snoozing in rocking chairs on front porches in the afternoon.

From Tincup, a white-knuckle drive over Cumberland Pass takes you through the heart of the old mining operation before dropping down to sensible elevations near a third mining town, Pitkin.

Between scenic drives, you can also drive a golf ball or two. There are two courses from which to choose. If that isn't enough activity, there's always hiking, biking, and horseback riding.

Camping choices are abundant here. Decide on your favorite activity, and then find the camp closest to it; everything else is just a short drive away.

**For More Information:**

Gunnison Chamber of Commerce
500 E. Tomichi Avenue
P.O. Box 36
Gunnison, CO 81230
970-641-1501
www.gunnison-co.com
e-mail: guncham@rmii.com

Crested Butte Chamber of Commerce
P.O. Box 1288
Crested Butte, CO 81224
970-349-6438
www.cbinteractive.com
e-mail: cbutte@rm1.net

# Commercial

## 210  Mesa Campground

**Location:** West of Gunnison.
**Affiliations:** Good Sam; AAA; Colorado Association of Campgrounds, Cabins, and Lodges.
**Contact:** 970-641-3186.
**Reservations:** 800-482-4384.
**Amenities:** Dump station, laundry, showers, store, public phone, playground, picnic tables, patios, grills.
**Sites:** 116, 100 full hookups.
**Price per night:** $14.95 to $19.95.
**Elevation:** 7,700 feet.
**Finding the campground:** From the junction of U.S. Highway 50, and Colorado Highway 135 in Gunnison, travel west on US 50 about 3 miles to the campground.

**The campground:** If you want to take advantage of the recreation at Curecanti National Recreation Area but prefer to camp in the shade and retain all the amenities, this is the place to stay. From here you can walk to the Gunnison River or drive to the lakes at Curecanti National Recreation Area. Golf and horseback riding are just minutes away as well.

## 211  Monarch Valley Ranch

**Location:** East of Gunnison.
**Affiliations:** Colorado Association of Campgrounds, Cabins, and Lodges.
**Contact:** 970-641-0626.
**Amenities:** Dump station, laundry, public phone, store, picnic tables, grills, private lakes, restaurant, hot tub.
**Sites:** 80, 70 full hookups.
**Price per night:** $15.
**Elevation:** 8,300 feet.
**Season:** Year-round.
**Finding the campground:** From Gunnison, travel east on U.S. Highway 50, about 25 miles to the ranch.

**The campground:** This working ranch comes with all the amenities of a full-service RV park. Fish in Tomichi Creek or one of the private lakes on the ranch. Horses are provided, or you can bring your own. Sites range from those that are side by side on open pasture to those that are scattered among the trees near the creek. In addition to being a great family destination, the ranch makes a perfect stopover for travelers along US 50.

## 212 Tall Texan Campground

**Location:** North of Gunnison.
**Affiliations:** Colorado Association of Campgrounds, Cabins, and Lodges.
**Contact:** 970-641-2927.
**Amenities:** Dump station, laundry, showers, public phone, playground, cabins, picnic tables, patios, grills, fishing pond.
**Sites:** 116, 60 full hookups.
**Price per night:** $13.50 to $18.
**Elevation:** 7,700 feet.
**Finding the campground:** From Gunnison, travel north on Colorado Highway 135, about 2 miles to County Road 11. The campground is about 200 yards to the east.

**The campground:** This quiet and pretty park provides easy access to everything the Gunnison area has to offer. Some sites are shaded, some have cement patios, and all are neat. From the park it's just minutes to the Gunnison National Forest, which boasts miles of hiking trails and some of the best trophy fishing in the state.

## 213 Three Rivers Resort

**Location:** North of Gunnison.
**Affiliations:** Colorado Association of Campgrounds, Cabins, and Lodges.
**Contact:** 970-641-1303, fax 970-641-1317.
**Amenities:** Dump station, public phone, laundry, showers, store, picnic tables, grills, patios, playground.
**Sites:** 48, 26 full hookups.
**Price per night:** $16.
**Elevation:** 8,000 feet.
**Season:** Year-round.
**Finding the campground:** From Gunnison, travel north on Colorado Highway 135, about 11 miles to County Road 742.

**The campground:** Three Rivers has quite a bit to offer from a recreational standpoint if you don't mind close quarters in the campground. There really are three rivers, so fishing, rafting, and kayaking are the main attractions. The resort is close enough to Gunnison to allow a day of golfing or a night out at a restaurant.

# Public

## 214 Curecanti National Recreation Area: Dry Gulch

**Location:** West of Gunnison.

**Facilities:** Central water, fire rings, picnic tables, flush toilets, corral.
**Sites:** 10.
**Fee:** $6.
**Elevation:** 7,519 feet.
**Road conditions:** two lane, dirt.
**Management:** National Park Service, 970-641-2337.
**Activities:** Fishing, hiking, biking, horseback riding, four-wheel driving
**Finding the campground:** From Gunnison, travel west on U.S. Highway 50 about 17 miles. Follow the signs to the campground on the north side of US 50.

**The campground:** If you want to stay near the water but have a bit of privacy, a smattering of shade, and access to hiking and saddle trails, Dry Gulch is your best choice. The camp is small and traffic noise could be a problem, but the cottonwood grove should help muffle the sound. Trails lead out the back side of camp into the Sapinero Wildlife Area. Before you set out either on foot or horseback, remember that the area is harsh and unforgiving. Carry plenty of water, and let someone know your itinerary.

## 215 Curecanti National Recreation Area: Elk Creek

**Location:** West of Gunnison.
**Facilities:** Central water, fire rings, picnic tables, flush toilets, showers, boat ramp, marina.
**Sites:** 179.
**Fee:** $6.
**Elevation:** 7,519 feet.
**Road conditions:** two lane, dirt.
**Management:** National Park Service, 970-641-2337.
**Activities:** Fishing, hiking, horseback riding, four-wheel driving, water sports.
**Finding the campground:** From Gunnison, travel west on U.S. Highway 50 about 16 miles.

**The campground:** Elk Creek is the grandest granddaddy of all the campgrounds here: it's huge. Sites are crowded, but the camp has everything you need for a vacation on the water. It is the only campground in the recreation area with showers.

## 216 Curecanti National Recreation Area: Gateview

**Location:** West of Gunnison.
**Facilities:** Central water, fire rings, picnic tables, vault toilets.
**Sites:** 7.
**Fee:** $6.
**Elevation:** 7,519 feet.
**Road conditions:** one lane, dirt.
**Management:** National Park Service, 970-641-2337.
**Activities:** Fishing, hiking, horseback riding, four-wheel driving.

**Finding the campground:** From Gunnison, travel west on U.S. Highway 50, about 5 miles to Colorado Highway 149. Turn south and travel about 26 miles to Gateview. Turn north on County Road 25 and go about 6 miles to the campground.

**The campground:** This is about as remote as it gets in the recreation area. The campground is near the southern tip of the Lake Fork arm of Blue Mesa. The only problem here is that since all sites are first-come, first-serve, you'd better hope that seven other campers didn't get these spots first.

## 217 Curecanti National Recreation Area: Lake Fork

**Location:** West of Gunnison.
**Facilities:** Central water, fire rings, picnic tables, flush toilets, boat ramp, marina, dump station.
**Sites:** 87.
**Fee:** $6.
**Elevation:** 7,519 feet.
**Road conditions:** two lane, dirt.
**Management:** National Park Service, 970-641-2337.
**Activities:** Fishing, hiking, horseback riding, four-wheel driving.
**Finding the campground:** From Gunnison, travel west on U.S. Highway 50, about 27 miles to the campground.

**The campground:** Lake Fork is a large campground designed specifically for water lovers. It has direct access to Blue Mesa Reservoir and nearby access to Morrow Point. The rugged rock walls surrounding the lakes make a beautiful backdrop, and sunsets are incredible here.

## 218 Curecanti National Recreation Area: Ponderosa

**Location:** West of Gunnison.
**Facilities:** Central water, fire rings, picnic tables, flush toilets, corral, boat ramp.
**Sites:** 16.
**Fee:** $6.
**Elevation:** 7,519 feet.
**Road conditions:** two lane, dirt.
**Management:** National Park Service, 970-641-2337.
**Activities:** Fishing, hiking, horseback riding, four-wheel driving.
**Finding the campground:** From Gunnison, travel west on U.S. Highway 50 about 28 miles to Soap Creek Road/ Forest Service Road 721. Turn north and go about 7 miles to the campground.

**The campground:** Ponderosa combines all of the best features of the recreation area: it is somewhat isolated, it has lake access, and it has wilderness access. The campsites are near the Soap Creek arm of Blue Mesa, which is small compared to the open waters of the rest of the reservoir but still navigable. Forest Service Road 721 becomes a four-wheel-drive-only route just above the campground.

## 219 Curecanti National Recreation Area: Red Creek

**Location:** West of Gunnison.
**Facilities:** Central water, fire rings, picnic tables, flush toilets.
**Sites:** 7.
**Fee:** $6.
**Elevation:** 7,519 feet.
**Road conditions:** two lane, dirt.
**Management:** National Park Service, 970-641-2337.
**Activities:** Fishing, hiking, horseback riding, four-wheel driving.
**Finding the campground:** From Gunnison, travel west on U.S. Highway 50, about 19 miles to Forest Service Road 723. Turn north to reach the campground.

**The campground:** Red Creek is a tiny camp offering the seclusion that the huge lakeside campgrounds lack. There are a few trees here, plus the trickle of Red Creek. Forest Service Road 723 continues north beyond the camp, eventually dwindling to a system of trails in the West Elk Wilderness.

## 220 Curecanti National Recreation Area: Stevens Creek

**Location:** West of Gunnison.
**Facilities:** Central water, fire rings, picnic tables, flush toilets, boat ramp.
**Sites:** 54.
**Fee:** $6.
**Elevation:** 7,519 feet.
**Road conditions:** two lane, dirt.
**Management:** National Park Service, 970-641-2337.
**Activities:** Fishing, hiking, biking, four-wheel driving, campfire ranger programs.
**Finding the campground:** From Gunnison, travel west on U.S. Highway 50 about 12 miles. Follow the signs to the campground.

**The campground:** Stevens Creek sprawls along the treeless north shore of Blue Mesa Reservoir. The boat ramp is limited to small boats, making this a good campground for sailing, sailboarding, and canoeing. Don't look for much in the way of amenities here, but the rangers do hold campfire programs throughout the summer.

## 221 Almont

**Location:** North of Gunnison.
**Facilities:** Central water, fire rings, picnic tables, vault toilets.

**Sites:** 10.
**Fee:** $6.
**Elevation:** 8,000 feet.
**Road conditions:** Paved.
**Management:** Gunnison National Forest, 970-641-0471.
**Activities:** Fishing.
**Finding the campground:** From Gunnison, travel north on Colorado Highway 135 about 11 miles to the campground.

**The campground:** Almont is a tiny fishing camp that could also serve as a stopover along the way to Crested Butte. The river is subject to strict Gold Medal fishing limits, which are designed to provide trophy-sized catches while protecting native fish. The restrictions include a bag limit of two brown trout and prohibit the taking of rainbow trout. Be sure to read all posted rules before wetting your hook.

There is considerable traffic noise at this campground, but the chance to wake up in the morning and catch your limit in the roaring Gunnison River before heading out just might make up for a restless night.

## 222 | Buffalo Pass

**Location:** Northwest of Saguache.
**Facilities:** Central water, fire rings, picnic tables, vault toilets.
**Sites:** 26.
**Fee:** $5.
**Elevation:** 9,100 feet.
**Road conditions:** one lane, gravel.
**Management:** Rio Grande National Forest, 791-655-2533.
**Activities:** Hiking, four-wheel driving.
**Finding the campground:** From Saguache, travel 27.6 miles northwest on Colorado Highway 114 to Forest Service Road 775. Turn north to the campground.

**The campground:** Buffalo Pass is a pretty campground that seems to be all but forgotten. It has widely spaced sites in a light pine forest and makes a wonderful stopover. Four-wheel-drive roads abound in this lonely area, many of them leading to excellent fishing opportunities.

## 223 | Cement Creek

**Location:** Northeast of Gunnison.
**Facilities:** Central water, fire rings, picnic tables, vault toilets.
**Sites:** 13.
**Fee:** $6.
**Elevation:** 9,000 feet.
**Road conditions:** One-and-a-half lane, washboard, gravel.
**Management:** Gunnison National Forest, 970-641-0471.

**Activities:** Hiking, fishing, dirt biking, horseback riding.
**Finding the campground**: From Gunnison, travel about 20 miles north on Colorado Highway 135, and then 4 miles east on Forest Service Road 740.

**The campground:** Cement Creek is a small campground with a lot going for it. It's close to the charming resort town of Crested Butte, where shopping and dining are the featured activities during summer months. The campground itself is situated along Cement Creek with easy access to trails of various types. Several are open to motorbikes. Two hot springs are located on the creek, one north and one south of camp. A bit of exploring along the creek could turn up others.

## 224 | Gold Creek

**Location:** North of Ohio City.
**Facilities**: Corral, fire rings, picnic tables, vault toilets; no water.
**Sites:** 4 trailer sites, 2 tent sites.
**Fee:** $4.
**Elevation:** 10,000 feet.
**Road conditions:** one lane, dirt, rocky.
**Management:** Gunnison National Forest, 970-641-0471.
**Activities**: Hiking, horseback riding, fishing.
**Restrictions:** 12-foot maximum trailer length.
**Finding the campground**: Ohio City is on County Road 76 northeast of Gunnison. In Ohio City, turn north on Forest Service Road 771. Travel about 8 miles to the campground.

**The campground:** Gold Creek is a beautiful but remote campground, accessible only to trailers less than 12 feet long. The drive along FSR 771 is a trip through history. The road passes mines, miner's cabins, and piles of rusted equipment. If you choose to explore, be sure not to trespass on private property. Do not collect any rocks from nearby dumps without first obtaining permission because some of the mines are still being worked.

The campground is beautifully set in a dense pine and spruce forest. You may have neighbors, but the camp is a quiet one. The real drawing card here is the trail system. Pack/saddle Trail 428 leaves the camp headed north through Gunsight Pass, ending at the Lottis Creek Campground (Campground 232) in Taylor Canyon. Anytime you spend along this trail is worth the effort.

## 225 | Lake Irwin

**Location:** Northwest of Crested Butte.
**Facilities**: Central water, fire rings, picnic tables, vault toilets.
**Sites:** 32.
**Fee:** $8.
**Elevation:** 10,000 feet.
**Road conditions:** One-and-a-half lane, gravel, some washboarding.

**Management**: Gunnison National Forest, 970-641-0471.
**Reservations**: 800-280-CAMP, www.nrrc.com, $8.65 fee.
**Activities**: Fishing, hiking.
**Finding the campground**: From Crested Butte, travel west on County Road 12 about 7 miles. Turn north onto Forest Service Road 826 and travel about 2.5 miles to the campground.
**The campground**: If the campgrounds in this book were listed in order by scenic beauty, Lake Irwin would be very near the front of the book. The crystal-clear lake begs your attention at all hours. The campground graces the western tip, allowing views of the spectacular sunrises reflected in the water. Because there is an abundance of camping in the Gunnison area, Lake Irwin sees slightly lower usage than you would expect from a camp this beautiful. Fishing is possible both on the lake and on the stream that feeds it. A hiking trail begins and ends near the summit of Ruby Peak (12,644 feet).

## 226 Mirror Lake

**Location**: Southeast of Tincup.
**Facilities**: Central water, fire rings, picnic tables, vault toilets.
**Sites**: 10.
**Fee**: $6.
**Elevation**: 11,100 feet.
**Road conditions**: One-and-a-half lane, rocky.
**Management**: Gunnison National Forest, 970-641-0471.
**Activities**: Fishing, hiking, horseback riding, four-wheel driving, scenic driving
**Finding the campground**: Tincup is southeast of Taylor Park Reservoir on Forest Service Road 765. From Tincup, travel southeast about 3 miles on FSR 267 to the campground.

**The campground**: Mirror Lake perches right at the timberline, allowing vehicle campers their only opportunity in the state to camp in alpine tundra and subalpine forest. It is important to note that at this elevation, the weather is unpredictable, so you should pack accordingly. The campsites are widely spaced at the edge of the lake. The campground is small, but spots for primitive camping line FSR 267.

Like many Colorado mining communities, Tincup draws its share of vacationers. What's different here, though, is the complete lack of antique stores, coffee shops, and brew pubs. The attraction is the place itself. The drive over Cumberland Pass is stunning but requires nerves of steel. Tincup Pass is four-wheel-drive only. The easiest way in and out of the area is via Taylor Canyon (FSR 742).

## 227 Pitkin

**Location**: Northeast of Ohio City.
**Facilities**: Central water, fire rings, wheelchair-accessible sites, picnic tables,

vault toilets.
**Sites:** 22.
**Fee:** $10.
**Elevation:** 9,400 feet.
**Road conditions:** two lane, gravel.
**Management:** Gunnison National Forest, 970-641-0471.
**Activities:** Fishing, hiking, dirt biking, antique shopping, four-wheel driving.
**Finding the campground:** Ohio City is on County Road 76, northeast of Gunnison. From Ohio City, continue northeast on CR 76 to the town of Pitkin. Go through town and travel about 1 mile northeast on Forest Service Road 765 to the campground.

**The campground:** Some say that the Texans know all the good campgrounds in Colorado. If that's true, this is a good one, because there's usually no shortage of Texas license plates here. The sites are moderately spaced in a light pine and spruce forest. There are some pull-throughs. Trails and four-wheel-drive roads fan out in all direction from camp. Many of the roads lead past abandoned mines that date back to the turn of the century. Use extreme caution if you choose to explore any of these, and take care not to trespass on private property.
Pitkin is an old mining town turned antique market. It provides another entertaining way to pass the day. FSR 765 continues over Cumberland Pass. It narrows to one lane of dirt and reaches an elevation of over 12,000 feet. The drive is incredible, and a juicy burger at the local hangout in Tincup awaits you if you have the nerve to go that far.

## 228 Quartz

**Location:** Northeast of Ohio City.
**Facilities:** Central water, fire rings, picnic tables, vault toilets.
**Sites:** 10.
**Fee:** $6.
**Elevation:** 9,800 feet.
**Road conditions:** One-and-a-half lane, dirt with washboarding.
**Management:** Gunnison National Forest, 970-641-0471.
**Activities:** Fishing, four-wheel driving, scenic driving.
**Finding the campground:** Ohio City is on County Road 76, northeast of Gunnison. From Ohio City, continue northeast on CR 76 to the town of Pitkin. Go through town and travel about 4 miles northeast on Forest Service Road 765 to the campground.

**The campground:** Quartz is a wonderful home base for exploring this mining area by four-wheel-drive vehicle. It's surprising that some enterprising soul hasn't opened a jeep rental operation in Pitkin or Ohio City. These seem to be popular in other parts of the state with a similar abundance of old mine roads. Unfortunately, here you'll have to bring your own wheels. Dirt bikers may also enjoy some of the lower roads, but they should avoid the passes (Cumberland and Tincup in particular), which are steep and narrow with no room for error on slick gravel. Fishing is a popular pastime here; North Quartz Creek runs through the campground.

## 229 Soap Creek

**Location:** West of Gunnison.
**Facilities:** Central water, fire rings, picnic tables, vault toilets.
**Sites:** 21.
**Fee:** $7.
**Elevation:** 7,700 feet.
**Road conditions:** two lane, gravel.
**Management:** Gunnison National Forest, 970-641-0471.
**Activities:** Fishing, hiking, horseback riding.
**Finding the campground:** From Gunnison, travel about 26 miles west on U.S. Highway 50 to Colorado Highway 92. Turn northwest and travel about 0.5 mile to Forest Service Road 721. Turn north and travel about 7 miles to FSR 824. Turn east and continue another 0.5 mile to the campground.

**The campground:** Easy access to the West Elk Wilderness via hiking and pack/saddle trails is the main feature of this rugged camp. Soap Creek is remote and sees fairly low usage due to its proximity to more popular campgrounds in the Curecanti National Recreation Area. Fishing is possible on Soap Creek or back down the road at Blue Mesa Reservoir.

## 230 Taylor Canyon Area: Cold Spring

**Location:** Northeast of Gunnison.
**Facilities:** Central water, fire rings, picnic tables, vault toilets.
**Sites:** 6.
**Fee:** $6.
**Elevation:** 9,000 feet.
**Road conditions:** Paved.
**Management:** Gunnison National Forest, 970-641-0471.
**Activities:** Fishing, river sports.
**Restrictions:** Tents only.
**Finding the campground:** From Gunnison, travel north on Colorado Highway 135, about 11 miles to Almont. Turn northeast onto Forest Service Road 742. The campground is 16.1 miles from Almont.

**The campground:** Cold Spring is the smallest campground along the Taylor River. The spaces here are widely spaced amid a pine forest. Trailers are not recommended because there is no room to turn around. The river is across the road.

## 231 | Taylor Canyon Area: Lodgepole/Gunnison

**Location:** Northeast of Gunnison.
**Facilities:** Central water, fire rings, picnic tables, vault toilets.
**Sites:** 16.
**Fee:** $8.
**Elevation:** 8,800 feet.
**Road conditions:** Paved.
**Management:** Gunnison National Forest, 970-641-0471.
**Reservations:** 800-280-CAMP, www.nrrc.com, $8.65 fee.
**Activities:** Fishing, hiking, river sports, horseback riding.
**Finding the campground:** From Gunnison, travel north on Colorado Highway 135 about 11 miles to Almont. Turn northeast onto Forest Service Road 742. The campground is 14.7 miles from Almont.

**The campground:** Lodgepole/Gunnison takes its name from the towering lodgepole pines that dot the campground. They provide a canopy of shade without creating that dense, dark atmosphere that can be claustrophobic to some. The sites are moderately spaced. Access to the Taylor River is across the road. Lodgepole is the closest campground to Trail 430, which crosses Fossil Ridge at around 12,000 feet. Pack/saddle animals are allowed on the trail but not in camp.

## 232 | Taylor Canyon Area: Lottis Creek

**Location:** Northeast of Gunnison.
**Facilities:** Central water, fire rings, picnic tables, vault toilets, wheelchair-accessible site.
**Sites:** 27.
**Fee:** $10.
**Elevation:** 9,000 feet.
**Road conditions:** Paved.
**Management:** Gunnison National Forest, 970-641-0471.
**Activities:** Fishing, hiking, river sports, horseback riding.
**Finding the campground:** From Gunnison, travel north on Colorado Highway 135 about 11 miles to Almont. Turn northeast onto Forest Service Road 742. The campground is 17.5 miles from Almont.

**The campground:** Lottis Creek is the last of the campgrounds in Taylor Canyon. If you get here and still haven't found a campground to your liking, try Taylor Park Reservoir just a few miles farther down the road. Fishing options here include both the Taylor River and Lottis Creek. Hiking and horseback riding are possible on several trails that leave the camp. A relatively easy hike will take you through Union Park to Taylor Park Reservoir. Take Trail 758 from camp, and then branch north onto Trail 752. Be sure to check with rangers regarding trail conditions.

## 233 Taylor Canyon Area: North Bank

**Location:** Northeast of Gunnison.
**Facilities:** Central water, fire rings, picnic tables, vault toilets.
**Sites:** 17.
**Fee:** $8.
**Elevation:** 8,600 feet.
**Road conditions:** Paved.
**Management:** Gunnison National Forest, 970-641-0471.
**Activities:** Fishing, river sports.
**Finding the campground:** From Gunnison, travel north on Colorado Highway 135, about 11 miles to Almont. Turn northeast onto Forest Service Road 742. The campground is 7.7 miles from Almont.

**The campground:** Though the campsites are tightly spaced, North Bank provides direct access to Taylor River, which is not available at many of the campgrounds in the canyon. The sites are squeezed onto the hillside amid a dense pine and spruce forest. Trails allow river access for sites away from the river.

## 234 Taylor Canyon Area: One Mile

**Location:** Northeast of Gunnison.
**Facilities:** Central water, fire rings, picnic tables, vault toilets, electricity.
**Sites:** 27.
**Fee:** $12.
**Elevation:** 8,600 feet.
**Road conditions:** Paved.
**Management:** Gunnison National Forest, 970-641-0471.
**Reservations:** 800-280-CAMP, www.nrrc.com, $8.65 fee.
**Activities:** Fishing, hiking, river sports, four-wheel driving.
**Finding the campground:** From Gunnison, travel north on Colorado Highway 135, about 11 miles to Almont. Turn northeast onto Forest Service Road 742. The campground is about 8 miles from Almont.

**The campground:** This thoroughly modern campground has paved roads throughout and electricity at many sites. Most of the campsites are widely spaced, some amid towering trees, some in open meadows. All are beautiful. Hiking and four-wheel-drive trails branch off to the south, so after you catch your limit, you can seek other adventures.

## 235 Taylor Canyon Area: Rosy Lane

**Location:** Northeast of Gunnison.
**Facilities:** Central water, fire rings, wheelchair-accessible site, picnic tables, vault toilets.
**Sites:** 19.

**Fee:** $10.
**Elevation:** 8,600 feet.
**Road conditions:** Paved.
**Management:** Gunnison National Forest, 970-641-0471.
**Reservations:** 800-280-CAMP, www.nrrc.com, $8.65 fee.
**Activities:** Fishing, river sports.
**Finding the campground:** From Gunnison, travel north on Colorado Highway 135, about 11 miles to Almont. Turn northeast onto Forest Service Road 742. The campground is just before mile marker 9.

**The campground:** As the name implies, this peaceful campground is one of the nicest in the canyon. It has been completely remodeled with modern toilets and paved bike trails. The sites are set amid pines and aspens and some have direct access to Taylor River. Break out the hammock for this one, because you won't want to leave unless you run low on bait.

## 236 | Taylor Canyon Area: Spring Creek

**Location:** Northeast of Gunnison.
**Facilities:** Central water, fire rings, picnic tables, vault toilets.
**Sites:** 12.
**Fee:** $7.
**Elevation:** 8,600 feet.
**Road conditions:** two lane, gravel.
**Management:** Gunnison National Forest, 970-641-0471.
**Activities:** Fishing, river sports.
**Finding the campground:** From Gunnison, travel north on Colorado Highway 135, about 11 miles to Almont. Turn northeast onto Forest Service Road 742. Travel 7.2 miles to FSR 744. Turn north and travel about 2 miles to the campground.

**The campground:** If you prefer to stay one step ahead of the crowd, this campground is for you. It isn't actually located in Taylor Canyon, but rather, is 2 miles north on Spring Creek. The sites are just as pretty, and not quite as likely to be full as those lining the Taylor River.

## 237 | Taylor Park Reservoir: Lakeview/Gunnison

**Location:** Northeast of Gunnison.
**Facilities:** Central water, fire rings, picnic tables, vault toilets.
**Sites:** 46.
**Fee:** $10.
**Elevation:** 9,400 feet.
**Road conditions:** Paved.
**Management:** Gunnison National Forest, 970-641-0471.
**Reservations:** 800-280-CAMP, www.nrrc.com, $8.65 fee.
**Activities:** Fishing, hiking, scenic driving.

**Finding the campground:** From Gunnison, travel north on Colorado Highway 135, about 11 miles to Almont. Turn northeast onto Forest Service Road 742 and go 23 miles to the reservoir.

**The campground:** Taylor Park Reservoir is like the cherry on top of an ice cream sundae: you don't really have to have it, but it sure is nice. The campsites here offer moderate to tight spacing, but most have beautiful views of the lake. If you've made it through Taylor Canyon without finding a campsite to your liking, one is bound to be waiting for you here.

The reservoir has a second campground, River's End, but it's not much more than an open parking lot, and the access road is so rough that it's like driving on railroad tracks.

# Additional Campgrounds in the Gunnison Area

| | Type* | Contact | Location |
|---|---|---|---|
| 7-11 Ranch | P (6) | 970-641-0666 | CR 76 in Parlin |
| Crystal Meadows Ranch | P (23) | 970-929-5656 | E of Somerset off CO 133 |
| Gunnison KOA | P (124) | 800-562-1248 | W of Gunnison off US 50 |
| Rockey River Resort | P (27) | 970-641-0174 | 4359 CR 10 in Gunnison |
| Rowe's RV Park | P (8) | 970-641-4272 | Main Street in Ohio City |
| Shady Island Resort | P (42) | 970-641-0416 | N of Gunnison on CO 135 |
| Sunnyside Campground | P (122) | 970-641-0477 | W of Gunnison on US 50 |
| Comanche | NF (4) | 970-641-0471 | N of Ohio City on FSR 771 |
| Commissary | NF (7) | 970-641-0471 | NW of Gunnison on FSR 72 |
| Dinner Station | NF (22) | 970-641-0471 | NE of Almont on FSR 742 |
| Dorchester | NF (10) | 970-641-0471 | NE on Almont on FSR 742 |
| Erickson Spring | NF (18) | 970-527-4131 | NE of Delto on CR 12 |
| Gothic | NF (4) | 970-641-0471 | N of Crested Butte on FSR 317 |
| Lost Lake | NF (11) | 970-527-4131 | W of Crested Butte on FSR 706 |
| Luders Creek | NF (6) | 719-655-2553 | NW of Saguache on FSR 750 |
| Middle Quart | NF (7) | 970-641-0471 | NE of Parlin on FSR 767 |
| Mosca | NF (16) | 970-641-0471 | NE of Almont on FSR 742 |
| River's End | NF (15) | 970-641-0471 | N side of Taylor Park Reservoir |
| Taylor Canyon Tent | NF (7) | 970-641-0471 | NE of Gunnison on FSR 742 |
| The Gate | BLM (8) | 970-641-0471 | N of Lake City on CO 149 |
| Red Bridge | BLM (7) | 970-641-0471 | N of Lake City on CO 149 |
| Cebolla Creek | SWA (3) | 970-641-0471 | SW of Gunnison on CR 27 |
| Dome Lakes | SWA DSP | 970-249-3431 | SE of Gunnison on CO 114 |

* See "Key to Abbreviations" p.22—(# of sites)

# Area 21: Cortez

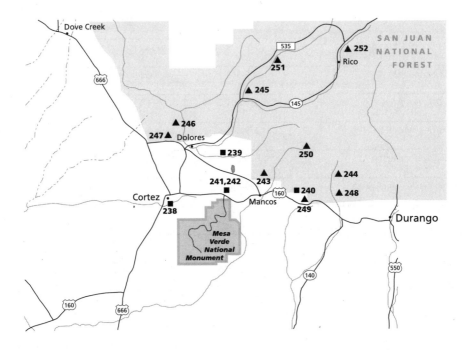

## CORTEZ

Cortez is the gateway to this corner of the state. All major roads from the south and west pass through here. Like much of the western edge of Colorado, the area surrounding Cortez is a blend of green mountains and unforgiving desert.

The focal point of this area is Mesa Verde National Park. Hidden atop a piñon-covered mesa are the incredibly well-preserved ruins of the Anasazi, or "ancient ones." Artifacts of their culture date back as far as A.D. 550. The monument provides a fascinating glimpse into the lives of these people, who disappeared from what is now Colorado around A.D. 1300. Additional artifacts and ruins can be viewed at the Anasazi Heritage Center near Dolores, and at Hovenweep National Monument on the Colorado-Utah border.

In addition to the ruins, the area overflows with opportunities for outdoor recreation. Choose from the standard fare of fishing, hiking, scenic driving, water sports, horseback riding, and golf. Or, for a real change of pace, try digging for artifacts at the Crow Canyon Archeological Center.

Camping in the area is as diverse as the land. There is no shortage of commercial campgrounds, including a guest ranch or two. National forest camps are equally plentiful. For those looking for a more primitive experience, try one of the state wildlife areas, such as Miramonte or even Ground Hog if you can stand the high elevation.

**For More Information:**

Cortez Welcome Center
928 E. Main St.
P.O. Box 968
Cortez, CO 81321
970-565-3414
e-mail: cacc@fone.net

Dolores Chamber of Commerce
P.O. Box 602
Dolores, CO 81323
970-882-4018

Mancos Visitor Center
P.O. Box 494
Mancos, CO 81328
970-533-7434 or 800-873-3310
www.swcolo.org

Crow Canyon Archeological Center
800-422-8975

# Commercial

## 238 Cortez KOA

**Location:** Cortez.
**Affiliations:** KOA; Colorado Association of Campgrounds, Cabins, and Lodges.
**Contact:** 970-565-9301, fax 970-565-2107.
**Amenities:** Dump station, laundry, showers, store, pool, whirlpool, public phone, playground, cabins, picnic tables, fire rings, grills.
**Sites:** 73, 28 full hookups.
**Price per night:** $24.
**Elevation:** 6,200 feet.
**Finding the campground:** Located on the east side of Cortez on U.S. Highway 160.

**The campground:** There aren't many surprises here. The facilities are easy to reach and in near-perfect condition. The location allows for easy exploration of Mesa Verde National Park, as well as the casino at Sleeping Ute.

## 239 Dolores River RV Park & Cabins

**Location:** East of Dolores.
**Affiliations:** Good Sam; Colorado Association of Campgrounds, Cabins, and

189

Lodges.
**Contact:** 970-882-7761, fax 970-882-4829.
**Reservations:** 800-200-2399.
**Amenities:** Dump station, laundry, showers, store, public phone, playground, cabins, picnic tables, fire rings, grills.
**Sites:** 93, 63 full hookups.
**Price per night:** $11 to $20.
**Elevation:** 7,000 feet.
**Season:** Year-round.
**Finding the campground:** From the junction of Colorado Highways 184 and 145, travel northeast on CO 145, about 4 miles to the park.

**The campground:** Dolores is a pretty little town sandwiched between the rolling desert of far western Colorado and the jagged mountains of the San Juan National Forest. If you're looking for a full-service RV park in the Dolores area, this is a good choice. Its sites are shaded by towering cottonwoods along the Dolores River. The central location allows you to spend time fishing in the river or in McPhee Reservoir, plus it's a short drive to Telluride for a day of shopping and taking in the sites.

## 240  Echo Basin RV & Guest Ranch

**Location:** Between Durango and Cortez.
**Affiliations:** Colorado Association of Campgrounds, Cabins, and Lodges.
**Contact:** 970-533-7000.
**Reservations:** 800-426-1890.
**Amenities:** Dump station, laundry, showers, store, pool, public phone, playground, cabins, restaurant, picnic tables, fishing lakes, hiking trails, horse rental.
**Sites:** 102, 50 full hookups.
**Price per night:** $19.
**Elevation:** 7,800 feet.
**Season:** Year-round.
**Finding the campground:** From Mancos, between Durango and Cortez, travel east on U.S. Highway 160, about 2 miles to Echo Basin Road. Turn north and go about 3 miles to the ranch.

**The campground:** This is one of the few true guest ranches with an RV park. The ranch comprises 600 pine-covered acres and three fishing lakes. With all the available activities, you may not want to leave, but the location is an easy drive from other activities in the southwest corner of the state. This is the kind of place you'll want to bring the family back to year after year.

## 241  Mesa Verde Point Kampark

**Location:** East of Mesa Verde National Park.
**Affiliations:** Good Sam; AAA; Colorado Association of Campgrounds, Cabins, and Lodges.

**Contact:** 970-533-7421.
**Reservations:** 800-776-7421.
**Amenities:** Dump station, laundry, showers, store, pool, whirlpool, public phone, playground, picnic tables, grills.
**Sites:** 44, 18 full hookups.
**Price per night:** $20 to $23.
**Elevation:** 6,995 feet.
**Finding the campground:** From the park entrance, go 0.5 mile east on U.S. Highway 160.

**The campground:** If you've come this far to see Mesa Verde, you might as well stay in comfort, right? If that's your plan, then this is a great choice for a campground. The pool is incredibly tempting after a hot afternoon trekking through the Anasazi ruins. The showers are within walking distance of your camp instead of driving distance as they are at the campground inside the park. In addition, your hosts can help you arrange rafting or horseback riding nearby. The sites are grassy, shaded, and inviting.

# Public

## 242 Mesa Verde National Park: Morefield Campground

**Location:** East of Cortez.
**Facilities:** Dump station, laundry, showers, store, public phone, restaurant, picnic tables, grills.
**Sites:** 440, 15 full hookups.
**Fee:** $12 to $19.
**Elevation:** 8,000 feet.
**Road conditions:** Paved.
**Management:** ARAMARK (concessionaire), 970-565-2133 (summer); 970-533-7731 (winter); fax 970-533-7831.
**Activities:** Hiking, tours of ruins.
**Finding the campground:** From the park entrance, travel 4 miles south to the campground.

**The campground:** So you're going to drive a long way to see the archeological and geological wonders of Mesa Verde, and you think, "What better place to stay than inside the park?" Sorry folks, but this isn't Disney World. Though well managed and maintained, the campground here is not a pretty sight. It seems a shame to camp amid the stubby scrub oaks and sagebrush when aspen-covered mountains are a short drive away. The only advantage here is that you can be first in line to get the tickets necessary to tour the best of the ruins.

*To keep crowds manageable, the best ruins at Mesa Verde National Park are accessible only to ticketed tours.*

## 243 Mancos State Park

**Location:** North of Mancos.
**Facilities:** Dump station, boat ramp, trails, picnic tables, grills, central water, wheelchair-accessible site.
**Sites:** 33.
**Fee:** $6, plus $4 daily or $40 annual vehicle pass.
**Elevation:** 7,800 feet.
**Road conditions:** two lane, gravel.
**Management:** Colorado Department of Parks and Outdoor Recreation, 970-883-2203.
**Reservations:** 800-678-CAMP, $7 fee.
**Activities:** Fishing, hiking.
**Season:** Year-round.
**Finding the campground:** Mancos is 27 miles west of Durango on U.S. Highway 160. From Mancos, go north on Colorado Highway 184, about 0.25 mile to County Road 42/Forest Service Road 561. Turn north and go 4 miles to CR N. Turn right to the park entrance.

**The campground:** Mancos is one of the smallest state parks in the system: Twenty-four of the campsites are grouped together and separated from a small lake by a dense pine and oak forest. There are also nine lakeside tent sites on the northeast corner of the lake with no drinking water available. Only wake-less boating is allowed on the 216-acre lake. Sites are well spaced and pretty, but the campground is next to a busy guest ranch that runs a herd of horses back from their overnight pasture every morning at 6 A.M. If you don't mind waking up to thundering hooves and yipping cowhands, this is a nice place to stay.

## 244 Kroeger

**Location:** Northwest of Durango.
**Facilities:** Central water, fire rings, picnic tables, vault toilets.
**Sites:** 10.
**Fee:** $8.
**Elevation:** 9,000 feet.
**Road conditions:** One-and-a-half lane, dirt, rocky.
**Management:** San Juan National Forest, 970-882-7296.
**Activities:** Fishing, hiking.
**Finding the campground:** From Durango, travel west on U.S. Highway 160, about 11 miles to Hesperus. Turn north onto Forest Service Road 571 and go about 7 miles to the campground.

**The campground:** If you make it to Kroeger, you will be well rewarded by its beauty. This lonely camp offers well-spaced, stream-side sites. But the road is rough; 7 miles seem like 70. If you dare to go farther, FSR 571 allows access to the Colorado Trail on the north side of Snowstorm Peak, which is the beautiful peak you glimpsed while fighting the rocks in the road. The good news here is that the condition of the road will likely keep a great number of people away.

## 245 Mavreeso

**Location:** Northeast of Dolores.
**Facilities:** Central water, fire rings, picnic tables, vault toilets.
**Sites:** 13.
**Fee:** $8.
**Elevation:** 7,600 feet.
**Road conditions:** Paved.
**Management:** San Juan National Forest, 970-882-7296.
**Activities:** Fishing, hiking, horseback riding.
**Finding the campground:** From Dolores, travel northeast on Colorado Highway 145, about 13 miles to Forest Service Road 535. Turn and continue northeast about 6 miles to the campground.

**The campground:** Mavreeso is one of the prettiest campgrounds in the area. It perches on the banks of the West Dolores River in a dense forest of spruce and fir. About half the sites are actually on the river. The sites are well spaced, allowing more privacy than is often found in riverside camps. Access to the Stoner Mesa Trail is about 2.5 miles southwest of the camp. The trail across this 9,000-foot mesa presents an ideal way to enjoy the San Juan National Forest—after you've caught your limit of trout, of course.

## 246 McPhee Reservoir: House Creek

**Location:** West of Dolores.
**Facilities:** Central water, fire rings, picnic tables, vault toilets, dump station, showers, boat ramp, electricity, wheelchair-accessible sites.
**Sites:** 51.
**Fee:** $10 to $12, plus fee for second vehicle.
**Elevation:** 6,924 feet.
**Road conditions:** two lane, gravel.
**Management:** San Juan National Forest, 970-882-7296.
**Reservations:** 800-280-CAMP, www.nrrc.com, $8.65 fee.
**Activities:** Fishing, water sports.
**Finding the campground:** From Dolores, travel 6 miles north on Forest Service Road 526 to FSR 528. Turn southwest and go another 6 miles to the campground.

**The campground:** Your love for water sports can be easily satisfied at McPhee Reservoir. This large lake can accommodate both skiers and anglers. The House Creek Campground sprawls across a point overlooking the widest part of the lake. Sites are closely spaced, but not too close for comfort. The vegetation is primarily piñon and scrub oak, which provide very little shade, but some sites have shelters over the picnic tables. There are only a few sites with electricity, and the showers aren't free, but they are welcome after a long day of activity.

## 247 | McPhee Reservoir: McPhee

**Location:** West of Dolores.
**Facilities:** Central water, fire rings, picnic tables, vault toilets, dump station, showers, boat ramp, electricity, wheelchair-accessible sites.
**Sites:** 65.
**Fee:** $8 to $12, plus fee for second vehicle.
**Elevation:** 6,924 feet.
**Road conditions:** Paved.
**Management:** San Juan National Forest, 970-882-7296.
**Reservations:** 800-280-CAMP, www.nrrc.com, $8.65 fee.
**Activities:** Fishing, water sports.
**Finding the campground:** From Dolores, travel 2.5 miles west on U.S. Highway 145 to Colorado Highway 184. Turn northwest and go 4.5 miles to Forest Service Road 271. Turn northeast and go 2.5 miles to the campground.

**The campground:** McPhee Campground is very nice. The sites are scattered among the piñons and scrub oak far enough apart to give some measure of privacy. Some of the sites have extra parking for boat trailers, but there is an overflow lot for those that do not. In addition to the trailer sites, there are some nice walk-in tent sites. The only problem here is the lack of direct access to the reservoir.

## 248 | Snowslide

**Location:** North of Hesperus.
**Facilities:** Fire rings, picnic tables, vault toilets; no water.
**Sites:** 12.
**Fee:** $6.
**Elevation:** 9,000 feet.
**Road conditions:** One-and-a-half lane, dirt, rocky.
**Management:** San Juan National Forest, 970-533-7716.
**Activities:** Fishing, hiking.
**Finding the campground:** From Durango, travel west on U.S. Highway 160, about 11 miles to Hesperus. Turn north onto Forest Service Road 571 and go 6.5 miles to the campground.

**The campground:** The drive to Snowslide will give you some insight into this campground's former name, "Potato Patch." The road is very rocky and gets worse as you go. But if you can manage to look up from the road, the views of Snowstorm Peak are the kind you see in paintings and on postcards. Fishing along the La Plata River is possible right from camp.

## 249 | Target Tree

**Location:** East of Mancos.
**Facilities:** Central water, fire rings, picnic tables, vault toilets.

**Sites:** 25.
**Fee:** $8.
**Elevation:** 7,800 feet.
**Road conditions:** Paved.
**Management:** San Juan National Forest, 970-533-7716.
**Activities:** Hiking, scenic driving.
**Finding the campground:** From Mancos, travel east on U.S. Highway 160, about 7 miles to the campground.

**The campground:** Target Tree is a one-night-stand campground. There really aren't any reasons to stay here longer, unless you like staying in national forest campgrounds with easy access to the highway. If that's the case, then you can reach all of southwestern Colorado from U.S. Highway 160. The campsites here are scattered among a lush pine and oak forest, which helps reduce the traffic noise somewhat.

## 250 Transfer

**Location:** Northeast of Mancos.
**Facilities:** Central water, fire rings, picnic tables, vault toilets, corral.
**Sites:** 13.
**Fee:** $9.
**Elevation:** 8,500 feet.
**Road conditions:** two lane, gravel.
**Management:** San Juan National Forest, 970-533-7716.
**Activities:** Hiking, horseback riding.
**Finding the campground:** From Mancos, go about 200 yards north on Colorado Highway 145 to Forest Service Road 535. Turn northeast and go 7.5 miles to the campground.

**The campground:** Transfer is for hikers, horse lovers, and anybody else who wants to get away from the bustle of civilization. The large corral across the road from camp was built by and is occasionally shared by the wranglers at Lake Mancos Ranch, a guest ranch near Mancos State Park (Campground 243). There are miles of trails and roads to cover both on horseback and on foot. And what a campground to come home to at the end of the day! Sites are set in a lush aspen forest with a ground cover of wild pink roses and columbine. The view from camp is of the La Plata Mountains west of Durango. If you don't mind the lack of fishing opportunities, it doesn't get much better than this anywhere in the state.

## 251 West Dolores

**Location:** Northeast of Dolores.
**Facilities:** Central water, fire rings, picnic tables, vault toilets.
**Sites:** 11.

**Fee:** $8.
**Elevation:** 7,800 feet.
**Road conditions:** Paved.
**Management:** San Juan National Forest, 970-882-7296.
**Activities:** Fishing, hiking, horseback riding.
**Finding the campground:** From Dolores, travel northeast on Colorado Highway 145, about 13 miles to Forest Service Road 535. Turn left and continue northeast, 7.5 miles to the campground.

**The campground:** These 11 campsites seem to have attracted a regular following, making it difficult to find an open site here. But if you manage to get one, you won't be disappointed. The camp is prettier than most fishing camps. The trees are dense and the sites widely spaced.

If West Dolores is full, the next campground on this road is Burro Bridge. If you brave the road, which deteriorates into near non-existence before you reach the camp, you should have the place all to yourself. The brave and the foolhardy will enjoy the drive.

## Additional Campgrounds in the Cortez Area

| | Type* | Contact | Location |
|---|---|---|---|
| A & A Mesa Verde RV Park & Resort | P (85) | 970-565-3517 | Mesa Verde National Park entrance on US 160 |
| Cozy Comfort RV Park | P (11) | 970-882-2483 | 1501 Central in Dolores |
| LaMesa RV Park | P (41) | 970-565-3610 | CO 145 & US 160 |
| Lazy G Campground | P (79) | 970-565-8577 | CO 145 & US 160 |
| McPhee Mobile Home & RV Park | P (50) | 970-882-4901 | W of Dolores on CO 184 |
| Mesa Oasis Campground | P (89) | 970-565-8716 | S of Cortez on US 160/166 |
| Outpost Motel & RV Park | P (14) | 970-882-7271 | HWY 145 in Dolores |
| Priest Gulch Campground & RV Park & Resort | P (30) | 970-562-3810 | N of Dolores on CO 145 |
| Sleeping Ute RV Park & RV Park & Resort | P (84) | 800-565-9136 | S of Cortez on US 160/166 |
| Stoner Creek RV Park | P (44) | 970-882-2204 | CO 145 in Stoner |
| Sundance RV Park | P (78) | 970-565-0997 | E Main in Cortez |
| Wild Wild Rset | P (30) | 970-533-9747 | Mesa Verde National Park entrance on US 160 |
| Williams RV Park | P (19) | 970-565-9413 | S of Cortez on US 160/166 |
| Burro Bridge | NF (14) | 970-882-7296 | NE of Dolores on CR 535 |
| Cabin Canyon | NF (11) | 970-882-7296 | N of Cortez on FSR 504 |
| Ferris Canyon | NF (6) | 970-882-7296 | N of Cortez on FSR 504 |
| Bradfield | BLM (22) | 970-247-4082 | E of Cahone on Dolores River |
| Mountain Sheep Point | BLM (3) | 970-247-4082 | E of Dove Creek on River Access Road |
| Groundhog | SWA (13) | 970-249-3431 | N of Dolores on FSR 533 |
| Lone Cone | SWA DSP | 970-249-3431 | SE of Norwood on FSR 610 |
| Miramonte | SWA | 970-249-3431 | SE of Norwood on FSR 610 |

* See "Key to Abbreviations" p.22—(# of sites)

# Area 22: Telluride

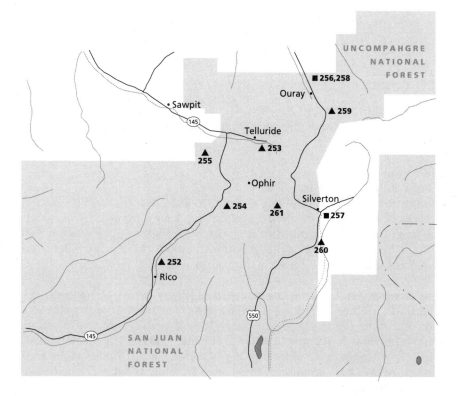

## TELLURIDE

If you are looking for an area that guarantees beautiful scenery in every direction, this is it. There's not an ugly patch of ground between Dolores and Telluride. Of course there's not much to do in between except fish and look at the scenery, but most visitors don't seem to mind.

If you really must spend the daylight hours doing something, head to Telluride, where shopping, dining, tennis, swimming, and ski-lift rides await.

Camping in the area is all of the public nature: six national forest camps, plus Town Park Campground operated by the city of Telluride. Unfortunately, only the Matterhorn (Campground 254) takes reservations.

**For More Information:**

Telluride Chamber Resort Association
666 W. Colorado Avenue
Box 653
Telluride, CO 81435

970-728-3041
e-mail: telluride_info@infozone.org

---

# Public

## 252 Cayton

**Location:** Northeast of Rico.
**Facilities:** Central water, fire rings, picnic tables, vault toilets.
**Sites:** 27.
**Fee:** $9.
**Elevation:** 9,400 feet.
**Road conditions:** two lane, gravel.
**Management:** San Juan National Forest, 970-882-7296.
**Activities:** Fishing, hiking, four-wheel driving, scenic driving.
**Finding the campground:** Rico is on Colorado Highway 145 between Telluride and Dolores. From Rico, travel northeast on CO 145, about 6 miles to Forest Service Road 578. Turn east to the campground.

**The campground:** Cayton is a secluded hideaway below Lizard Head Pass, where you will find fishing in the Dolores River and nearby access to the Colorado Trail. Sites are nicely spaced among towering pines and spruces, and the camp is far enough from the highway to eliminate the traffic noise. Trout Lake, which is one of the prettiest lakes in all of Colorado, is just 7 miles to the north. Cayton makes a nice destination to get away from the crowds, or a convenient stopover on your way north or south.

## 253 City of Telluride

**Location:** Telluride.
**Facilities:** Central water, picnic tables, vault toilets, tennis courts, pool, playground, children's fishing pond.
**Sites:** 30.
**Fee:** $10.
**Elevation:** 9,000 feet.
**Road conditions:** Paved.
**Management:** City of Telluride.
**Activities:** Fishing, hiking, biking, shopping, tennis, swimming.
**Finding the campground:** Travel through town heading east. Turn south at the city park near the end of town.

**The campground:** Telluride is probably the most renovated and celebrated mining town in Colorado. It's a glitzy mix of 1890s style and 1990s cash. You can wine, dine, and shop for antiques along almost any block in town. The city park is the only place to camp in town, since there are no RV parks. Sites are shady and scattered along a stream. They are available first-come, first-served, though, and the park stays fairly busy throughout the summer. If you are lucky enough to find an open site, the list of things to do is almost endless. If your luck doesn't hold, the next closest campground is Sunshine (Campground 255).

## 254 Matterhorn

**Location:** Southwest of Telluride.
**Facilities:** Central water, fire rings, wheelchair-accessible site, picnic tables, flush toilets, electricity, showers.
**Sites:** 23.
**Fee:** $10 to $14.
**Elevation:** 9,480 feet.
**Road conditions:** Paved.
**Management:** Uncompahgre National Forest, 303-327-4261.
**Activities:** Fishing, hiking, scenic driving, four-wheel driving.
**Finding the campground:** From Telluride, travel south on Colorado Highway 145, about 10 miles to the campground entrance.

**The campground:** Many campers would agree that the hot shower available here is worth the camping fee. Matterhorn is aptly named for its views of jagged Vermilion Peak to the southeast. Fishing at nearby Trout Lake is a joy. Vermilion Peak and Sheep Mountain stand watch over the crystal-clear lake. These two 13,000-foot-plus peaks are snowcapped most of the year. Matterhorn makes either a great destination (the second closest national forest camp to Telluride) or one of the prettiest stopovers in the state.

## 255 Sunshine

**Location:** Southwest of Telluride.
**Facilities:** Central water, fire rings, picnic tables, vault toilets.
**Sites:** 15.
**Fee:** $10.
**Elevation:** 9,500 feet.
**Road conditions:** Paved.
**Management:** Uncompahgre National Forest, 970-327-4261.
**Activities:** Fishing, hiking, biking, shopping, scenic driving, four-wheel driving.
**Finding the campground:** From Telluride, travel southwest on Colorado Highway 145, about 8 miles to the campground entrance.

**The campground:** You can't get any closer to Telluride and stay in a national forest campground. Sunshine is near Cushman Lake and several trails suitable for hiking or biking. The sites are well spaced amid a mixed forest of aspens and evergreens. The camp is heavily used by both travelers passing through and those who plan to spend time exploring the area. So early arrival on weekends is the only way to ensure that a site will be available.

## Additional Campgrounds in the Telluride Area

|  | Type* | Contact | Location |
|---|---|---|---|
| Sheep Corral | NF (9) | 970-327-4261 | SW of Telluride on FSR 623 |
| Alta Lakes | NF DSP | 970-327-4261 | NE of Ophir |

* See "Key to Abbreviations" p.22—(# of sites)

# Area 23: Silverton

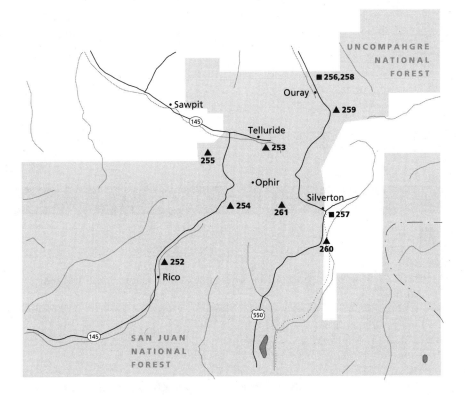

## SILVERTON

Silverton and Ouray are a package deal; if you've traveled far enough to visit one, don't miss the other. Both are mining towns at the northern end of the Animas River Valley, along which is an unparalleled scenic drive.

In Silverton, the big attraction is the narrow-gauge railroad, which runs from here to Durango. It chugs along the valley, belching black smoke and allowing you views that can only be seen from the cars of the train. Bus transportation is provided to complete the round trip.

Ouray is another of Colorado's hot-springs hot spots. The pools here include a lap pool, a shallow soaking pool, and a children's goldfish pond, plus shower and exercise facilities. There are few things better in life than relaxing in a hot mineral pool surrounded by the beauty of the Rocky Mountains.

Camping in the area is almost all commercially operated. There are RV parks in both towns. There are only two national forest camps, one near Silverton and the other near Ouray, plus one city park south of Silverton.

**For More Information:**

Silverton Chamber of Commerce
P.O. Box 565
Silverton, CO 81433
970-387-5654 or 800-752-4494
www.silverton.org

Ouray Chamber of Commerce
P.O. Box 145
Ouray, CO 81427
970-325-4743 or 800-228-1876
www.ouraycolorado.com

# Commercial

## 256  4J+1+1 Campground

**Location:** Ouray.
**Affiliations:** Colorado Association of Campgrounds, Cabins, and Lodges.
**Contact:** 970-325-4418.
**Amenities:** Laundry, showers, public phone, playground, cabins, picnic tables, fire rings, grills, patios.
**Sites:** 68, 50 full hookups.
**Price per night:** $16 to $22.
**Elevation:** 7,800 feet.
**Finding the campground:** In Ouray, turn west on 7th Avenue. Go about 2 blocks and then turn right on Oak Street.

**The campground:** Ouray is known as the "Switzerland of America," and this RV park is in the heart of town. The park is within walking distance of shops, restaurants, and hot springs. There are two preferred pastimes here: soaking in the hot mineral springs and driving the old mining roads in rented jeeps. There are so many places to rent jeeps here that you would think the Chrysler Corporation built the town. If you don't feel like driving, you can arrange a tour. Though there are many roads to choose from, the most popular is the Alpine Loop Backcountry Byway, which connects Ouray, Silverton, and Lake City via the famed Engineers Pass.

## 257  Silver Summit RV Park

**Location:** Silverton.
**Affiliations:** Colorado Association of Campgrounds, Cabins, and Lodges.
**Contact:** 970-387-0240, fax 970-387-5820, e-mail slvrsmmt@frontier.net.
**Amenities:** Dump station, laundry, showers, store, hot tub, public phone, helicopter tours, jeep rentals, picnic tables, grills.

**Sites:** 39, all full hookups.
**Price per night:** $15 to $20.
**Elevation:** 9,300 feet.
**Finding the campground:** In Silverton, turn east on 7th Street. Go 2 blocks to the campground.

**The campground:** There are two things you've got to do in Silverton: rent a jeep in which to go exploring, and ride the narrow-gauge railroad to Durango. Other than that, a visit here could include anything from shopping and dining to fishing and rockhounding. This is a nice park from which to do it all.

## 258 Timber Ridge

**Location:** Ouray.
**Affiliations:** Colorado Association of Campgrounds, Cabins, and Lodges.
**Contact:** 970-325-4523.
**Amenities:** Dump station, laundry, showers, public phone, restaurant, picnic tables, fire rings.
**Sites:** 70, 60 full hookups.
**Price per night:** $16 to $20.
**Elevation:** 7,800 feet.
**Finding the campground:** In Ouray, go 0.25 mile north of the hot-springs pool to the campground.

**The campground:** This parking-lot-style RV park is located on the Uncompahgre River. It is within walking distance of the hot-springs pool, which is a must-do activity in Ouray. If you don't "take in the waters," you've missed a real treat. The highway location also allows you to make a day trip to Ridgeway State Park for fishing if you like. If you reached Ouray from the north, be sure to make the drive south to Silverton part of your stay here. It is one of the most beautiful drives in the state.

## Public

## 259 Amphitheater

**Location:** South of Ouray.
**Facilities:** Central water, fire rings, picnic tables, vault toilets.
**Sites:** 30.
**Fee:** $12, plus fee for second vehicle.
**Elevation:** 8,400 feet.
**Road conditions:** Paved.
**Management:** Uncompahgre National Forest, 970-249-3711.
**Reservations:** 800-280-CAMP, www.nrrc.com, $8.65 fee.

**Activities:** Hiking, scenic driving, four-wheel driving, rockhounding.

**Finding the campground:** From Ouray, travel south on U.S. Highway 550, about 0.5 mile to Forest Service Road 885. Turn east and go 0.5 mile to the campground.

**The campground:** Amphitheater is the only national forest campground close to Ouray. The sites are widely spaced in a thick forest of pine and mixed deciduous trees. Hiking trails are near the camp, as well as throughout the Ouray area. Rockhounds will find plenty of spots to keep them busy, both north and south of Ouray. Places to start include the Senorita Mine, the Bullion King Mine, and the Brooklyn Mine. Amphitheater also makes the perfect stopover if you reach Ouray from the north near dark. You don't want to miss one of the most scenic drives in the state by driving from Ouray to Silverton at night.

## 260 | Molas Lake Park

**Location:** South of Silverton.

**Facilities:** Dump station, store, picnic tables, fire rings, grills, showers, cabins, laundry, hiking trails.

**Sites:** 60.

**Fee:** $12.

**Elevation:** 10,515 feet.

**Road conditions:** Paved.

**Management:** Town of Silverton, 970-387-5848.

**Activities:** Fishing, hiking, horseback riding, scenic driving, four-wheel driving.

**Finding the campground:** From Silverton, travel south on U.S. Highway 550, about 0.5 mile to the campground.

**The campground:** Wow! That pretty much sums up this breathtaking little lake. At least that's what you're likely to think the first time you round the bend in the road and see it for the first time. The lake is almost as pretty as Trout Lake on the road to Telluride, and it has a campground on its western and northern shore. Most sites are wooded and spaced far enough apart to allow some privacy. This is a nice cross between an RV park and a national forest campground.

## 261 | South Mineral

**Location:** West of Silverton.

**Facilities:** Central water, fire rings, picnic tables, vault toilets.

**Sites:** 23.

**Fee:** $8.

**Elevation:** 10,000 feet.

**Road conditions:** One-and-a-half lane, dirt.

**Management:** San Juan National Forest, 970-247-4874.

**Activities:** Fishing, hiking, horseback riding, four-wheel driving.

**Finding the campground:** From Silverton, travel northwest on U.S. Highway

550, about 4 miles to Forest Service Road 585. Turn southwest and go about 5 miles to the campground.

**The campground:** South Mineral is the closest national forest campground to Silverton, but it is still some distance away. Some sites are open, while some are wooded. A few sites are streamside. All are moderately spaced. There is also unimproved, dispersed camping possible along FSR 585. Trails nearby lead to several small lakes north and west of camp. The road becomes passable only to four-wheel-drive vehicles just beyond the campground, as it leads up the east slope of Rolling Mountain to the Bandora Mine. If you like peace and quiet but with activities reasonably close by, South Mineral is a campground to consider.

## Additional Campgrounds in the Silverton Area

| | Type* | Contact | Location |
|---|---|---|---|
| Ouray KOA | P (123) | 970-325-4736 | N of Ouray on CR 230 |
| Red Mountain Lodges & Campground | P (20) | 970-387-5512 | N of Silverton on CO 110 |
| Silverton Lakes Campground | P | 970-387-5721 | E of Silverton on CO 110 |

* See "Key to Abbreviations" p.22—(# of sites)

# Area 24: Lake City

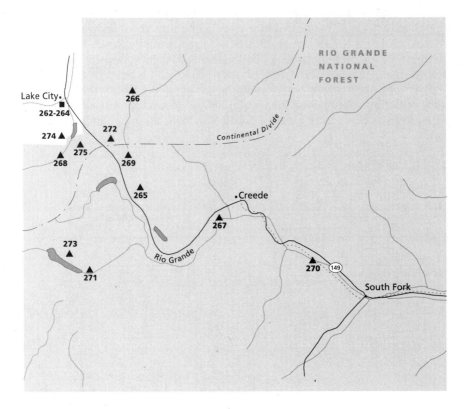

## LAKE CITY

Nobody ends up in Lake City by accident because not only is it difficult to reach, but it isn't on the way to anywhere else. If you do visit, you'll find a friendly town with a beautiful lake in its backyard. The mountains surrounding the town and lake are just short of magnificent.

Activity throughout this area centers on fishing. In Lake City, you have a choice of Lake San Cristobal or any number of streams that feed into the Lake Fork of the Gunnison. Between Creede and Lake City, the Rio Grande begins its journey southward to the Gulf of Mexico, and it attracts a huge number of fishermen.

The Lake City area also seems to attract some people with its quiet, small-town atmosphere. A large number of people have summer homes in the area. The weather is mild, the scenery enchanting, and the road is "one less traveled."

If you should suffer an attack of wanderlust, you can always rent a jeep and meander over the famed Engineer and Cinnamon passes, which are on the National Alpine Loop Backcountry Byway. The loop connects Lake City, Silverton, and Telluride, which probably accounts for the name given to Engineer Pass. One look at a topographical map makes it clear that it would take a real feat of engineering to connect these three towns.

Camping accommodations include several outstanding RV resorts on the lake and upriver from it. There are also shady RV parks in town that cater to both the one-nighter (though why would anyone go to Lake City for one night?) and the long-term guest. National forest camps are scattered throughout the area, including the highest in the state: Slumgullion (Campground 272).

**For More Information:**

Lake City Chamber of Commerce
P.O. Box 430
Lake City, CO 81235
970-944-2527

Creede/Mineral County Chamber of Commerce
P.O. Box 580
Creede, CO 81130
719-658-2374
www.creede.com
e-mail: creede@amigo.net

# Commercial

## 262 Castle Lakes Campground Resort

**Location:** Southwest of Lake City.
**Affiliations:** Colorado Association of Campgrounds, Cabins, and Lodges.
**Contact:** 970-944-2622.
**Amenities:** Laundry, showers, store, public phone, playground, cabins, restaurant, picnic tables, fire rings, grills, private fishing lakes, hiking trails, jeep rentals, horse rentals, trailer rentals.
**Sites:** 47, 29 full hookups.
**Price per night:** $12 to $17.
**Elevation:** 9,200 feet.
**Finding the campground:** From Lake City, travel south on Colorado Highway 149, about 2 miles to Lake San Cristobal Road/County Road 30. When the pavement ends, turn right and continue about 4 miles to the campground.

**The campground:** Castle Lakes isn't the easiest campground to find, but it's well worth the effort. Sites are widely spaced among the pines so that it resembles a national forest campground more than the typical RV park. There are plenty of activities, making this a relaxing family retreat far from the rush of traffic and the business of everyday life. The real beauty is, you don't even have to have your own trailer. You can rent one on site.

## 263 Lakeview Resort

**Location:** Lake San Cristobal.
**Affiliations:** None.
**Contact:** 970-944-2401, fax 970-944-2925, e-mail lvrmurphy@youngminds.com.
**Amenities:** Store, public phone, cabins, marina, picnic tables, grills, horse rentals, jeep rentals, boat rentals, fishing and hunting guides.
**Sites:** 10, all full hookups.
**Price per night:** $18.
**Elevation:** 9,100 feet.
**Finding the campground:** From Lake City, travel southwest on Colorado Highway 149, about 2 miles to Lake San Cristobal Road/County Road 30. Go 1.5 miles to CR 33, turn left and go about 0.5 mile to the resort. The office is at the marina.

**The campground:** Though it has only ten sites, the RV park at this resort is spacious and allows you to take advantage of the many recreational opportunities offered. Lake San Cristobal is large and surrounded by pine-covered peaks. You won't have to compete for space with the rest of the world at this destination.

## 264 Woodlake Park

**Location:** South of Lake City.
**Affiliations:** None.
**Contact:** 970-944-2283.
**Reservations:** 800-201-2694.
**Amenities:** Showers, public phone, cabins.
**Sites:** 19, 13 full hookups.
**Price per night:** $16.
**Elevation:** 9,000 feet.
**Finding the campground:** From Lake City, travel 2.5 miles south on Colorado Highway 149. The campground is between mileposts 69 and 70.

**The campground:** This RV park with shady, widely spaced sites along Slumgullion Creek is an easily accessible base from which to explore the treasures of the Lake City area. Four-wheel-driving—either in rented jeeps, in your own four-wheel-drive vehicle, or on guided tours—is the activity that brings many people here. The Alpine Loop Backcountry Byway is a round trip that you won't soon forget.

| Public |
| --- |

## 265 Bristol Head

**Location:** West of Creede.
**Facilities:** Central water, fire rings, picnic tables, vault toilets.
**Sites:** 16.
**Fee:** $7.
**Elevation:** 9,500 feet.
**Road conditions:** two lane, gravel.
**Management:** Rio Grande National Forest, 719-658-2556.
**Activities:** Fishing.
**Finding the campground:** From Creede, travel 27.5 miles west on Colorado Highway 149 to Forest Service Road 510. Turn north and go 0.5 mile to the campground.

**The campground:** Bristol Head is a little-used camp that makes a good stopover or base camp from which to test the waters at several lakes, rivers, and streams in the surrounding area. If none of those suit you, the Rio Grande is a short drive away. The campsites are widely spaced along the edge of a meadow. The scenery is pretty, especially when you consider that you may have the place all to yourself.

## 266 Deer Lakes

**Location:** East of Lake City.
**Facilities:** Central water, fire rings, picnic tables, vault toilets.
**Sites:** 12.
**Fee:** $7.
**Elevation:** 10,400 feet.
**Road conditions:** two lane, gravel.
**Management:** Gunnison National Forest, 970-641-0471.
**Activities:** Fishing, hiking, horseback riding, four-wheel driving.
**Finding the campground:** From Lake City, travel southeast on Colorado Highway 149, about 9 miles to Forest Service Road 788. Turn northeast and go about 4 miles to the campground.

**The campground:** Deer Lakes is the first of a string of small and lonely camps bordering the La Garita Wilderness Area. Accessibility with trailers dwindles the farther up Forest Service Road 788 you go, but you can get to Deer Lakes pulling anything up to 30 feet long. The sites are well spaced on a rocky hillside near Cebolla Creek. Pack/saddle trails are abundant throughout the area. If the high altitude suits you, this is an outstanding destination where you can really get away from it all.

## 267 | Marshall Park

**Location:** Southwest of Creede.
**Facilities:** Central water, fire rings, picnic tables, vault toilets.
**Sites:** 15.
**Fee:** $10.
**Elevation:** 8,800 feet.
**Road conditions:** Paved.
**Management:** Rio Grande National Forest, 719-658-2556.
**Activities:** Fishing.
**Reservations:** 800-280-CAMP, www.nrrc.com, $8.65 fee.
**Finding the campground:** From Creede, travel southwest on Colorado Highway 149, about 7 miles to the campground.

**The campground:** This fishing camp on the Rio Grande could also serve as a stopover to enjoy the wide, open range surrounding Creede. All the sites are on the river and moderately spaced, but none have trees or vegetation over 1 foot high. The place seems to attract a crowd, so the fishing must be good.

## 268 | Mill Creek

**Location:** South of Lake City.
**Facilities:** Central water, fire rings, picnic tables, vault toilets.
**Sites:** 22.
**Fee:** $6.
**Elevation:** 9,500 feet.
**Road conditions:** One-and-a-half lane, dirt.
**Management:** Bureau of Land Management, 970-641-0471.
**Activities:** Fishing, hiking, four-wheel driving.
**Finding the campground:** From Lake City, travel south on Colorado Highway 149, about 3 miles to Bureau of Land Management Road 3306/County Road 30. Turn southwest and go about 11 miles to the campground.

**The campground:** Mill Creek is one of the few mid-sized campgrounds in the state that is managed by the Bureau of Land Management. Though larger and more developed than most of its cousins, it is like most BLM camps, hard to reach. Without a four-wheel-drive vehicle, the campground is about as far as you can travel on BLM Road 3306. The road is part of the Alpine Loop National Backcountry Byway, so besides fishing, driving is the recreation of choice for most campers here.

## 269 | North Clear Creek

**Location:** West of Creede.
**Facilities:** Central water, fire rings, picnic tables, vault toilets.
**Sites:** 25.
**Fee:** $9.

*These thundering falls are a short drive from the North Clear Creek Campground.*

**Elevation:** 9,900 feet.
**Road conditions:** One-and-a-half lane, dirt.
**Management:** Rio Grande National Forest, 719-658-2556.
**Activities:** Fishing, four-wheel driving, photography.
**Finding the campground:** From Creede, travel southwest on Colorado Highway 149, about 33 miles. Turn south on Forest Service Road 509 and go about 3 miles to the campground.

**The campground:** North Clear Creek is far enough off the road to give you the feel of being in the backcountry. Add to that the fact that usage is fairly low, and this campground becomes a nice place to spend time. The sites are a mix of light aspen and spruce forest and open meadow. The waterfall farther along this road offers an outstanding photographic opportunity with no hiking involved. A parking area is just steps from an overlook that allows a clear view of the falls as they plunge over an abrupt break in the rolling parkland.

## 270 Palisade

**Location:** Northwest of South Fork.
**Facilities:** Central water, fire rings, picnic tables, vault toilets.
**Sites:** 12.
**Fee:** $10.
**Elevation:** 8,300 feet.
**Road conditions:** Paved.
**Management:** Rio Grande National Forest, 719-658-2556.
**Activities:** Fishing, river sports.
**Finding the campground:** From South Fork, travel northwest on Colorado Highway 149, about 9 miles to the campground.

**The campground:** If you're looking for a fishing or rafting camp along the Rio Grande, this is a spot to consider. More than half of the sites are on the river. Most of them are in the open, but there are a few trees scattered throughout the camp. Weekday usage is low, but expect a crowd on weekends. The views of the Rio Grande Palisades across the road are an incredible bonus.

## 271 River Hill

**Location:** Southwest of Creede.
**Facilities:** Central water, fire rings, picnic tables, vault toilets.
**Sites:** 20.
**Fee:** $9, plus fee for second vehicle.
**Elevation:** 9,200 feet.
**Road conditions:** two lane, dirt, rough in places.
**Management:** Rio Grande National Forest, 719-658-2556.
**Reservations:** 800-280-CAMP, www.nrrc.com, $8.65.
**Activities:** Fishing, river sports.
**Finding the campground:** From Creede, travel southwest on Colorado High-

way 149, about 25 miles to Forest Service Road 520. Turn south and continue about 10 miles to the campground.

**The campground:** River Hill is probably the best fishing camp on this portion of the Rio Grande. It has river access but is removed from the highway. Some of the campsites are a bit close together, but others are spaced better. The camp is lightly forested and very pretty. An added bonus is the Rio Grande Reservoir, which is most beautiful at peak capacity after the spring runoff.

## 272 Slumgullion

**Location:** Southeast of Lake City.
**Facilities:** Central water, fire rings, picnic tables, vault toilets.
**Sites:** 19.
**Fee:** $6.
**Elevation:** 11,200 feet.
**Road conditions:** Paved.
**Management:** Gunnison National Forest, 970-641-0471.
**Activities:** Hiking, scenic driving.
**Finding the campground:** From Lake City, travel southeast on Colorado Highway 149, about 9 miles to Forest Service Road 788. The campground is on both sides of the road, about 200 yards off the highway.

**The campground:** Slumgullion is a nice stopover in a lush spruce forest. It is the highest improved campground in the state. That fact will likely make it attractive to some and rule it out for others. Activities at the campground itself are rather limited, but fishing is just a short drive away. Between fishing trips, try hiking one of the nearby trails into the La Garita Wilderness. If you can stand this extreme altitude, Slumgullion makes a good stopover or destination spot close to Lake City.

## 273 Thirty Mile

**Location:** Southwest of Creede.
**Facilities:** Central water, fire rings, picnic tables, vault toilets.
**Sites:** 35.
**Fee:** $9, plus $4.50 for second vehicle.
**Elevation:** 9,450 feet.
**Road conditions:** two lane, dirt, rough in places.
**Management:** Rio Grande National Forest, 719-658-2556.
**Reservations:** 800-280-CAMP, www.nrrc.com, $8.65 fee.
**Activities:** Fishing, hiking, river sports, horseback riding.
**Finding the campground:** From Creede, travel southwest on Colorado Highway 149, about 25 miles to Forest Service Road 520. Turn south and continue about 12 miles to the campground.

The campground: Thirty Mile is a beautiful campground that sees heavy usage when the reservoir is full from spring runoff, but low usage in late summer and early fall. Sites are widely spaced in a pretty evergreen forest. Trails suitable for hiking or horseback riding head south from camp toward the Continental Divide and the Weminuche Wilderness.

## 274  Williams Creek/Gunnison

**Location:** South of Lake City.
**Facilities:** Central water, fire rings, picnic tables, vault toilets.
**Sites:** 23.
**Fee:** $8.
**Elevation:** 9,200 feet.
**Road conditions:** One-and-a-half lane, dirt.
**Management:** Gunnison National Forest, 970-641-0471.
**Activities:** Fishing, biking, hiking, four-wheel driving.
**Finding the campground:** From Lake City, travel 2.5 miles south on Colorado Highway 149 to Bureau of Land Management Road 3306/County Road 30. Turn south and go about 7 miles to the campground.

The campground: There are two campgrounds in the state named Williams Creek (see Campground 302). This one is situated on the Lake Fork of the Gunnison River, above Lake San Cristobal. Sites are well spaced, and usage is fairly low. The camp boasts mountain views, river access, and a thick aspen and spruce forest. Fishing and hiking opportunities abound. The camp also is on the Alpine Loop Backcountry Byway, a four-wheel-drive road, so there's plenty to do here. When you've done it all, just hang the hammock.

## 275  Wupperman

**Location:** South of Lake City.
**Facilities:** Central water, fire rings, picnic tables, vault toilets.
**Sites:** 40.
**Fee:** $8.
**Elevation:** 8,000 feet.
**Road conditions:** one lane, dirt.
**Management:** Hinsdale County, 970-944-2225.
**Activities:** Fishing, four-wheel driving.
**Finding the campground:** From Lake City, travel 2.5 miles south on Colorado Highway 149 to County Road 30. Turn south and go about 1 mile, continuing around the south end of the lake to the eastern shore.

The campground: Lake San Cristobal is a gleaming jewel set among the mountains near Lake City. If you want a campground from which you can see the whole lake this is the place. Some sites perch on high, open cliffs, while others take shelter among the spruce trees. Almost all are good choices for either fishing or basking in the cool mountain air.

# Additional Campgrounds in the Lake City Area

| | Type* | Contact | Location |
|---|---|---|---|
| Broadacres Travlin Tepee | P (22) | 719-658-2291 | SW of Creede on CO 149 |
| Clear Creek Guest Ranch | P | 719-658-2491 | 1786 FSR 510, Creede |
| Henson Creek RV Park | P (33) | 970-944-2394 | S of Lake City on CO 149 |
| Highlander RV Park | P (24) | 970-944-2878 | SW of Lake City on Lake San Cristobal Road |
| Lake City Campground | P | 970-944-2287 | 713 N Bluff in Lake City |
| Mining Camp RV Resort & Fishing | P (83) | 719-658-2814 | SW of Creede off CO 149 |
| River Fork Camper & Trailer Park | P (87) | 970-944-2389 | Off CO 149 in Lake City |
| Cebolla | NF (5) | 970-641-0471 | SE of Lake City on FSR 788 |
| Hidden Valley | NF (3) | 970-641-0471 | SE of Lake City on FSR 788 |
| Ivy Creek | NF (4) | 719-658-2556 | SW of Creede on FSR 256 |
| Lost Trail | NF (7) | 719-658-2556 | SW of Creede on FSR 520 |
| Rio Grande | NF (4) | 719-658-2556 | SW of Creede on River Road |
| Road Canyon | NF (6) | 719-658-2556 | SW of Creede on FSR 520 |
| Silver Thread | NF (11) | 719-658-2556 | SW of Creede on FSR 515 |
| Spruce | NF (9) | 970-641-0471 | SE of Lake City on FSR 788 |
| Stone Cellar | NF (11) | 719-655-2553 | SE of Gunnison on FSR 804 |

* See "Key to Abbreviations" p.22—(# of sites)

# Area 25: Durango

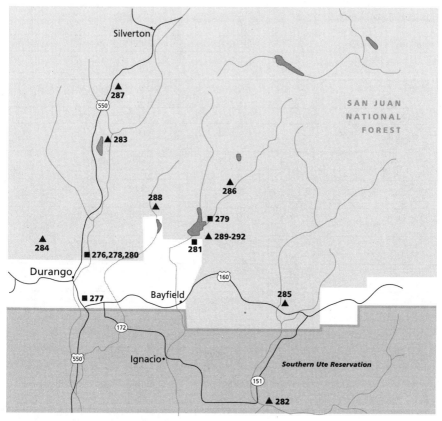

Silverton

▲ 287
⑤⑤⓪

▲ 283

288
▲

▲ 286

■ 279

289-292
▲

281
■

SAN JUAN
NATIONAL
FOREST

▲
284

■ 276, 278, 280

Durango

■ 277

Bayfield

160

⑤⑤⓪

172

550

Ignacio

285
▲

Southern Ute Reservation

151

▲ 282

NEW MEXICO

## DURANGO

Durango owes its origin to industry, namely smelting the ore brought down the Las Animas River Valley from Ouray. Though tourism is now the main source of revenue in the area, the town still carries an air of hard work. A hint of soot still graces its buildings. Though the town has no direct views of soaring peaks, a short drive in any direction, but south, will add those views to the skyline.

The big draw here is the Durango and Silverton Narrow Gauge Railroad, which hauls 200,000 travelers a year through the San Juan Mountains. If you're looking for a unique experience, check out the RailCamp, which allows you to "camp" in the wilderness in a modified railroad car parked off the main line.

Southern Colorado's finest dining can be found among the restaurants of Durango. Other activities include swimming in the municipal pool, playing tennis, touring museums, golfing, and soaking in the hot springs. For something to do outside the confines of the city, look for rafting trips, glider soaring, four-wheel driving, and horseback riding. There's enough here to keep a family occupied for a week or more.

To the northeast of town lies the lovely Vallecito Reservoir, which offers a wealth of activities all its own. Water sports such as skiing, tubing, and boating rule, but the lake has been known to produce some trophy-sized fish.

There is no shortage of campsites in the area. RV parks line U.S. Highways 160 and 550, all of them good choices for people who don't want to miss out on the action. Navajo State Park straddles the New Mexico border and adds seventy-one sites to the mix of national forest camps found throughout the area.

**For More Information:**

Durango Area Chamber Resort Association
111 S. Camino del Rio
P.O. Box 2587
Durango, CO 81302
970-247-0312 or 800-525-8855
www.durango.org
e-mail: durango@frontier.net

Durango & Silverton Narrow Gauge Railroad Co.
479 Main Ave.
Durango, CO 81301
970-247-2733

# Commercial

## 276 Alpen Rose RV Park

**Location:** North of Durango.
**Affiliations:** Good Sam; Colorado Association of Campgrounds, Cabins, and Lodges.
**Contact:** 970-259-8938.
**Amenities:** Dump station, laundry, showers, store, pool, public phone, playground, fishing pond, tours.
**Sites:** 100, all full hookups.
**Price per night:** $25 to $28.
**Elevation:** 6,700 feet.
**Finding the campground:** From Durango, travel north on U.S. Highway 550, about 6 miles to the campground.

**The campground:** The Animas River Valley north of Durango is part of what has been called the most scenic drive in all of Colorado. Alpen Rose RV Park allows you to take advantage of that and everything else there is to see and do in the area, including the narrow-gauge railroad to Silverton. Sixty of the sites here are shaded. The other 40 take advantage of the beautiful mountain views.

## 277  Durango East KOA

**Location:** East of Durango.
**Affiliations:** KOA.
**Contact:** 970-247-0783, fax 970-247-3655.
**Amenities:** Dump station, laundry, showers, store, pool, public phone, playground, cabins, breakfast served.
**Sites:** 93, 39 full hookups.
**Price per night:** $19 to $26.
**Elevation:** 7,000 feet.
**Finding the campground:** From the east junction of U.S. Highways 160 and 550, travel 2.5 miles east on US 160.

**The campground:** Perched on a 7,000-foot mesa, this pretty KOA is a convenient and comfortable place to stay in the Durango/Cortez area. Many sites have trees for shade and privacy. The train depot is just 7 miles away. Families will enjoy exploring the area knowing there's a pleasant place to return to at the end of the day. This campground also makes an excellent stopover along US 60.

## 278  Durango North KOA

**Location:** North of Durango.
**Affiliations:** KOA; Colorado Association of Campgrounds, Cabins, and Lodges.
**Contact:** 970-247-4499.
**Amenities:** Dump station, laundry, public phone, pool, picnic tables, fire rings, grills, river/pond fishing, playground, trails.
**Sites:** 150, 41 full hookups.
**Price per night:** $17.50 to $23.
**Elevation:** 7,000 feet.
**Finding the campground:** From Durango, travel north on U.S. Highway 550 about 16 miles to the campground.

**The campground:** This particularly pretty KOA offers all the usual amenities plus shady, riverside sites. It's close enough to town to allow you to enjoy everything Durango has to offer, but far enough away to give the feeling of country camping. There's also a public golf course nearby.

## 279  Five Branches Camper Park

**Location:** Northeast of Bayfield.
**Affiliations:** Colorado Association of Campgrounds, Cabins, and Lodges.
**Contact:** 970-884-2582, fax 970-884-9765.
**Reservations:** 800-582-9580.
**Amenities:** RV rentals, cabins, showers, laundry, public phone, picnic tables, fire rings, grills, hiking trails, horseback-riding trails, boat rentals, boat dock.
**Sites:** 123, 95 full hookups.

**Price per night:** $13 to $22.
**Elevation:** 7,650 feet.
**Finding the campground:** From Bayfield, travel north on County Road 501 about 14 miles. At the directory sign below the dam, stay to the left, continuing on CR 501 on the west side of the lake through Elk Point, then down the hill to the campground.

**The campground:** Vallecito Reservoir is an unusual mountain lake in that it is warm enough for water sports yet set amid a dense pine forest. If you want all the amenities of a privately owned RV park while still camping at the lake, this is a good choice. Sites range from wooded spots tucked along the Los Pinos River to open sites on the lakeshore. The views across the lake from here are nothing short of astounding.

## 280 Hermosa Meadows Camper Park

**Location:** North of Durango.
**Affiliations:** Good Sam; AAA; Colorado Association of Campgrounds, Cabins, and Lodges.
**Contact:** 970-247-3055.
**Reservations:** 800-748-2853.
**Amenities:** Dump station, laundry, showers, store, public phone, playground, river/pond fishing, bike rentals, picnic tables, fire rings, grills.
**Sites:** 150, 59 full hookups.
**Price per night:** $16 to $24.
**Elevation:** 6,600 feet.
**Season:** Year-round.
**Finding the campground:** From Durango, travel north on U.S. Highway 550, about 8 miles to Hermosa Meadows Road. Turn east and go about 0.5 mile to the campground.

**The campground:** Hermosa Meadows is another good choice for family accommodations in the Animas River Valley north of Durango. The park is pretty and the area is scenic and brimming with activities. In the immediate vicinity, you can choose from horseback riding, golf, hot springs, and chuck wagon dinners.

## 281 Vallecito Resort RV Park

**Location:** North of Bayfield.
**Affiliations:** Colorado Association of Campgrounds, Cabins, and Lodges.
**Contact:** 970-884-9458.
**Reservations:** 800-258-9458.
**Amenities:** Dump station, showers, laundry, playground, store, river fishing, picnic tables, grills.
**Sites:** 200, all full hookups.
**Price per night:** Not available.

**Elevation:** 7,600 feet.
**Finding the campground:** From Bayfield, travel north on County Road 501 about 14 miles.

**The campground:** You will find this pleasant park just below Vallecito Reservoir on the Los Pinos River. The sites are closely spaced, but there is plenty of shade. The campground has a community feel to it, as though everyone is welcome to pull in, put their feet up, and join in a game of checkers. Lake access is a short drive away, and this could be a nice place to avoid the noisy crowd at the lake.

# Public

## 282 Navajo State Recreation Area

**Location:** Southeast of Durango.
**Facilities:** Dump station, electricity, showers, snack bar, boat ramp, marina, boat rental, trails, picnic tables, fire rings, central water, flush toilets, playground.
**Sites:** 71.
**Fee:** $4 to $7, plus $4 daily or $40 annual vehicle pass.
**Elevation:** 6,100 feet.
**Road conditions:** Paved.
**Management:** Colorado Department of Parks and Outdoor Recreation, 970-883-2208.
**Activities:** Fishing, water sports, hiking, biking.
**Season:** Year-round.
**Finding the campground:** From Durango, travel east on U.S. Highway 160 about 47 miles to Colorado Highway 151. Turn south and go about 18 miles to the town of Arboles. Continue south on County Road 982 to the park.

**The campground:** Navajo State Recreation Area is unique in that it straddles the Colorado–New Mexico border. The largest part of Navajo Reservoir is south of the border. The setting is pure desert Southwest: rolling hills and low mesas dotted with low-growing sage and piñons. The campground is thoroughly modern and dedicated to those who come to enjoy the water. Campsites are close together, but there is enough room for boat trailers. The lake is deep and the marina is home to a number of large houseboats. The boat ramp is large enough to handle almost any watercraft. Navajo is a beautiful destination for families who love to play in and on the water.

## 283 Haviland Lake

**Location:** North of Durango.
**Facilities:** Central water, fire rings, picnic tables, vault toilets, boat dock.
**Sites:** 45.
**Fee:** $8.

**Elevation:** 8,000 feet.
**Road conditions:** Paved.
**Management:** San Juan National Forest, 970-247-4874.
**Reservations:** 800-280-CAMP, www.nrrc.com, $8.65 fee.
**Activities:** Fishing, scenic driving.
**Restrictions:** Slated for reconstruction during the summer of 1998.
**Finding the campground:** From Durango, travel 16.5 miles north on Colorado Highway 550 to Forest Service Road 671. The campground is to the left.

**The campground:** Haviland Lake is a vacation spot that even non-fishermen will love because of its sheer beauty. The campsites are terraced above the lake, with the lower loops set in a pine forest and the upper loop hiding in dense aspen and scrub oak. Sites 36-42 have beautiful views of the lake. Boats with electric motors are allowed. The drive north on CO 550 would rank near the top of any list of magnificent drives in Colorado. The best part is that, until you near Silverton, it isn't even what you would call a "white-knuckle" drive.

## 284 Junction Creek

**Location:** Northwest of Durango.
**Facilities:** Central water, fire rings, picnic tables, vault toilets.
**Sites:** 34.
**Fee:** $9.
**Elevation:** 7,500 feet.
**Road conditions:** two lane, gravel.
**Management:** San Juan National Forest, 970-247-4874.
**Activities:** Hiking, fishing, four-wheel driving, horseback riding.
**Finding the campground:** From Durango, travel north on Colorado Highway 550, about 1 mile to County Road 204. Turn northwest and go 3.5 miles, until the road becomes Forest Service Road 171. The campground is another mile to the northwest.

**The campground:** Junction Creek Campground is adjacent to the southern trailhead of the Colorado Trail. This makes it a busy place throughout the summer, when hundreds of hikers, bikers, and horseback riders begin or end their treks along this 470-mile recreational trail across the state. Several jeep trails also begin near the campground and head north into the San Juan National Forest.

   The campground is set in a pine forest with sites well spaced. This is a good campground in which to relax, since many visitors are gone by noon, leaving you alone with the serenity of the pines.

## 285 Lower Piedra

**Location:** East of Bayfield.
**Facilities:** Picnic tables, fire rings, vault toilets; no water.
**Sites:** 17.

**Fee:** $6.
**Elevation:** 7,200 feet.
**Road conditions:** one lane, dirt.
**Management:** San Juan National Forest, 970-264-2268.
**Activities:** Fishing.
**Finding the campground:** From Bayfield, travel east on U.S. Highway 160 about 20 miles, then northeast on the frontage road (Chimney Rock Court), and then immediately north on Forest Service Road 621 to the camp.

**The campground:** Lower Piedra is tucked away in a lush oak and pine forest. Don't be surprised to find it deserted; it doesn't seem to get much use. Campsites are widely to moderately spaced with some on the river. Lower Piedra is far enough from the highway to escape much of the traffic noise, making this a quiet stopover along the route between Durango and Pagosa. It would also make an excellent base if you want to spend time in both places. Don't forget to bring your own supply of water.

## 286 Pine River

**Location:** Northeast of Bayfield.
**Facilities:** Fire rings, picnic tables, vault toilets; no water.
**Sites:** 6.
**Fee:** $7.
**Elevation:** 8,100 feet.
**Road conditions:** one lane, dirt, rough.
**Management:** San Juan National Forest, 970-884-2512.
**Activities:** Fishing, hiking.
**Finding the campground:** From Bayfield, travel north on County Road 501 to Vallecito Reservoir. Turn right on Forest Service Road 603 to follow the southeastern lakeshore. Travel through the privately owned campgrounds. Just past the entrance to Middle Mountain (Campground 290), turn right onto FRS 602. Travel northeast 3.5 miles to the campground.

**The campground:** If you don't find a campground to your liking at Vallecito Reservoir, this out-of-the-way camp might be the one to make your heart sing. It's small, gets little use, and is close to the Los Pinos River. A trail leads north from camp into the Weminuche Wilderness.

## 287 Purgatory

**Location:** Southwest of Silverton.
**Facilities:** Central water, fire rings, picnic tables, vault toilets.
**Sites:** 14.
**Fee:** $8.
**Elevation:** 8,800 feet.
**Road conditions:** Paved.
**Management:** San Juan National Forest, 970-247-4874.

**Activities:** Hiking, scenic driving.
**Finding the campground:** From Silverton, travel south on U.S. Highway 550, about 22 miles to the campground.

**The campground:** This campground is opposite the Purgatory Ski Resort. Unfortunately, it's closed during ski season. The resort is usually open during the summer though, offering lift rides that will give you a panoramic view of the Animas River Valley. The campsites are widely spaced in a pretty spruce forest, but they are not very large. The other big attraction here is a trail that wanders along Lime Creek before it joins the Animas River, paralleling the Durango-Silverton Narrow Gauge Railroad tracks for about 6 miles. The campground also makes a convenient stopover between Durango and Silverton.

## 288 Transfer Park

**Location:** Northeast of Durango.
**Facilities:** Central water, fire rings, picnic tables, vault toilets.
**Sites:** 25.
**Fee:** $8.
**Elevation:** 8,200 feet.
**Road conditions:** One-and-a-half lane, gravel.
**Management:** San Juan National Forest, 970-884-2512.
**Reservations:** 800-280-CAMP, www.nrrc.com, $8.65 fee.
**Activities:** Fishing, hiking.
**Restrictions:** Slated for tree removal in 1998; may be closed.
**Finding the campground:** From Durango, travel northeast on Florida Road (County Road 240), about 14 miles to County Road 243. Turn north and travel about 8 miles, past Lemon Reservoir to the campground.

**The campground:** The highlight of this pretty campground in the pines is its proximity to Lemon Reservoir and the Weminuche Wilderness trailhead. The campground sees moderately low usage on weekdays but can fill on weekends, so plan accordingly. Fishing in the Florida River is possible near camp.

## 289 Vallecito Reservoir: Graham Creek/Old Timers

**Location:** Northeast of Bayfield.
**Facilities:** Boat ramp, central water, fire rings, picnic tables, vault toilets.
**Sites:** 35.
**Fee:** $8.
**Elevation:** 7,750 feet.
**Road conditions:** One-and-a-half lane, gravel, rough in places.
**Management:** San Juan National Forest, 970-884-2512.
**Activities:** Fishing, water sports, hiking.
**Finding the campground:** From Bayfield, travel north on County Road 501 about 14 miles. Turn right to follow the southeastern lakeshore. Old Timers is the first campground; Graham Creek is the second.

The campground: Vallecito is possibly the only large reservoir in the state that allows you to combine the tranquility of camping in the woods with the fun of water sports. These two campgrounds are set in a dense forest of pine and aspen. Sites are widely spaced; most have views of the water. If you come for the fishing, try visiting in early fall when the number of water skiers drops with the water temperature. Some campsites remain open through October. Anglers can pursue rainbow and German brown trout, plus kokanee salmon and northern pike. In fact, the state record pike (30 pounds, 1 ounce, 48.25 inches) was caught here.

## 290 Vallecito Reservoir: Middle Mountain

**Location:** Northeast of Bayfield.
**Facilities:** Central water, fire rings, picnic tables, vault toilets.
**Sites:** 24.
**Fee:** $8.
**Elevation:** 7,750 feet.
**Road conditions:** One-and-a-half lane, gravel, rough in places.
**Management:** San Juan National Forest, 970-884-2512.
**Activities:** Fishing, water sports, hiking.
**Finding the campground:** From Bayfield, travel north on County Road 501 about 14 miles. Turn right to follow the southeastern lakeshore. Middle Mountain is beyond the privately owned campgrounds. Go through Five Branches Camper Park (Campground 279), across the bridge, and through the Elk Point Lodge area. The campground is on the left.

The campground: Middle Mountain is less heavily wooded than the camps on the eastern shore, but it still has a good complement of aspen and pine. Sites are widely spaced. The real reason to camp here is a full view of the lake, which reminds you why you wanted to get away from home. Bring your camera to capture the sunsets mirrored in the water.

## 291 Vallecito Reservoir: North Canyon

**Location:** Northeast of Bayfield.
**Facilities:** Central water, fire rings, picnic tables, vault toilets.
**Sites:** 21.
**Fee:** $8.
**Elevation:** 7,750 feet.
**Road conditions:** One-and-a-half lane, gravel, rough in places.
**Management:** San Juan National Forest, 970-884-2512.
**Activities:** Fishing, water sports, hiking.
**Finding the campground:** From Bayfield, travel north on County Road 501 about 14 miles. Turn right to follow the southeastern lakeshore. North Canyon is the third campground along the lake.

The campground: The sites here stretch along the lakeshore, offering direct access to the water in several places. They are spaced widely enough to allow privacy when the campground fills on busy weekends. This campground closes earlier than the rest, usually in September. A wilderness trailhead is just across the road from camp, if you have any energy left after water skiing.

## 292 | Vallecito Reservoir: Pine Point

**Location:** Northeast of Bayfield.
**Facilities:** Central water, fire rings, picnic tables, vault toilets.
**Sites:** 30.
**Fee:** $8.
**Elevation:** 7,750 feet.
**Road conditions:** One-and-a-half lane, gravel, rough in places.
**Management:** San Juan National Forest, 970-884-2512.
**Activities:** Fishing, water sports, hiking.
**Finding the campground:** From Bayfield, travel north on County Road 501 about 14 miles. Turn right to follow the southeastern lakeshore. Pine Point is the fourth campground along the lake.

**The campground:** The only difference between Pine Point and the other Vallecito campgrounds is that the shoreline is slightly elevated, which makes access to the water a bit more difficult. The camp is just as pretty as the others, though. Horse and boat rentals are available just around the bend, so if those activities suit your tastes, this may be the best choice for you. This also may be the last camp to fill on weekends. It is unfortunate that you can't make reservations at any of the Vallecito campgrounds. This forces you to time your arrival before Friday evening to ensure a spot.

## Additional Campgrounds in the Durango Area

| | Type* | Contact | Location |
|---|---|---|---|
| Blue Spruce | P (107) | 970-884-2641 | Near Lake Vallecito on CR 500 |
| Butch's Beach | P | 970-247-3404 | Durango |
| Chimney Rock Campground | P (44) | 970-731-5237 | W of Bayfield on US 160 |
| Cottonwood Camper Park | P (73) | 970-247-1977 | W of Durango on US 160 |
| Lightner Creek Campground | P (97) | 970-247-5406 | NW of Durango on CR 207 |
| Riverside RV Park | P (81) | 970-884-2475 | W of Bayfield on US 160 |
| United Camground of Durango | P (192) | 970-247-3853 | N of Durango on US 550 |
| Miller Creek | NF (12) | 970-884-2512 | NE of Durango on CR 243 |
| Sig Creek | NF (9) | 970-247-4874 | |
| Vallecito | NF | 970-884-2512 | Closed in 1997, call |

* See "Key to Abbreviations" p.22—(# of sites)

# Area 26: Pagosa Springs

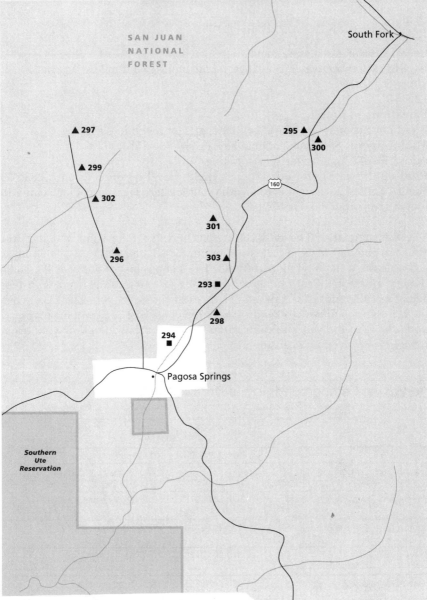

SAN JUAN
NATIONAL
FOREST

South Fork

▲ 297

295 ▲
▲ 300

▲ 299

▲ 302

160

▲
301

▲
296

303 ▲

293 ■

▲
298

294
■

• Pagosa Springs

*Southern
Ute
Reservation*

NEW MEXICO

# Pagosa Springs

If Durango feels like the industrial town it once was, Pagosa Springs is one big playground—from the Wolf Creek Ski Area to the Fairfield Pagosa golf resort. Few towns in the state can match the mountain views found here. Whether you are teeing off on one of the 27 championship holes or soaking your cares away in the hot-springs downtown, you're always within sight of the jagged San Juan Mountains.

Activities in town seem to center around eating. There are several fine restaurants, many with patios that allow you to enjoy the view. There are also a few shops, but people spend a lot of time here just milling about along the San Juan River. The best way to enjoy the river, though, is to float in it.

Visitors to the hot-springs pools on the southern banks of the San Juan at the center of town can cool off in the icy river. One popular plunge takes you from the hottest of the pools, known as "The Lobster Pot," right into the river for a short float in its gentle current. For a cool experience that's a bit less shocking to the system, ease into the river at a point where the hot mineral pools overflow and mix with the cold river water.

Even if a Swedish-style, heart-stopping plunge isn't for you, you should not rule out the hot-springs facility. It is first class, with clean showers and creative landscaping. There are plenty of pools of varying temperatures to choose from, including one maintained at around 99 degrees, which is cool enough for the kids. The pools are open around the clock; late evening is the prime time to soak before turning in for the night.

Many visitors hope to camp close enough to town to enjoy the food, the river, the golf course, and the hot springs. Unfortunately, there never seems to be quite enough commercial RV space to accommodate everyone. The logical solution is to stay in one of three national forest campgrounds east of town.

For those who appreciate a slower pace, the area northwest of Pagosa offers some of the most striking and least-used campgrounds in the state. From them, you can combine camping in the deep woods with an occasional trip back to town to eat, soak, and buy T-shirts.

**For More Information:**

Pagosa Springs Area Chamber of Commerce
P.O. Box 787
Pagosa Springs, CO 81147
970-264-2360 or 800-252-2204

# Commercial

## 293 Bruce Spruce Ranch

**Location:** East of Pagosa Springs.
**Affiliations:** Good Sam; Colorado Association of Campgrounds, Cabins, and Lodges.
**Contact:** 970-264-5374 or 806-622-1346 (November-April).
**Amenities:** Laundry, showers, public phone, playground, cabins, stables, fishing pond, picnic tables, fire rings.
**Sites:** 38, 28 full hookups.
**Price per night:** $13 to $15.
**Elevation:** 8,200 feet.
**Finding the campground:** The campground entrance is on the south side of U.S. Highway 60, near milepost 158, between Pagosa Springs and Wolf Creek Pass.

**The campground:** This rustic getaway borders the San Juan National Forest at the base of Wolf Creek Pass. The ranch offers trail rides into the mountains, fishing, and hiking. The campsites are scattered, some in a clearing, some with shade. If you're looking for a private RV park that feels a little more like a public camp, this is a good choice.

## 294 Elk Meadows Campground

**Location:** East of Pagosa Springs.
**Affiliations:** AAA; Colorado Association of Campgrounds, Cabins, and Lodges.
**Contact:** 970-264-5482.
**Amenities:** Dump station, laundry, showers, store, public phone, playground, cabins, grills, fire rings, picnic tables.
**Sites:** 43, 19 full hookups.
**Price per night:** $14 to $17.
**Elevation:** 7,900 feet.
**Finding the campground:** From the junction of U.S. Highways 160 and 84 at the east end of Pagosa Springs, travel east on US 160, about 5 miles to the campground entrance.

**The campground:** What this RV park offers most is an excellent location. It is just minutes from the bustle of town, yet it still allows you to enjoy the great outdoors. Some sites are shaded; others are open. The campground is on the San Juan River and has fishing access. If you prefer the conveniences of RV parks over the more primitive national forest campgrounds, Elk Meadows is a good choice.

# Public

## 295 Big Meadows

**Location:** Southwest of South Fork.
**Facilities:** Central water, fire rings, picnic tables, vault toilets, wheelchair-accessible sites.
**Sites:** 56.
**Fee:** $10.
**Elevation:** 9,200 feet.
**Road conditions:** two lane, dirt,
**Management:** Rio Grande National Forest, 719-654-3321.
**Reservations:** 800-280-CAMP, www.nrrc.com, $8.65 fee.
**Activities:** Fishing, hiking, horseback riding.
**Finding the campground:** From South Fork, travel 12.5 miles southwest on U.S. Highway 160 to Forest Service Road 410. Turn left and travel about 1 mile to the campground.

**The campground:** This campground is situated in a thick spruce forest above a reservoir of the same name that does, indeed, occupy a "big meadow." Sites are terraced up the hillside; all are just a short hike from the lake. Spacing is ideal, and some sites extend deep into the woods. The campground has been updated recently with new toilets and tables. There is a short trail to Cascade Falls that begins from the upper loop. This is a true destination spot that will allow you to forget that the rest of the world is rushing by without you.

## 296 Bridge

**Location:** Northwest of Pagosa Springs.
**Facilities:** Central water, fire rings, picnic tables, vault toilets.
**Sites:** 19.
**Fee:** $8.
**Elevation:** 7,800 feet.
**Road conditions:** two lane, gravel.
**Management:** San Juan National Forest, 970-264-2268.
**Activities:** Fishing, hiking, biking.
**Finding the campground:** From Pagosa Springs, travel west on U.S. Highway 160, about 3 miles to Piedra Road (Forest Service Road 631). Turn north and travel about 17 miles to the northwest, bearing left at all forks.

**The campground:** Bridge is a campground for lovers of rushing rivers and wide-open spaces. The trees are sparse, but the sites are so widely spaced that trees aren't needed for privacy. This is also a beautiful place to stretch out in a lounge chair and enjoy the afternoon sun (after you've caught dinner, of course). Trails for hiking and biking are abundant near camp.

## 297 | Cimarrona

**Location:** Northwest of Pagosa Springs.
**Facilities:** Central water, fire rings, picnic tables, vault toilets.
**Sites:** 21.
**Fee:** $8.50.
**Elevation:** 8,400 feet.
**Road conditions:** One-and-a-half lane, smooth, gravel.
**Management:** San Juan National Forest, 970-264-2268.
**Activities:** Fishing, hiking.
**Finding the campground:** From Pagosa Springs, travel west on U.S. Highway 160, about 3 miles to Piedra Road (Forest Service Road 631). Turn north and travel about 22 miles northwest to FSR 640. Go north about 4 miles to the campground.

**The campground:** Cimarrona is the uppermost camp on Williams Creek; it sits above Williams Creek Reservoir. More aspens grow here than at the lower campgrounds along the creek, so this is a good spot if you're hoping to catch some early color change before the campgrounds close with the October snows. The sites are nicely spaced; some offer glimpses of the mountains between the trees. Cimarrona Creek passes the camp on its way to the reservoir. Hiking trails head north from camp toward the Continental Divide.

## 298 | East Fork

**Location:** East of Pagosa Springs.
**Facilities:** Central water, fire rings, picnic tables, vault toilets.
**Sites:** 26.
**Fee:** $8.
**Elevation:** 7,600 feet.
**Road conditions:** One-and-a-half lane, gravel.
**Management:** San Juan National Forest, 970-264-2268.
**Activities:** Hiking, shopping, scenic driving, golfing, mineral baths.
**Finding the campground:** From Pagosa Springs, travel 9.7 miles northeast on U.S. Highway 160 to Forest Service Road 667. Turn southeast and go 0.8 mile to the campground.

**The campground:** If you prefer national forest camping but want to stay close enough to Pagosa Springs to enjoy its shopping, dining, and lounging in the hot springs, this is your best choice. The campground is densely forested with aspen and a mix of evergreens. The sites are widely spaced, and the camp is far enough off the road to escape most of the traffic noise. Easy access to a fishing hole is the only thing missing.

## 299 Teal

**Location:** Northwest of Pagosa Springs.
**Facilities:** Central water, fire rings, picnic tables, vault toilets.
**Sites:** 16.
**Fee:** $9.
**Elevation:** 8,300 feet.
**Road conditions:** one lane, gravel with turnouts.
**Management:** San Juan National Forest, 970-264-2268.
**Activities:** Fishing, hiking.
**Finding the campground:** From Pagosa Springs, travel west on U.S. Highway 160, about 3 miles to Piedra Road (Forest Service Road 631). Turn north and travel about 22 miles northwest to FSR 640. Go about 2 miles north to the campground.

**The campground:** If you enjoy lake fishing, Teal is your best choice of campgrounds among the four camps scattered along Williams Creek. It languishes along the southern shore of Williams Creek Reservoir, which is set in a wide meadow against a mountain backdrop. The campground is lightly forested with a mix of aspen and spruce. And even though the sites are spaced a little too close together, it's hard to complain when you can wake every morning to a place this beautiful. Motorized boats are allowed on the lake to help you catch your limit.

## 300 Tucker Ponds

**Location:** Southwest of South Fork.
**Facilities:** Central water, fire rings, picnic tables, vault toilets.
**Sites:** 16.
**Fee:** $8.
**Elevation:** 9,700 feet.
**Road conditions:** One-and-a-half lane, gravel.
**Management:** Rio Grande National Forest, 719-657-3321.
**Activities:** Fishing, hiking, scenic driving, four-wheel driving.
**Finding the campground:** From South Fork, travel about 14 miles southwest on U.S. Highway 160 to Forest Service Road 390. Turn south and go 2.6 miles to the campground.

**The campground:** The campsites here are widely spaced and heavily forested. The ponds are just across the road from camp. Forest Service Road 390 continues several miles beyond the campground, becoming a jeep trail as it climbs. There is access to Wolf Creek all along the road. This is a nice place to stop for the night if you're traveling US 160, particularly if you are headed west over the pass and it's near nightfall. But don't rule out this camp for lengthy stays, either.

## 301 West Fork

**Location:** East of Pagosa Springs.
**Facilities:** Central water, fire rings, picnic tables, vault toilets.
**Sites:** 28.
**Fee:** $8.
**Elevation:** 8,000 feet.
**Road conditions:** One-and-a-half lane, smooth. gravel.
**Management:** San Juan National Forest, 970-264-2268.
**Activities:** Hiking, scenic driving, horseback riding.
**Finding the campground:** From Pagosa Springs, travel east on U.S. Highway 160, about 12 miles to Forest Service Road 648. Turn north and go about 3 miles to the campground (past Wolf Creek Campground).

**The campground:** West Fork is a lovely campground that gets surprisingly low usage. The sites are wide to moderately spaced in a light pine forest. Pack/saddle Trail 561 heads north from near the camp. The trail passes hot springs, falls, and a lake on its way to the Continental Divide. The hot springs are several miles up, so this is not an easy stroll in the woods. If you aren't up to a strenuous hike, head to Pagosa for the hot water.

## 302 Williams Creek/San Juan

**Location:** Northwest of Pagosa Springs.
**Facilities:** Central water, fire rings, picnic tables, vault toilets.
**Sites:** 66.
**Fee:** $9.
**Elevation:** 8,200 feet.
**Road conditions:** One-and-a-half lane, gravel.
**Management:** San Juan National Forest, 970-264-2268.
**Reservations:** 800-280-CAMP, www.nrrc.com, $8.65 fee.
**Activities:** Fishing, hiking.
**Finding the campground:** From Pagosa Springs, travel west on U.S. Highway 160, about 3 miles to Piedra Road (Forest Service Road 631). Turn north and travel about 22 miles northwest to FSR 640. Go north about half a mile to the campground.

**The campground:** This book isn't supposed to be about the author's personal favorites. But because so many people have asked which campground would top my list, here it is: Williams Fork. It has everything I look for, including a nice mix of aspen, blue spruce, and pine, accented by open meadows that allow views of the surrounding peaks. A river runs through it, and some sites hug its banks. The camp gets relatively little use. (I was there on Labor Day weekend and found the camp almost empty.) In addition to all that, there is a lodge just a bit farther up FSR 640 that offers hot showers for a modest fee. And whenever it strikes your fancy, you can drive back to Pagosa Springs for a meal, a round of golf, and a soak in the hot springs.

## 303 | Wolf Creek

**Location:** East of Pagosa Springs.
**Facilities:** Central water, fire rings, picnic tables, vault toilets.
**Sites:** 26.
**Fee:** $8.
**Elevation:** 8,000 feet.
**Road conditions:** One-and-a-half lane, smooth, gravel.
**Management:** San Juan National Forest, 970-264-2268.
**Activities:** Hiking, fishing.
**Finding the campground:** From Pagosa Springs, travel east on U.S. Highway 160, about 12 miles to Forest Service Road 648. Turn north and go about 0.5 mile to the campground.

**The campground:** Wolf Creek makes a nice stopover close to Pagosa, but if you plan to stay more than a night or two, you may want to head farther up FSR 648 to West Fork (Campground 301) to avoid the traffic noise. The sites at Wolf Creek are well spaced in a dense pine forest, so they get a bit more shade than the sites at West Fork. Usage here is moderate, and between the two camps there are fifty-four sites that rarely fill to capacity. On your excursions out of camp, be sure to stop at Treasure Falls and take the short hike up to the lookout.

## Additional Campgrounds in the Pagosa Springs Area

|  | Type* | Contact | Location |
|---|---|---|---|
| Chromo Merchantile RV Park | P (15) | 970-264-4583 | CO 84 in Chromo |
| Happy Camper RV Park | P (83) | 970-731-5822 | W of Pagosa Springs on US 160 |
| Hide-a-way RV Park & Campground | P (29) | 970-731-2115 | W of Pagosa Springs on US 160 |
| Pagosa Riverside Campground | P (86) | 970-264-5874 | NE of Pagosa Springs on US 160 |
| Sportsman's Supply & Campground | P (32) | — | N of Pagosa Springs on FSR ? |
| Wolf Creek Valley Country Store & Campground | P (23) | 970-264-4853 | E of Pagosa Springs on US 160 |
| Blanco River | NF (6) | 970-264-2268 | 14.9 miles SE of Pagosa Springs on FSR 656 |

*·See "Key to Abbreviations" p.22—(# of sites)

# Area 27: South Fork and Platoro

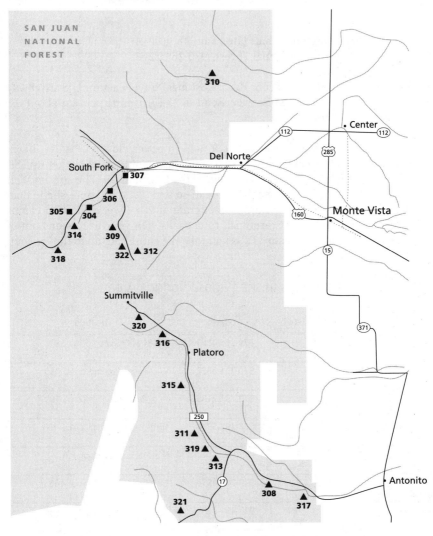

## SOUTH FORK AND PLATORO

Don't be confused by the grouping of these two towns into one section of the book. Geographically they look rather close, but getting from one to the other is one of those Colorado shortcuts that is best avoided unless you intend to take a scenic drive. The roads are rough, winding, and very close to deserving a four-wheel-drive designation.

South Fork serves as a gateway to the San Juan Mountains and all the recreation found therein. Because of that, RV parks offering everything from swimming pools to mini-golf to overnight pack trips are in great supply. Parks on the Rio Grande or its South Fork are among the best choices.

In contrast, Platoro is barely a town at all. No more than a few ramshackle houses and a store, it is a fishing destination hidden away, below the mining community of Summitville.

What the two communities do have in common are a large number of national forest campgrounds that put you right in the heart of the San Juan Mountains.

**For More Information:**

South Fork Chamber of Commerce
P.O. Box 12
South Fork, CO 81154
719-873-5512

# Commercial

## 304 Fun Valley

**Location:** Southwest of South Fork.
**Contact:** 719-873-5566.
**Finding the campground:** From South Fork, travel southwest on U.S. Highway 160 about 5 miles.

**The campground:** Fun Valley looks like an interesting place to stay, but detailed information wasn't forthcoming from the proprietors. The place sprawls along the South Fork of the Rio Grande with what looks like enough sites to house an army division. Some are shaded and beside the river, while others are in open meadow. The recreational opportunities appear extensive, but you'll have to call to find out more.

## 305 Moon Valley

**Location:** Southwest of South Fork.
**Affiliations:** Colorado Association of Campgrounds, Cabins, and Lodges.
**Contact:** 719-873-5216.
**Amenities:** Dump station, laundry, showers, store, public phone, playground, RV rentals, picnic tables, fire rings, grills, fishing pond.
**Sites:** 55, 50 full hookups.
**Price per night:** $14.
**Elevation:** 8,300 feet.
**Finding the campground:** From South Fork, travel southwest on U.S. Highway 160, about 6 miles to the campground.

**The campground:** This roadside park offers a nice place to stay if you want to explore the South Fork area. Sites are grassy; some are shaded. There are ten lakes and streams to fish within a fifteen-minute drive from the park. The hosts here also offer horseback riding, including overnight wilderness trips.

## 306 Riverbend Resort

**Location:** Southwest of South Fork.
**Affiliations:** Good Sam; Wheelers; Coachmen; Colorado Association of Campgrounds, Cabins, and Lodges.
**Contact:** 719-873-5344, www.riverbend-resort.com.
**Reservations:** 800-621-6512.
**Amenities:** Laundry, showers, public phone, playground, cabins, whirlpool, picnic tables, grills, river fishing.
**Sites:** 64, 58 full hookups.
**Price per night:** $15 to $19.
**Elevation:** 8,300 feet.
**Season:** Year-round.
**Finding the campground:** From South Fork, travel southwest on U.S. Highway 160, about 3 miles to the campground.

**The campground:** To check out this campground, go to your local video store and rent *National Lampoon's Vacation*, starring Chevy Chase. The resort was known as "Kamp Komfort" in the movie. The sites are somewhat close together and lack shade, but this would be a good place to stay to enjoy the vast array of recreational offerings in the South Fork area or to park for the night if you're just passing through.

## 307 Spruce Ski Lodge & RV Park

**Location:** South Fork.
**Affiliations:** Colorado Association of Campgrounds, Cabins, and Lodges.
**Contact:** 719-873-5605.
**Reservations:** 800-228-5605.
**Amenities:** Laundry, showers, whirlpool, public phone, playground, cabins, restaurant, miniature golf, picnic tables, fire rings, grills, rafting.
**Sites:** 12, all full hookups.
**Price per night:** $6 to $12.
**Elevation:** 8,300 feet.
**Finding the campground:** From the junction of Colorado Highway 149 and U.S. Highway 160, travel east about 0.75 mile to the campground.

**The campground:** These campsites adjacent to a full-service lodge make a fun and convenient place to spend time in the South Fork area. You can spend your morning rafting the Rio Grande, your afternoon playing miniature golf, and your evening soaking in the hot tub.

# Public

## 308 Aspen Glade

**Location:** West of Antonito.
**Facilities:** Central water, fire rings, picnic tables, vault toilets.
**Sites:** 34.
**Fee:** $9.
**Elevation:** 8,500 feet.
**Road conditions:** Paved.
**Management:** Rio Grande National Forest, 719-274-8971.
**Reservations:** 800-280-CAMP, www.nrrc.com, $8.65 fee.
**Activities:** Fishing, hiking, four-wheel driving.
**Finding the campground:** From Antonito, travel west on Colorado Highway 17, about 18 miles to the campground.

**The campground:** The campgrounds along CO 17 are all very pretty and see relatively low weekday usage. But they do fill on the weekends, so keep the reservation number in mind. Aspen Glade is easy to reach, so it will be one of the first to fill. It has moderately spaced sites in a light aspen and pine forest. Fishing is subject to restrictions along some parts of the Conejos River, so be sure to check posted regulations. The entire area is crisscrossed with mining roads that make it a four-wheel-drive paradise.

## 309 Beaver Creek

**Location:** Southwest of South Fork.
**Facilities:** Central water, fire rings, picnic tables, vault toilets.
**Sites:** 19.
**Fee:** $10.
**Elevation:** 8,850 feet.
**Road conditions:** Paved.
**Management:** Rio Grande National Forest, 719-657-3321.
**Activities:** Fishing, hiking, scenic driving, four-wheel driving.
**Finding the campground:** From South Fork, travel 2.4 miles southwest on U.S. Highway 160. Turn south onto Beaver Creek Road (Forest Service Road 360) and go about 3 miles, then turn left on FSR 355 to the campground.

**The campground:** This pretty spot amid a light pine, aspen, and spruce forest has widely spaced sites and fishing access to Beaver Creek. The crowds seem to prefer camping closer to the reservoir, so you may find this camp empty except on holiday weekends. Hiking trails nearby will take you almost to the top of Cattle Mountain and Grouse Mountain in a day. There are also numerous old mining camps in the area surrounding South Fork that you can explore in a four-wheel-drive vehicle.

## 310 | Cathedral

**Location:** Northwest of Del Norte.
**Facilities:** Central water, fire rings, picnic tables, vault toilets.
**Sites:** 33.
**Fee:** $9.
**Elevation:** 9,400 feet.
**Road conditions:** One-and-a-half lane, gravel.
**Management:** Rio Grande National Forest, 719-274-8971.
**Activities:** Fishing, hiking, four-wheel driving.
**Finding the campground:** From Del Norte, travel west on U.S. Highway 160, about 9 miles to County Road 18. Turn north and go 1.5 miles to Forest Service Road 650. Continue north about 3 miles to FSR 640. Turn northwest and go about 7 miles to the campground.

**The campground:** Cathedral is another pretty campground that few people seem to know. It isn't easy to reach, but it's the kind of place that makes you want to stay put once you get there. If you do get the itch to get out of camp, the surrounding mountains offer numerous hiking and four-wheel-drive challenges. And day trips either to Pagosa Springs or Gunnison are not entirely out of the question if you start craving civilization. Fishing Embargo Creek is possible near camp.

## 311 | Conejos

**Location:** Northwest of Antonito.
**Facilities:** Central water, fire rings, picnic tables, vault toilets.
**Sites:** 16.
**Fee:** $8.
**Elevation:** 8,700 feet.
**Road conditions:** two lane, gravel.
**Management:** Rio Grande National Forest, 719-274-8971.
**Activities:** Fishing, hiking.
**Finding the campground:** From Antonito, travel west on Colorado Highway 17 about 23 miles. Turn northwest onto Forest Service Road 250 and go about 7 miles to the campground.

**The campground:** With sites tightly spaced in a light pine forest, this isn't the prettiest of the campgrounds along the Conejos River. But it does provide fishing and hiking access to the South San Juan Wilderness. It also satisfies the strong urge many people seem to have to be near Platoro. Like many spots in Colorado where people leave their hearts, Platoro casts a selective spell. Some can drive out of the valley without ever looking back, but those who lack immunity will forever hear a call to return.

## 312 Cross Creek

**Location:** Southwest of South Fork.
**Facilities:** Central water, fire rings, picnic tables, vault toilets.
**Sites:** 12.
**Fee:** $9.
**Elevation:** 8,800 feet.
**Road conditions:** One-and-a-half lane, gravel.
**Management:** Rio Grande National Forest, 719-657-3321.
**Activities:** Fishing, four-wheel driving.
**Finding the campground:** From South Fork, travel 2.4 miles southwest on U.S. Highway 160. Turn south onto Beaver Creek Road (Forest Service Road 360) and go about 6 miles to the campground.

**The campground:** Because its sites are so tightly spaced, Cross Creek can handle only small trailers and tents. The views across Beaver Creek Reservoir make this a wonderful place to stay, whether you fish or not. The lake has boat ramps, and you can use motorized boats at wakeless speeds. After you catch your limit, try driving farther south on Forest Service Road 360. Between here and Summitville, you'll find some of the most pristine land in southern Colorado. You'll need detailed maps, though, and the road may be passable only to four-wheel-drive vehicles, depending on weather conditions.

## 313 Elk Creek

**Location:** West of Antonito.
**Facilities:** Central water, fire rings, picnic tables, vault toilets.
**Sites:** 45.
**Fee:** $10.
**Elevation:** 8,500 feet.
**Road conditions:** One-and-a-half lane, dirt.
**Management:** Rio Grande National Forest, 719-274-8971.
**Reservations:** 800-280-CAMP, www.nrrc.com, $8.65 fee.
**Activities:** Fishing, scenic driving, hiking, four-wheel driving.
**Restrictions:** No ATVs in the campground.
**Finding the campground:** From Antonito, travel west on Colorado Highway 17 about 23 miles. Turn southwest onto Forest Service Road 128 and go about 1 mile to the campground.

**The campground:** Elk Creek is a good place to spend some time. The campsites are well spaced in a light forest of birch and spruce. Though the creek itself runs near camp, there is no direct access to it. Fishing is possible in the Conejos River just a short hike away. There are also several small lakes to the west that are within easy hiking distance. Travelers along Colorado Highway 17 can use Elk Creek as a stopover between Antonito and Chama, New Mexico, because of its easy access and abundance of sites.

## 314 | Highway Springs

**Location:** Southwest of South Fork.
**Facilities:** Fire rings, picnic tables, vault toilets; no water.
**Sites:** 11.
**Fee:** $5.
**Elevation:** $8,400 feet.
**Road conditions:** two lane, dirt, rough and rocky.
**Management:** Rio Grande National Forest, 719-657-3321.
**Activities:** Four-wheel driving, scenic driving.
**Finding the campground:** From South Fork, travel 5.2 miles southwest on U.S. Highway 160 to Forest Service Road 380. Turn south to reach the campground.

**The campground:** Highway Springs Campground is a lightly forested, rather primitive camp that can be used either as a stopover or a base camp for those wanting to explore the mining camps to the south by four-wheel-drive. FSR 380 eventually connects with FSR 330 near Summitville, an abandoned mining camp. This spectacular drive is often possible in two-wheel-drive vehicles, depending upon weather conditions.

## 315 | Lake Fork

**Location:** South of Platoro.
**Facilities:** Central water, fire rings, picnic tables, vault toilets.
**Sites:** 18.
**Fee:** $8.
**Elevation:** 8,800 feet.
**Road conditions:** two lane, dirt, rough.
**Management:** Rio Grande National Forest, 719-274-8971.
**Reservations:** 800-280-CAMP, www.nrrc.com, $8.65 fee.
**Activities:** Fishing, scenic driving.
**Finding the campground:** From Antonito, travel west on Colorado Highway 17 about 23 miles. Turn northwest onto Forest Service Road 250 and go about 16 miles to the campground.

**The campground:** These 18 sites are as good as it gets in the Platoro area. From here you can fish two rivers and the lakes north of Platoro, drive up to Summitville, or string up your hammock for an afternoon nap. Sites are widely spaced in a light forest of aspen and spruce interspersed with areas of open meadow. This campground is probably the best place from which to sample the magic that draws people to this valley.

## 316 Mix Lake

**Location:** North of Platoro.
**Facilities:** Central water, fire rings, picnic tables, vault toilets.
**Sites:** 22.
**Fee:** $9.
**Elevation:** 10,035 feet.
**Road conditions:** two lane, gravel.
**Management:** Rio Grande National Forest, 719-274-8971.
**Activities:** Fishing, four-wheel driving.
**Finding the campground:** From Antonito, travel west on Colorado Highway 17 about 23 miles. Turn northwest onto Forest Service Road 250 and go 21.6 miles to FSR 250B. Turn west and go about 0.75 mile to the campground.

**The campground:** Because there are no campgrounds on Platoro Reservoir, this is where everyone stays. Mix Lake is tiny compared to Platoro, but it's still worth casting a line here. The area around Platoro is becoming a haven for Texans, so the crowds can get thick. The campground itself offers nicely spaced sites set on a hillside. Some sites are wooded, others open. Almost all have views of the surrounding mountains.

It is important to note that although some maps show the road from Colorado Highway 17 to Del Norte via Platoro and Summitville as a through route, it is a difficult drive. You can get through most of the time, but this drive is best reserved for scenic pleasure, not destination travel. Perhaps the fact that you can't pass through Platoro on your way to somewhere else is part of the magic spell the community casts.

## 317 Mogote

**Location:** West of Antonito.
**Facilities:** Central water, fire rings, picnic tables, vault toilets.
**Sites:** 41.
**Fee:** $10.
**Elevation:** 8,400 feet.
**Road conditions:** Paved.
**Management:** Rio Grande National Forest, 719-274-8971.
**Reservations:** 800-280-CAMP, www.nrrc.com, $8.65 fee.
**Activities:** Fishing, four-wheel driving.
**Restrictions:** No ATVs in the campground.
**Finding the campground:** From Antonito, travel west on Colorado Highway 17, about 15 miles to the campground.

**The campground:** This heavily used campground is pretty, easily accessible, and at the hub of a vast array of jeep trails heading both north and south. Don't plan to stay here on a weekend without reservations. You'd hate to arrive at midnight and find no room in camp.

## 318 | Park Creek

**Location:** Southwest of South Fork.
**Facilities:** Central water, fire rings, picnic tables, vault toilets.
**Sites:** 13.
**Fee:** $9.
**Elevation:** 8,500 feet.
**Road conditions:** Paved.
**Management:** Rio Grande National Forest, 719-657-3321.
**Activities:** Fishing, hiking.
**Finding the campground:** From South Fork, travel 8.9 miles southwest on U.S. Highway 160 to the campground.

**The campground:** Park Creek is a riverside camp with somewhat narrow spacing, heavy usage, and potential traffic noise, but it is very pretty and makes a convenient stopover before or after crossing Wolf Creek Pass. There is also a good network of trails north of camp that is worth exploring.

## 319 | Spectacle Lake

**Location:** South of Platoro.
**Facilities:** Central water, fire rings, picnic tables, vault toilets.
**Sites:** 24.
**Fee:** $8.
**Elevation:** 8,700 feet.
**Road conditions** two lane, dirt.
**Management:** Rio Grande National Forest, 719-274-8971.
**Activities:** Fishing, hiking.
**Finding the campground:** From Antonito, travel west on Colorado Highway 17 about 23 miles. Turn northwest onto Forest Service Road 250 and go about 7 miles to the campground.

**The campground:** Spectacle Lake Campground is lightly forested. Many sites are in the open, allowing views of the surrounding river valley. Fishing in the Conejos River is possible from camp, and trails nearby lead into the South San Juan Wilderness. Usage here is slightly lower than at camps closer to Platoro, so this may be a good alternative if the others are full.

## 320 | Stunner

**Location:** Northwest of Platoro.
**Facilities:** Central water, fire rings, picnic tables, vault toilets.
**Sites:** 10.
**Fee:** None.
**Elevation:** 9,700 feet.
**Road conditions:** one lane, rough and rocky.
**Management:** Rio Grande National Forest, 719-274-8971.

**Activities:** Fishing, hiking, four-wheel driving.
**Finding the campground:** From Antonito, travel west on Colorado Highway 17 about 23 miles. Turn northwest onto Forest Service Road 250 and go about 26 miles to FSR 380. Turn west and go about 0.25 mile to the campground.

**The campground:** Stunner is a pretty camp set in a thick aspen forest. Most people find it too difficult to reach, but if you dislike the crowds at lower elevations, this is a great spot to try. Be sure to check posted fishing regulations. To the north of this camp there are mine dumps that leach heavy metals into some of the streams, making both the water and the fish unsafe for consumption. The affected streams are well marked, but if in doubt, don't partake.

## 321 | Trujillo Meadows

**Location:** West of Antonito.
**Facilities:** Central water, fire rings, picnic tables, vault toilets, wheelchair-accessible sites.
**Sites:** 50.
**Fee:** $9.
**Elevation:** 9,700 feet.
**Road conditions:** One-and-a-half lane, gravel.
**Management:** Rio Grande National Forest, 719-274-8971.
**Activities:** Fishing, scenic driving, four-wheel driving, hiking.
**Finding the campground:** From Antonito, travel west on Colorado Highway 17 about 32 miles. Turn north onto Forest Service Road 116 and go about 3 miles to the campground.

**The campground:** This beautiful campground is a bit off the beaten path, but it still sees a good deal of traffic. It is the best place to camp and still drive into Chama, New Mexico, to ride the narrow gauge train there. The campground has widely spaced sites—some open, some wooded. All are a short walk from crystal blue Trujillo Lake. With a choice of activities in and around camp that will satisfy everyone, this is a terrific family vacation spot.

## 322 | Upper Beaver Creek

**Location:** Southwest of South Fork.
**Facilities:** Central water, fire rings, picnic tables, vault toilets.
**Sites:** 15.
**Fee:** $9.
**Elevation:** 8,500 feet.
**Road conditions:** Paved.
**Management:** Rio Grande National Forest, 719-657-3321.
**Activities:** Fishing, hiking, four-wheel driving.
**Finding the campground:** From South Fork, travel 2.4 miles southwest on U.S. Highway 160. Turn south onto Beaver Creek Road (Forest Service Road 360) and go about 4 miles to the campground.

*The wildlife is undoubtedly a part of the magic many people find in Platoro.*

**The campground:** Upper Beaver Creek Campground is about a mile south of Beaver Creek Reservoir, making lake fishing the preferred activity of most campers. The lake has boat ramps, but only wakeless boating is allowed. The sites in camp are well spaced amid a dense pine forest. This is a beautiful place to vacation, but you should expect weekend crowds.

## Additional Campgrounds in the South Fork and Platoro Areas

|  | Type* | Contact | Location |
|---|---|---|---|
| Alamosa KOA | P (52) | 719-562-9157 | E of Alamosa on US 160 |
| Aspen Ridge | P NA | 719-873-5921 | CO 149 in South Fork |
| Blue Creek Cabins & Campground | P (34) | 719-658-2479 | Off CO 149 between mileposts 11 & 12 |
| Conejos River Campground | P (58) | 719-376-5943 | W of Antonito on CO 17 |
| Cottonwood Cone Lodge & Cabins | P (8) | 719-658-2248 | NW of South Fork on CO 149 |
| Gold Pan Acres Campground | P (20) | 719-376-2246 | Antonito |
| Grandview Cabins & RV Park | P (60) | 719-873-5541 | N of South Fork on CO 149 |
| High Country RV Park | P (60) | 719-873-5863 | N of South Fork on CO 59 |

| | Type* | Contact | Location |
|---|---|---|---|
| Josey's Mogote Meadow | P (55) | 719-376-5774 | W of Antonito on CO 17 |
| Mobile Manor Overnite Park | P (36) | 719-852-5921 | W of Monte Vista on US 160 |
| Narrow Guage Railroad Inn & RV Park | P (8) | 719-376-5441 | Antonito |
| Navajo Trall Campground | P (46) | 719-589-9460 | W of Alamosa on US 160 |
| Ponderosa Campground | P (57) | 719-873-5993 | CO 17 in Antonito |
| Riversedge RV Resort | P (58) | 719-873-5993 | E of South Fork on US 160 |
| South Fork Campground & & RV Resort | P (58) | 719-237-7322 | E of South Fork on US 160 |
| Twin Rivers Cabins & RV Park | P (49) | 719-376-5710 | W of Antonito on CO 17 |
| Ute Bluff Lodge & RV Park | P (45) | 719-872-5595 | E of South Fork on US 160 |
| Alamosa | NF (10) | 719-274-8971 | SW of Monte Vista on FSR 250 |
| Comstock | NF (8) | 719-657-3321 | SW of Monte Vista on FSR 265 |
| Lake Fork | NF (18) | 719-274-8971 | W of Antonito on FSR 250 |
| Poso | NF (11) | 719-655-2547 | NW of La Garita on FSR 675 |
| Storm King | NF (11) | 719-655-2553 | NW of La Garita on FSR 690 |
| Penitente Canyon | BLM (10) | 719-589-4975 | NE of Del Norte on CR 33138 |
| LaJara Reservoir | SWA DSP | 970-249-3431 | SW of Monte Vista on RaJadero Canyon Road |

- * See "Key to Abbreviations" p.22—(# of sites)

# South Central

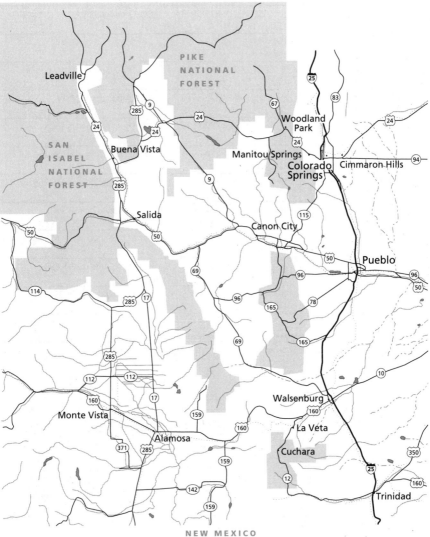

# Area 28: Buena Vista

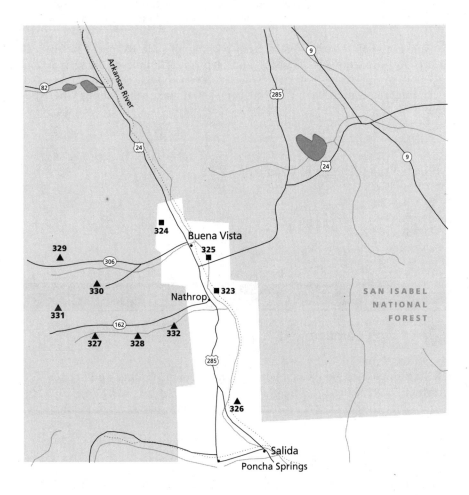

## BUENA VISTA

South-central Colorado is an outdoor playground that plays host to thousands of families every year. More than 150,000 people float the Arkansas River each year. Almost any place you choose to stay in the region will offer a multitude of fun things to do.

Buena Vista is no exception. With the Arkansas to the east and the 14,000-foot Collegiate Peaks to the west, it's hard to find time to take in all that the area has to offer. The town itself is a collection of motels, restaurants, and gas stations, with rafting companies squeezed in where there is room. There is a nine-hole golf course and even a drive-in theater that features first-run movies.

One reason the Arkansas is so popular is that it is one of the few whitewater rivers in the state for which you can arrange tours that include children as young as eight. Trips range from half a day to three days long, and no matter which you choose, you'll wish it were longer. Most rafting companies rent wetsuits, which are a necessity, and provide wool sweaters to help ward off the chill of the mountain water. If you've never rafted before, Buena Vista is an ideal place to give it a try.

Camping choices vary greatly, from parking-lot-style RV parks to full-scale resorts featuring horseback riding and jeep tours. Public camping is a good choice if you prefer to entertain yourself. Even though there are more than seven hundred campsites in the area, you should make reservations where possible.

**For More Information:**

Buena Vista Chamber of Commerce
343 Highway 24
P.O. Box 2021
Buena Vista, CO 81211
719-395-6612
www.fourteenernet.com

# Commercial

## 323 Brown's Campground

**Location:** Nathrop.
**Affiliations:** Colorado Association of Campgrounds, Cabins, and Lodges.
**Contact:** 719-395-8301.
**Amenities:** Dump station, laundry, showers, store, playground, picnic tables, grills, stream fishing.
**Sites:** 71, 15 full hookups.
**Price per night:** $13 to $17.
**Elevation:** 7,900 feet.
**Finding the campground:** From U.S. Highway 285 in Nathrop, travel about 50 feet on County Road 197 to the campground.

**The campground:** Brown's is a full-service RV park with some shaded sites located in the heart of rafting country on Chalk Creek. The sites are tightly spaced, but the lower loop is grassy and is shaded by towering cottonwoods. Some sites are on the creek. Rafting trips can be arranged across the road. Overall, this is a nice place to come home to after a day running the river.

## 324 Buena Vista KOA

**Location:** East of Buena Vista.
**Affiliations:** KOA; Colorado Association of Campgrounds, Cabins, and Lodges.

**Contact:** 719-395-8318.
**Reservations:** 800-562-2672.
**Amenities:** Dump station, laundry, showers, store, playground, picnic tables, grills, cabins, horseback riding, bike rentals, rafting guides, whirlpool, café, fire rings, public phone, hiking trails, stable.
**Sites:** 96, 21 full hookups.
**Price per night:** $17 to $22.
**Elevation:** 8,000 feet.
**Finding the campground:** From the junction of U.S. Highways 285 and 24, travel east on US 24/285 about 1.25 miles to County Road 303. Turn north and go about 0.25 mile to the campground.

**The campground:** This could be called a deluxe KOA because it has all the usual amenities, plus stables, trails, a rafting company, and a mountain view. It is hard to pass this place by, whether you are looking for a base from which to enjoy the Collegiate Peaks area or a one-night stop in your travels. Weekend reservations are a must. Don't expect a spot to be available on the spur of the moment.

## 325 Crazy Horse Campground

**Location:** North of Buena Vista.
**Affiliations:** Colorado Association of Campgrounds, Cabins, and Lodges.
**Contact:** 719-395-2323.
**Reservations:** 800-888-7320.
**Amenities:** Dump station, laundry, showers, store, playground, picnic tables, grills, cabins, horseback riding, jeep rentals, rafting guides, pool, miniature golf, fire rings, public phone.
**Sites:** 101, 34 full hookups.
**Price per night:** $17 to $19.
**Elevation:** 8,300 feet.
**Finding the campground:** From Buena Vista, travel about 8 miles north on U.S. Highway 24 to the campground.

**The campground:** Crazy Horse is a fun-filled family destination if ever there was one. The campsites are spread across a piñon-covered hillside. The hosts here offer just about every activity that people come to Buena Vista to enjoy. If Crazy Horse doesn't have it, they'll help you arrange it somewhere else. Tenters will appreciate the wooded sites away from the crowds. Crazy Horse also makes a convenient stopover point, but be aware that with all the recreational activities it will be hard to leave (especially if you have kids).

# Public

## 326 Arkansas Headwaters State Park

**Location:** Between Leadville and Pueblo.
**Facilities:** Fire rings, picnic tables, vault toilets; no water.
**Sites:** 60.
**Fee:** $2 to $6.
**Elevation:** 4,000 to 9,000 feet.
**Road conditions:** Varied.
**Management:** Colorado Department of Parks and Outdoor Recreation, 719-539-7289.
**Activities:** Fishing, river sports.
**Season:** Year-round.
**Finding the campground:** Campsites are located at the following recreation areas along the river: Five Points and Rincon, off U.S. Highway 50; Hecla Junction and Ruby Mountain, off US 285.

**The campground:** The Arkansas River is the most heavily traveled whitewater river in the United States. You can arrange rafting adventures for all ages and skill levels through commercial operations along the river, from Leadville all the way to the Royal Gorge. Floaters and anglers use these campgrounds along the river, which are part of the state park system. All of the camps are primitive; no drinking water is available.

## 327 Cascade

**Location:** West of Nathrop.
**Facilities:** Central water, fire rings, picnic tables, vault toilets.
**Sites:** 23.
**Fee:** $9.
**Elevation:** 8,700 feet.
**Road conditions:** two lane, gravel.
**Management:** San Isabel National Forest, 719-539-3591.
**Reservations:** 800-280-CAMP, www.nrrc.com, $8.65 fee.
**Activities:** Fishing, hiking.
**Finding the campground:** From Nathrop, travel about 0.5 mile south to County Road 162. Turn west and go 8.5 miles to the campground.

**The campground:** Lush pines, aspens, and wild roses greet visitors to this campground. The sites are well spaced with plenty of privacy. The one drawback is that the creek is across the road. A short trail connects this camp with the Colorado Trail as it passes the eastern face of the Collegiates. Any of the campgrounds along County Road 162 make good base camps for day hiking along the trail or rafting the Arkansas.

## 328 Chalk Lake

**Location:** West of Nathrop.
**Facilities:** Central water, fire rings, picnic tables, vault toilets.
**Sites:** 21.
**Fee:** $9.
**Elevation:** 8,700 feet.
**Road conditions:** Paved.
**Management:** San Isabel National Forest, 719-539-3591.
**Reservations:** 800-280-CAMP, www.nrrc.com, $8.65 fee.
**Activities:** Fishing, hiking.
**Finding the campground:** From Nathrop, travel about 0.5 mile south to County Road 162. Turn west and go 7.5 miles to the campground.

**The campground:** Tenters dream of campgrounds like this. There are walk-in sites at the water's edge on both sides of Chalk Creek. The sites are heavily shaded and well spaced. Some of the sites are suitable for trailers and RVs, but they are a distance from the creek and have no trees. As with the other campgrounds on County Road 162, access to the Colorado Trail is a prime reason for staying here. This is a popular segment of the trail, and side trails lead up many of the Collegiate Peaks.

## 329 Collegiate Peaks

**Location:** West of Buena Vista.
**Facilities:** Central water, fire rings, picnic tables, vault toilets.
**Sites:** 56.
**Fee:** $10.
**Elevation:** 9,800 feet.
**Road conditions:** Paved.
**Management:** San Isabel National Forest, 719-539-3591.
**Reservations:** 800-280-CAMP, www.nrrc.com, $8.65 fee.
**Activities:** Fishing, hiking, four-wheel driving.
**Finding the campground:** From Buena Vista, travel 10.6 miles west on County Road 306 to the campground.

**The campground:** Many people shy away from large campgrounds, but this one should not bother you if you plan ahead. In fact, it is the prettiest campground in the Buena Vista area. Most of the sites are well spaced; some are extremely deep and densely forested. But reservations are a must throughout most of the summer if you want the good sites. The river sites are the best.

The location of this campground will allow you to enjoy the entire area with ease. Rafting trips, access to the Colorado Trail, a riding stable, a hot-springs resort are all a short drive away. There is even a drive-in theater on the edge of town, in case you run out of campfire stories. All this combines to make Collegiate Peaks a premier family camping destination.

## 330  Cottonwood Lake

**Location:** West of Buena Vista.
**Facilities:** Central water, fire rings, picnic tables, vault toilets.
**Sites:** 28.
**Fee:** $9.
**Elevation:** 9,600 feet.
**Road conditions:** two lane, dirt.
**Management:** San Isabel National Forest, 719-539-3591.
**Activities:** Fishing.
**Finding the campground:** From Buena Vista, travel west on County Road 306, about 7 miles to CR 344. Turn southwest and continue about 3.5 miles to the campground.

**The campground:** This is a newly reforested campground that apparently has been moved from its original location to the shore of Cottonwood Lake. Campsites are well spaced, but the young aspens offer little shade. The lake is lovely, and there is shade along the shore. Only hand-powered boats are allowed, but this is the kind of place that makes you want to while away the afternoon paddling a canoe from one end to the other, whether you catch any fish or not.

## 331  Iron City

**Location:** West of Nathrop.
**Facilities:** Central water, fire rings, picnic tables, vault toilets.
**Sites:** 15.
**Fee:** $9.
**Elevation:** 9,900 feet.
**Road conditions:** two lane, gravel.
**Management:** San Isabel National Forest, 719-539-3591.
**Activities:** Fishing, hiking, four-wheel driving.
**Finding the campground:** From Nathrop, travel 0.5 mile south to County Road 162. Turn west and go about 15 miles to Forest Service Road 292. Turn north and go about 0.5 mile to the campground.

**The campground:** It's very difficult to get away from the crowds in the Buena Vista area, but if that's your goal, try Iron City Campground. It won't be empty, but the crowd will be limited by the size of the campground and its distance from the Arkansas River. The sites are well spaced among pines and aspens; some are creekside. Alpine Reservoir is nearby for those who like lake fishing.

## 332  Mount Princeton

**Location:** West of Nathrop.
**Facilities:** Central water, fire rings, picnic tables, vault toilets.
**Sites:** 17.
**Fee:** $9.

**Elevation:** 8,000 feet.
**Road conditions:** Paved.
**Management:** San Isabel National Forest, 719-539-3591.
**Reservations:** 800-280-CAMP, www.nrrc.com, $8.65 fee.
**Activities:** Fishing, hiking.
**Finding the campground:** From Nathrop, travel 0.5 mile south to County Road 162. Turn west and go about 7 miles to the campground.

**The campground:** Mount Princeton is a pretty campground, but if your accommodations involve sleeping on the ground, you may want to look farther up the road. The ground here is littered with large rocks. Trailer campers will enjoy the well spaced sites scattered amidst a light pine forest, provided they don't do much walking around in the dark. The campground gets heavy use due to the nearby access to the Colorado Trail.

## Additional Campgrounds in the Buena Vista Area

| | Type* | Contact | Location |
|---|---|---|---|
| Arkansas River Rim Campground & RV Park | P (63) | 719-395-8883 | N of Buena Vista on US 24 |
| Bergstrom's Court & Campsite | P (42) | 719-395-8481 | N of Buena Vista on US 24 |
| Buena Vista Family Campground & Resort | P (66) | 719-395-8318 | N of Buena Vista on US 24 |
| Collegiate Peaks Family Inn & RV | P (NA) | 719-395-2251 | US 24 in Buena Vista |
| Fisherman's Bridge Campground | P (12) | 719-539-8207 | 24070 CR 301 |
| Mount Princeton RV Park | P (44) | 719-395-6206 | N of Buena Vista on CR 383 |
| Bootleg | NF (7) | 719-539-3591 | W of Nathrop on CR 162 |
| Antero Reservoir | SWA DSP | 719-473-2945 | SW of Hartzel on US 24 |

- \* See "Key to Abbreviations" p.22—(# of sites)

# Area 29: Colorado Springs

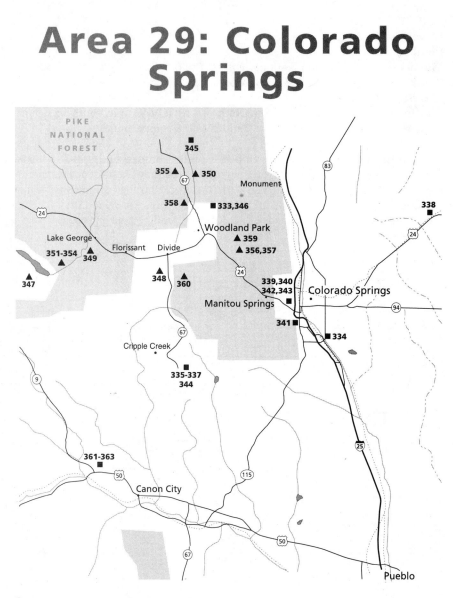

PIKE
NATIONAL
FOREST

■ 345

355 ▲  ▲ 350
67
Monument

358 ▲  ■ 333,346

338 ■

Woodland Park
▲ 359
▲ 356,357

24
Lake George
351-354 ▲  ▲
349  Florissant  Divide

347 ▲  348 ▲  ▲ 360

339,340
342,343 ■  Colorado Springs
Manitou Springs  ■

341 ■

■ 334
83
24
94

67
Cripple Creek

335-337 ■
344
9

361-363 ■
50
Canon City

115

25

50
67
Pueblo

## Colorado Springs

The Springs, as this town is affectionately called, sprawls along the side of the Rockies at an elevation of 5,900 feet. It feels much higher. Snowcapped Pikes Peak casts an ominous shadow across this second largest of Colorado cities. Though beautiful, the town looks like a child that has outgrown its clothing. Like elbows and knees bursting through tight fabric, vast housing developments stretch south and east through the confining foothills.

This is a town where tourism reigns; it's a carnival of attractions—enough to boggle the mind. Treat it like a carnival, though. Keep in mind that not all carnies hawk the truth.

*The quaint casinos in Cripple Creek are among the many attractions of the Colorado Springs area.*

Some of the highlights of this area include:

—**Garden of the Gods and Florissant Fossil Beds National Monument**, where you can learn geology and paleontology the fun way.

—**The Air Force Academy and the U.S. Olympic Training Center**, where tours will stir your patriotism.

—**Pikes Peak**, where the views will take your breath away.

—**Cheyenne Mountain Zoo**, where the small size of the facility is not an indication of its quality.

—**Cripple Creek,** where you can imagine yourself in the midst of a nine-teenth-century gold rush as you plunk coins into a modern slot machine.

For a little physical activity, there are golf courses, year-round ice skating rinks, public swimming pools, and tennis courts. Museums include the World Figure Skating Hall of Fame and Museum, the Pro Rodeo Hall of Champions, and the Hall of Presidents, among others.

Outside the city, fishing and hiking opportunities abound. Eleven Mile Reservoir and Rampart Reservoirs offer excellent, though crowded, lake fishing.

Where to camp? A lot depends on what you plan to do. There are nice RV parks in the city, many away from the interstate, but still convenient to attractions. If you prefer to get away from the bustle of the Springs, there are good commercial operations in both Woodland Park and Cripple Creek. For state park camping, try Eleven Mile Reservoir (Campground 347) or Mueller (Campground 348). National forest camps are scattered throughout the region. They are not the first choice of many visitors, so they tend to be less crowded.

**For More Information:**

Colorado Springs Convention and Visitors Bureau
104 S. Cascade Avenue Suite 104
Colorado Springs, CO 80903
719-635-7506, ext.0, or 800-DO-VISIT
www.coloradosprings-travel.com/cscvb/

Manitou Springs Chamber of Commerce
354 Manitou Avenue
Manitou Springs, CO 80829
719-685-5089 or 800-642-2567
www.pikes-peak.com/manitou

U.S. Air Force Academy
Exit 156B off Interstate 25
719-472-2025
www.usafa.af.mil/ah/

Cheyenne Mountain Zoo
4250 Cheyenne Mountain Zoo Road
Colorado Springs, CO 80906
719-633-9925

U.S. Olympic Complex
One Olympic Plaza
Colorado Springs, CO 80909
719-578-4644

Cripple Creek Chamber of Commerce
337 E. Bennett Avenue
P.O. Box 650
Cripple Creek, CO 80813
719-689-2169 or 800-526-8777

# Commercial

##  333  Campground at Woodland Park

**Location:** Woodland Park.
**Affiliations:** Colorado Association of Campgrounds, Cabins, and Lodges.
**Contact:** 719-687-7575.
**Reservations:** 800-808-CAMP.
**Amenities:** Dump station, laundry, showers, store, playground, picnic tables, grills, cabins, pool, miniature golf, fire rings, public phone, movies, ice cream socials.
**Sites:** 126, 55 full hookups.
**Price per night:** $17 to $22.50.
**Elevation:** 8,500 feet.
**Finding the campground:** From Exit 141 on Interstate 25 in Colorado Springs, travel west, about 18 miles on U.S. Highway 24 to Woodland Park. Turn right onto Colorado Highway 67. Travel about 0.5 mile, then turn left on Bowman. Go 3 blocks to the campground.

**The campground:** This campground is a pleasant surprise tucked away in the woods. The spacing of the sites is more like that found in a national forest campground than in a full-service RV park. All sites are heavily wooded. The park is far enough from the highway to escape almost all traffic noise, yet it is convenient enough to make it a good stopover or base from which to explore all of the attractions in the area surrounding the Springs. The only drawback here is that maintenance of the facilities doesn't seem to be high on the list of priorities. If you can overlook the run-down miniature golf course, it's a nice place to stay.

## 334  Colorado Springs South KOA

**Location:** South of Colorado Springs.
**Affiliations:** KOA.
**Contact:** 719-382-7575.
**Reservations:** 800-562-8609.

**Amenities:** Dump station, showers, laundry, picnic tables, grills, public phone, playground, miniature golf, indoor pool, whirlpool, car rentals, church service, kitchen, computer room, café, cabins, local tours.
**Sites:** 235, 126 full hookups.
**Price per night:** $15 to $23.
**Elevation:** 6,000 feet.
**Season:** Year-round.
**Finding the campground:** Take Exit 132 off Interstate 25.

**The campground:** The best word to describe this easy-in/easy-out RV park is huge. If you need a place to park in the area with access to the interstate, this is a good choice for any length of stay. You can start your day off with a flapjack breakfast, see the sights all day, and then wind down in the pool and hot tub. This is also the closest RV park to Pikes Peak International Raceway.

## 335 Cripple Creek Gold Campground

**Location:** Northeast of Cripple Creek.
**Affiliations:** Colorado Association of Campgrounds, Cabins, and Lodges.
**Contact:** 719-689-2342.
**Amenities:** Dump station, laundry, showers, store, cabins, playground, picnic tables, grills, horseback riding, fire rings.
**Sites:** 24, no full hookups.
**Price per night:** $14 to $15.
**Elevation:** 10,200 feet.
**Restrictions:** 30-foot maximum trailer length.
**Finding the campground:** From Cripple Creek, travel north on Colorado Highway, 67 about 5 miles to the campground.

**The campground:** Cripple Creek Gold is set in the woods away from town, making it a good place from which the family can enjoy both Cripple Creek and the San Isabel National Forest. Hiking trails lead right from camp. Other activities in the area include mine tours, trail rides, and outstanding scenic drives.

## 336 Cripple Creek Hospitality House & RV Park

**Location:** Cripple Creek.
**Affiliations:** Colorado Association of Campgrounds, Cabins, and Lodges.
**Contact:** 719-689-2513.
**Reservations:** 800-522-2513.
**Amenities:** Dump station, showers, laundry, picnic tables, grills, public phone, playground, whirlpool, hiking trails, casino shuttle.
**Sites:** 50, 48 full hookups.
**Price per night:** $14 to $18.
**Elevation:** 9,500 feet.
**Finding the campground:** Travel west through Cripple Creek on Bennett Avenue to B Street. Turn north and continue to the Hospitality House.

**The campground:** This is a park for people who want to be as close to the action as possible. The campground is located behind a beautifully restored hotel, steeping you in the sense of history that pervades Cripple Creek. It's not possible to walk down the street here without feeling the gold fever. (Of course, the clinking of nearby slot machines will remind you that the source of riches has changed in the past century.) For a change of pace, hit the street early in the morning. It's like stepping back in time. Only the arrival of the first tour bus shatters the illusion.

## 337 Cripple Creek KOA

**Location:** Northeast of Cripple Creek.
**Affiliations:** KOA.
**Contact:** 719-689-3376.
**Amenities:** Dump station, showers, laundry, picnic tables, grills, public phone.
**Sites:** 82, 34 full hookups.
**Price per night:** $18.50 to $22.50.
**Elevation:** 9,500 feet.
**Finding the campground:** From the junction of Colorado Highway 67 and County Road 81, travel south on CR 81 about 0.5 mile to the campground.

**The campground:** The open sites here allow you to take in the panoramic views of the mountains that surround this hillside meadow. The town of Cripple Creek is just around the bend, but Pike National Forest beckons almost as strongly. For four-wheel-drive enthusiasts, the old mine roads are a labyrinth just waiting to be explored.

## 338 Falcon Meadow Campground

**Location:** East of Colorado Springs.
**Affiliations:** Colorado Association of Campgrounds, Cabins, and Lodges.
**Contact:** 719-495-2694.
**Amenities:** Dump station, showers, laundry, picnic tables, grills, public phone, playground, hiking trails.
**Sites:** 30, 8 full hookups.
**Price per night:** $10 to $12.
**Elevation:** 6,800 feet.
**Season:** Year-round.
**Finding the campground:** On U.S. Highway 24 between Colorado Springs and Limon.

**The campground:** If you're looking for a place to avoid the crowds, this country spot is ideal. Located on the high plains, the campground has outstanding (though distant) views of Pikes Peak. This is a terrific stopover if you are arriving in Colorado Springs near dark. You can wake up to the splendor of the mountains before heading into the city traffic.

## 339 Fountain Creek RV Resort

**Location:** Colorado Springs.
**Affiliations:** Colorado Association of Campgrounds, Cabins, and Lodges.
**Contact:** 719-633-2192, fax 719-633-6612, e-mail fcrv@pcisys.net, www.fcrvpark.com.
**Amenities:** Dump station, showers, laundry, picnic tables, grills, patios, public phone.
**Sites:** 117, 33 full hookups.
**Price per night:** $17 to $22.
**Elevation:** 6,200 feet.
**Season:** Year-round.
**Finding the campground:** From Exit 141 on Interstate 25, go about 3 miles west on U.S. Highway 24 to 31st Street.

**The campground:** This quiet and shady RV park in town is a good place from which to enjoy the treasure trove of activities available in the area. Easy access to US 24 allows you to make day trips to Garden of the Gods, Cave of the Winds, Pikes Peak, and Cripple Creek.

## 340 Garden of the Gods Campground

**Location:** Northwest of Colorado Springs.
**Affiliations:** None.
**Contact:** 719-475-9450, fax 719-633-9643, e-mail gog@worldnet.att.net.
**Reservations:** 800-248-9451.
**Amenities:** Dump station, showers, laundry, picnic tables, grills, pool, whirlpool, store, public phone, playground, cabins, rafting trips, horseback riding, tour office.
**Sites:** 315, 200 full hookups.
**Price per night:** $25 to $30.
**Elevation:** 6,000 feet.
**Finding the campground:** From Exit 141 on Interstate 25, travel west on U.S. Highway 24, about 2.5 miles to 31st Street. Turn north and go 1 block to Colorado Avenue. Turn west and go 6 blocks to the entrance.

**The campground:** This landscaped RV park has special areas set aside for tenters, long-term guests, and large rigs. It is a family-oriented destination right in the heart of all the fun. Most sites are shaded and well spaced.

## 341 Golden Eagle Ranch RV Park & Campgrounds

**Location:** Southwest of Colorado Springs.
**Affiliations:** AAA; Colorado Association of Campgrounds, Cabins, and Lodges.
**Contact:** 719-576-0450.
**Reservations:** 800-666-3841.
**Amenities:** Dump station, showers, laundry, picnic tables, grills, public phone,

playground, museum, fishing pond, hiking trails.
**Sites:** 500, 200 full hookups.
**Price per night:** $15.50 to $17.50.
**Elevation:** 6,200 feet.
**Finding the campground:** From Exit 135 on Interstate 25, travel west on Academy, about 2 miles to Colorado Highway 115 (Nevada Avenue). Turn south and go about 5 miles to Rock Creek Canyon Road. Turn west and go about 1 mile to the campground.

**The campground:** What an incredible place! Campsites are bunched amid the hills of this 1,000-acre ranch. There is plenty of space for the kids to roam after they have toured the on-site museum, which features giant tropical insects. The real advantage to this park, though, is that it gets you away from the rush of traffic on I-25. Even if you plan to stay a single night, the peaceful mountain setting will work its magic on you.

## 342 Goldfield Campground

**Location:** Colorado Springs.
**Affiliations:** Colorado Association of Campgrounds, Cabins, and Lodges.
**Contact:** 719-471-0495.
**Amenities:** Dump station, showers, laundry, picnic tables, grills, public phone, store, local tours.
**Sites:** 65, 36 full hookups.
**Price per night:** $18.50 to $21.
**Elevation:** 6,000 feet.
**Season:** Year-round.
**Finding the campground:** From Exit 141 on Interstate 25, travel west on U.S. Highway 24, about 2 miles to 26th Street.

**The campground:** Goldfield is a quiet, wooded park and another of the lovely camping choices available in the heart of Colorado Springs. Access to US 24 makes sightseeing a breeze. You can even arrange guided tours right at the campground.

## 343 Lone Duck Campground

**Location:** Cascade.
**Affiliations:** AAA; Colorado Association of Campgrounds, Cabins, and Lodges.
**Contact:** 719-684-9907.
**Reservations:** 800-776-5925.
**Amenities:** Dump station, showers, laundry, picnic tables, grills, fire rings, pool, store, public phone, playground, hiking trails, fishing pond.
**Sites:** 60, 8 full hookups.
**Price per night:** $16 to $20.
**Elevation:** 7,500 feet.
**Finding the campground:** From Exit 141 on Interstate 25, travel west on U.S.

Highway 24, about 12 miles to the first Green Mountain Falls exit. Make a U-turn and go east on US 24 about 250 yards to the campground.

**The campground:** Lone Duck is tucked away in a valley with beautiful views of the surrounding mountains. There is plenty to do both in the immediate area and at the campground itself. This makes a great family base camp while you are in the Colorado Springs area.

## 344 Lost Burro Campground

**Location:** Northwest of Cripple Creek.
**Affiliations:** Colorado Association of Campgrounds, Cabins, and Lodges.
**Contact:** 719-689-2341.
**Amenities:** Dump station, showers, picnic tables, grills, public phone, playground, cabins, fire rings.
**Sites:** 36, no full hookups.
**Price per night:** $14 to $16.
**Elevation:** 8,600 feet.
**Season:** Year-round.
**Finding the campground:** From Cripple Creek, go about 8 miles northwest on County Road 1 to the campground.

**The campground:** Lost Burro is an out-of-the-way spot that may be just what you're looking for in the Cripple Creek area. It has all the advantages of being near town, and, at the same time, in the wooded countryside. Sites are scattered across 17 acres. There's even a stream in which you can pan for gold. An unusual feature here is the availability of portable pet enclosures, which you can set up at your campsite for your furry traveling companion while you are away from camp.

## 345 Rainbow Falls Park

**Location:** North of Woodland Park.
**Affiliations:** AAA; Good Sam; Colorado Association of Campgrounds, Cabins, and Lodges.
**Contact:** 719-687-9074, fax 719-687-9386.
**Amenities:** Dump station, showers, picnic tables, grills, public phone, fishing lakes, hay rides, horseback riding, hiking trails, chuck wagon suppers, church services, cabins.
**Sites:** 645, 45 full hookups.
**Price per night:** $12 to $15.
**Elevation:** 7,440 feet.
**Season:** Year-round.
**Finding the campground:** In Woodland Park, turn north on Colorado Highway 67 and go about 10 miles to County Road 49. Turn northeast and travel about 2 miles to the campground.

**The campground:** Though only 45 sites have hookups, and they are crowded closely together, the rest of the park is an astonishing cross between a national forest camp and a guest ranch. It's the kind of place you might bring the family for a weekend of fishing, horseback riding, and other fun with a Western theme. At selected pools, the pole and bait are provided, and even the fish you catch are cleaned for you. No state fishing license is required, even if you prefer stream fishing. The chuck wagon dinner and show is a treat for everyone.

## 346 Town & Country Resort & RV Park

**Location:** Woodland Park.
**Affiliations:** Colorado Association of Campgrounds, Cabins, and Lodges.
**Contact:** 719-687-9518.
**Amenities:** Dump station, showers, laundry, picnic tables, grills, public phone, whirlpool, cabins.
**Sites:** 50, all full hookups.
**Price per night:** $18 to $19.50.
**Elevation:** 8,500 feet.
**Restrictions:** No tents.
**Season:** Year-round.
**Finding the campground:** From Exit 141 on Interstate 25 in Colorado Springs, travel west about 18 miles on U.S. Highway 24 to Woodland Park. Turn right onto Colorado Highway 67. Travel about 0.5 mile to the campground.

**The campground:** Town and Country is an upscale, wooded RV park in a mountain setting. It is a pleasant place to spend time in the Woodland Park area, even during winter months. The sites are closely spaced amid aspen and pine trees. After a busy day exploring the area, the hot tub on the beautiful deck is a pleasure.

# Public

## 347 Eleven Mile State Park

**Location:** South of Lake George.
**Facilities:** Central water, fire rings, picnic tables, flush toilets, electricity, dump station, laundry, showers, boat ramps, hiking trails, biking trails.
**Sites:** 300.
**Fee:** $6 to $10.
**Elevation:** 8,600 feet.
**Road conditions:** Paved.
**Management:** Colorado Department of Parks and Outdoor Recreation, 719-471-0900.
**Reservations:** 800-678-CAMP, $7 fee.

**Activities:** Fishing, hiking, biking, boating, birding.
**Season:** Year-round.
**Finding the campground:** From the town of Lake George, travel west on Colorado Highway 24, about 1 mile to County Road 90. Follow the pavement about 10 miles to the park.

**The campground:** Camping is possible on both sides of Eleven Mile Reservoir. Sites on the southwestern shore are primitive and treeless, but at the water's edge. Facilities on the north shore are modern and offer shelter in the form of trees and boulders, but they are set back from the shore. The sprawling lake is beautiful in its parkland setting. It is a prime spot for anglers hoping to catch northern pike. Trout and kokanee salmon are also available. Bird watchers will find that the lake attracts a wide range of waterfowl, including pelicans, gulls, and Canada geese.

---

## 348 Mueller State Park

**Location:** South of Divide.
**Facilities:** Central water, fire rings, picnic tables, flush toilets, electricity, dump station, laundry, showers, trails, playground, public phone.
**Sites:** 90.
**Fee:** $7 to $10.
**Elevation:** 9,500 feet.
**Road conditions:** Paved.
**Management:** Colorado Department of Parks and Outdoor Recreation, 719-687-2366.
**Reservations:** 800-678-CAMP, $7 fee.
**Activities:** Fishing, hiking, biking, horseback riding, scenic driving.
**Season:** Year-round.
**Finding the campground:** From Divide, travel 3.5 miles south on Colorado Highway 67 to the park entrance.

**The campground:** Mueller is one of Colorado's finest state parks. It is the third largest in the system, but second in terms of backcountry acreage. There are more than 85 miles of hiking trails to challenge every level of ability. The camping facilities are new and well maintained. The sites are widely spaced amid a light forest of aspen, pine, and fir. Many have incredible views of Pikes Peak.

Mueller is an outstanding choice for family camping in the Colorado Springs area. The park is just a half hour away from attractions in the city, such as the zoo, museums, and ice rink. Florissant Fossil Beds National Monument is a short drive away, as are the casinos in Cripple Creek.

---

## 349 Blue Mountain

**Location:** Southwest of Lake George.
**Facilities:** Central water, fire rings, picnic tables, vault toilets.
**Sites:** 21.

**Fee:** $9.
**Elevation:** 8,200 feet.
**Road conditions:** two lane, gravel.
**Management:** Pike National Forest, 719-836-2031.
**Activities:** Hiking.
**Finding the campground:** From Lake George, travel 1.3 miles southwest on Forest Service Road 245 to FSR 240. Turn south and continue to the campground, about 0.5 mile.

**The campground:** There's not a lot here, including people, making Blue Mountain a quiet alternative to the crowded campgrounds in Eleven Mile Canyon. The sites are widely spaced in a dense pine forest. Fishing in Lake George and in the canyon are a short drive away. This is also the closest national forest campground to Florissant Fossil Beds National Monument and not a bad place to stay if you want to make day trips into Cripple Creek. Families looking for a quiet camping destination with an unusual mix of activities nearby may want to place this one high on their list.

## 350 Colorado

**Location:** North of Woodland Park.
**Facilities:** Central water, fire rings, picnic tables, vault toilets.
**Sites:** 81.
**Fee:** $10.
**Elevation:** 7,800 feet.
**Road conditions:** Paved.
**Management:** Pike National Forest, 719-636-1602.
**Activities:** Hiking, biking, fishing.
**Finding the campground:** From Woodland Park, travel 6.9 miles north on Colorado Highway 67 to the campground.

**The campground:** This large campground sprawls across a lightly forested hillside. Sites are moderately spaced, allowing just a bit of privacy. Colorado Campground looks like a great place to have a family reunion because there's plenty of room for everyone and lots to do. The paved Manitou Park Trail passes the camp, allowing bicycle enthusiasts the opportunity to pedal back to Woodland Park or out to 34-acre Manitou Park Lake.

## 351 Eleven Mile Canyon: Cove

**Location:** Southwest of Lake George.
**Facilities:** Central water, fire rings, picnic tables, vault toilets.
**Sites:** 4.
**Fee:** $9.
**Elevation:** 8,400 feet.
**Road conditions:** One-and-a-half lane, gravel.
**Management:** Pike National Forest, 719-836-2031.

**Activities:** Fishing, hiking, rock climbing.
**Finding the campground:** From Lake George, travel southwest on Forest Service Road 245, about 8 miles to the campground.

**The campground:** Eleven Mile Canyon surprises many people who are visiting for the first time. The surrounding area is made up of gently rounded hills that rise from a vast, flat parkland. Then you follow the South Platte upriver into this canyon. It's as dramatic a change as a clap of thunder on a sunny day. Granite walls tower over the crashing river, which tumbles more than 500 feet in elevation as it snakes through the canyon.

The incredible beauty of the landscape is what brings most people here. The fishing is good when water levels are high but only mediocre at other times. The road through the canyon appears narrow, but even large trailers seem to manage. Because the canyon is narrow, the campsites are necessarily small and tightly spaced. Cove is the smallest campground here, with only four sites, but they are good ones.

## 352 Eleven Mile Canyon: Riverside

**Location:** Southwest of Lake George.
**Facilities:** Central water, fire rings, picnic tables, vault toilets.
**Sites:** 19.
**Fee:** $9.
**Elevation:** 8,000 feet.
**Road conditions:** One-and-a-half lane, gravel.
**Management:** Pike National Forest, 719-836-2031.
**Activities:** Fishing, hiking, rock climbing.
**Finding the campground:** From Lake George, travel southwest on Forest Service Road 245, about 2.5 miles to the campground.

**The campground:** This is the first camp in the canyon, and though it has easy fishing access, there's not a lot to be said for its scenic qualities. There are no trees, but the sites are far enough apart to afford some privacy. The river is across the road. Riverside will do, though, if everything else is full.

## 353 Eleven Mile Canyon: Spillway

**Location:** Southwest of Lake George.
**Facilities:** Central water, fire rings, picnic tables, vault toilets.
**Sites:** 24.
**Fee:** $9.
**Elevation:** 8,500 feet.
**Road conditions:** One-and-a-half lane, gravel.
**Management:** Pike National Forest, 719-836-2031.
**Activities:** Fishing, hiking, rock climbing.
**Finding the campground:** From Lake George, travel 8.2 miles southwest on Forest Service Road 245 to the campground.

**The campground:** This is the last campground in the canyon—and perhaps the best. Some sites are tightly spaced and in the open, but a few farther up the hillside have both shade and privacy. There is a short overlook trail from the campground that gives you a view of Eleven Mile Reservoir, but a longer hike is required to gain access to the lake itself.

## 354 Eleven Mile Canyon: Springer Gulch

**Location:** Southwest of Lake George.
**Facilities:** Central water, fire rings, picnic tables, vault toilets.
**Sites:** 15.
**Fee:** $9.
**Elevation:** 8,300 feet.
**Road conditions:** One-and-a-half lane, gravel.
**Management:** Pike National Forest, 719-836-2031.
**Activities:** Fishing, hiking, rock climbing.
**Finding the campground:** From Lake George, travel 6.6 miles southwest on Forest Service Road 245 to the campground.

**The campground:** Sites here are moderately spaced amid huge boulders and trees. This is the prettiest campground in this canyon carved by the South Platte River, but you have to walk a ways to fish. There is a short but steep hiking trail up the side of the canyon, south of the campground.

## 355 Painted Rocks

**Location:** North of Woodland Park.
**Facilities:** Central water, fire rings, picnic tables, vault toilets.
**Sites:** 18.
**Fee:** $10.
**Elevation:** 7,900 feet.
**Road conditions:** Paved.
**Management:** Pike National Forest, 719-636-1602.
**Reservations:** 800-280-CAMP, www.nrrc.com, $8.65 fee.
**Activities:** Hiking, fishing, biking.
**Finding the campground:** From Woodland Park, travel north on Colorado Highway 67, about 8 miles to Forest Service Road 342. Turn west and go about 0.5 mile to the campground.

**The campground:** This quiet getaway is a real gem. It has the advantage of being close to all the fun and activity in the area, yet it's just far enough away to provide a real camping-in-the-woods experience. Fishing is nearby on Manitou Park Lake, which you can reach by car, bicycle, or foot along the paved Manitou Park Trail, which passes the campground. The large number of campsites available nearby make open sites at Painted Rocks a safe bet even on weekends.

## 356 | Rampart Reservoir: Meadow Ridge

**Location:** East of Woodland Park.
**Facilities:** Central water, fire rings, picnic tables, vault toilets, boat ramps.
**Sites:** 19.
**Fee:** $10.
**Elevation:** 9,200 feet.
**Road conditions:** two lane, gravel.
**Management:** Pike National Forest, 719-636-1602.
**Reservations:** 800-280-CAMP, www.nrrc.com, $8.65 fee.
**Activities:** Fishing, hiking, biking.
**Finding the campground:** From Woodland Park, travel about 3 miles northeast on Forest Service Road 393 to FSR 300 (Rampart Range Road). Turn southeast and go 1.5 miles to FSR 306. Turn northeast and go 2.5 miles to the campgrounds.

**The campground:** Rampart Reservoir is easily overlooked amid all the well-known, advertised attractions in the Colorado Springs area. The lake itself is clear blue and surrounded by thick stands of pine. The only unfortunate thing about the campgrounds here is that they aren't situated on the lakeshore but are perched high above it on a hillside. Don't let that stop you from coming; this is a wonderful place to bring the family. Most of the sites at Meadow Ridge are widely spaced and open, and some have mesmerizing views.

## 357 | Rampart Reservoir: Thunder Ridge

**Location:** East of Woodland Park.
**Facilities:** Central water, fire rings, picnic tables, vault toilets.
**Sites:** 21.
**Fee:** $10.
**Elevation:** 9,200 feet.
**Road conditions:** two lane, gravel.
**Management:** Pike National Forest, 719-636-1602.
**Reservations:** 800-280-CAMP, www.nrrc.com, $8.65 fee.
**Activities:** Fishing, hiking.
**Finding the campground:** From Woodland Park, travel about 3 miles northeast on Forest Service Road 393 to FSR 300 (Rampart Range Road). Turn southeast and go 1.5 miles to FSR 306. Turn northeast and go 2.5 miles to the campgrounds.

**The campground:** Thunder Ridge Campground overlooks Rampart Reservoir and offers moderately spaced sites and a substantial number of trees for shade and privacy. Trails suitable for hiking and mountain biking branch off from the recreation area. The trails lead to three other small lakes that are just as lovely as the main reservoir.

## 358 South Meadows

**Location:** North of Woodland Park.
**Facilities:** Central water, fire rings, picnic tables, vault toilets.
**Sites:** 18.
**Fee:** $10.
**Elevation:** 8,000 feet.
**Road conditions:** Paved.
**Management:** Pike National Forest, 719-636-1602.
**Reservations:** 800-280-CAMP, www.nrrc.com, $8.65 fee.
**Activities:** Hiking, biking, fishing.
**Finding the campground:** From Woodland Park, travel 5.8 miles north on Colorado Highway 67 to the campground.

**The campground:** South Meadows is the closest national forest campground to Woodland Park. It makes a convenient place to stay to take in all of the activities in the surrounding area. The sites are well spaced in a dense pine forest that provides plenty of privacy. The sites on the outside edge of the camp have wonderful meadow views, allowing you to watch an almost endless parade of deer every evening.

## 359 Springdale

**Location:** East of Woodland Park.
**Facilities:** Fire rings, tables, vault toilets; no water.
**Sites:** 14.
**Fee:** $9.
**Elevation:** 9,200 feet.
**Road conditions:** two lane, gravel.
**Management:** Pike National Forest, 719-636-1602.
**Activities:** Fishing, wildlife viewing.
**Finding the campground:** From Woodland Park, travel about 3 miles northeast on Forest Service Road 393 to FSR 300 (Rampart Range Road). Turn southeast and go 2.5 miles to the campground.

**The campground:** There isn't much to do here except watch the wildflowers grow, but if that's your idea of fun, this is a great place to do it. Spacing between the sites is moderate and this campground gets little use, so privacy is not a problem. The campground is heavily wooded but surrounded by open meadows on three sides. Rampart Reservoir is just down the road if you get tired of the view, but don't count on that happening.

## 360 The Crags

**Location:** Southeast of Divide.
**Facilities:** Central water, fire rings, picnic tables, vault toilets.
**Sites:** 17.

**Fee:** $9.
**Elevation:** 10,100 feet.
**Road conditions:** one lane, dirt, rough.
**Management:** Pike National Forest, 719-636-1602.
**Activities:** Fishing, hiking.
**Finding the campground:** From Divide, travel 4.25 miles south on Colorado Highway 67 to Forest Service Road 383. Turn east and go about 3 miles to the campground.

**The campground:** People pull trailers up this road, but it isn't recommended. There is very little space along the side of the road for passing, and some of the turns are narrow. With or without a trailer, if you make it to this campground you are in for a treat. This high-mountain camp offers widely spaced sites along a small stream and is near the trailhead to The Crags. The hike is a difficult one, especially at this elevation, but even inexperienced hikers can enjoy the level terrain at the beginning of the trail.

## Additional Campgrounds in the Colorado Springs Area

| | Type* | Contact | Location |
|---|---|---|---|
| Coachlight RV Park & Motel | P (69) | 719-687-8732 | E of Woodland Park on US 24 |
| Cripple Creek Travel Park | P (48) | 719-689-2513 | N B Street in Cripple Creek |
| Diamond Campground & RV Park | P (150) | 719-687-9684 | N of Woodland Park on US 24 |
| Lake of the Rockies | P (248) | 719-481-4227 | N of Colorado Springs, off I-25, exit 161 |
| Lone Duck Campground | P (64) | 800-776-5925 | US 24 in Cascade |
| Peak View Inn & RV Resort | P (143) | 800-551-CAMP | Off I-25, exit 148A |
| Pikes Peak RV Park & Campground | P (69) | 719-685-9459 | In Manitou Springs on Manitou Avenue |
| Prospector's RV Park | P (16) | 719-689-2006 | Cripple Creek on 2nd Street |
| RNK Park & Camp | P (25) | 719-689-3371 | N of Cripple Creek on CO 67S |
| Rocky Top Motel & Campground | P (77) | 719-684-9044 | W of Pikes Peak Entrance on US 24 |
| Wrangler RV Ranch & Motel | P (100) | 719-591-1402 | 6225 E US 24 in Colorado Springs |
| Yogi Bear's Jellystone Camp Resort at Alpine Lakes | P (140) | 719-687-7337 | N of Divide on CR 5 |
| Farish Recreation Area | MP (35) | 719-687-9098 | N of Woodland Park on Rampart Range Road |
| Big Turkey | NF (10) | 303-275-5610 | N of Woodland Park on FSR 360 |

\* See "Key to Abbreviations" p.22—(# of sites)

| | Type* | Contact | Location |
|---|---|---|---|
| Trail Creek | NF (7) | 719-636-1602 | NW of Woodland Park on CR 3 |
| Wildhorn | NF (9) | 719-636-1602 | N of Florissant on CR 3 |
| Skagway Reservoir | SWA DSP | 719-473-2945 | E of Victor on CR 441 |

- * See "Key to Abbreviations" p.22—(# of sites)

# Area 30: Canon City and Royal Gorge

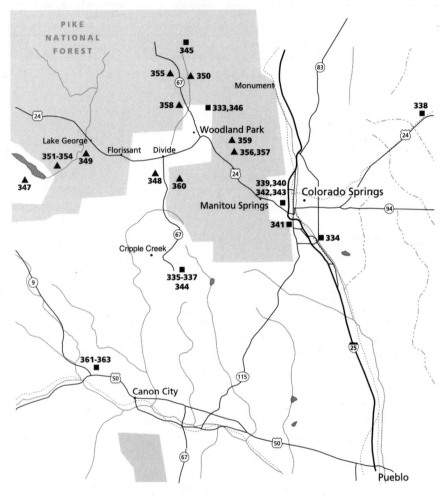

PIKE NATIONAL FOREST

■ 345

355 ▲  ▲ 350
67

358 ▲

■ 333,346

Monument

83

338 ■

24

24

. Woodland Park

▲ 359

▲ 356,357

Lake George
Florissant   Divide

351-354 ▲
▲ 349
347 ▲

348 ▲  ▲ 360

24

339,340
342,343
341 ■

Colorado Springs

Manitou Springs

94

334 ■

67

Cripple Creek

335-337
344 ■

9

115

361-363
■
50

Canon City

25

50

67

Pueblo

## CANON CITY AND ROYAL GORGE

The Royal Gorge is one of the most popular tourist attractions in the Southwestern United States, so keep that in mind if you plan a weekend getaway here. The gorge and the bridge across it are by no means overrated, but a visit to the area is likely to leave a hole in your wallet almost as large as the canyon. Admission to the city-owned park that encompasses the gorge is steep but includes all the rides, shows, and attractions that surround the bridge. There are shops and restaurants inside the park as well.

Surrounding the gorge are a variety of tour operators who offer everything from horseback rides and rafting trips to helicopter and hot-air balloon views of the canyon. There are also amusement parks and a western theme park called Buckskin Joe's. Don't forget that wallet.

Camping here is all commercially operated, but the choices are pretty good. Almost all of them are family oriented with on-site activities to help pass the time at less expense.

**For More Information:**

Canon City Chamber of Commerce
403 Royal Gorge Boulevard
Canon City, CO 81212
800-876-7922

Royal Gorge Bridge
P.O. Box 549
Canon City, CO 81215
719-275-7507

# Commercial

## 361 Fort Gorge Campground & RV Park

**Location:** West of Canon City.
**Affiliations:** Good Sam; Colorado Association of Campgrounds, Cabins, and Lodges.
**Contact:** 719-275-5111.
**Amenities:** Dump station, showers, laundry, picnic tables, grills, store, public phone, playground, cabins, rafting.
**Sites:** 53, 10 full hookups.
**Price per night:** $12 to $19.50.
**Elevation:** 6,330 feet.
**Finding the campground:** From Canon City, travel west on U.S. Highway 50, about 7 miles to the campground.

**The campground:** Situated just 0.25 mile from the Royal Gorge turnoff, this park is at the center of activity. Rafting trips can be arranged at camp. Horseback riding and helicopter rides can be arranged nearby. Views of the mountains are the icing on the cake.

## 362 Royal Gorge KOA

**Location:** West of Canon City.
**Affiliations:** KOA; Colorado Association of Campgrounds, Cabins, and Lodges.
**Contact:** 719-275-6116.
**Amenities:** Dump station, showers, laundry, picnic tables, grills, store, pool,

public phone, playground, cabins, miniature golf, amusement park, Dairy Queen.
**Sites:** 153, 37 full hookups.
**Price per night:** $17 to $21.50.
**Elevation:** 6,330 feet.
**Finding the campground:** From Canon City, travel west on U.S. Highway 50, about 8 miles to Royal Gorge Road. Turn south and go about 0.5 mile to the campground.

**The campground:** This is as close as you can camp to the gorge itself. After a day of sightseeing, you can come back to camp and continue the fun. The adjacent amusement park features a giant slide and a go-cart track. Horseback riding and rafting are available nearby. Reservations are necessary on weekends, and if you'd like a Kamper Kabin on a weekend, be sure you reserve it well in advance.

## 363  Yogi Bear's Jellystone Park Camp

**Location:** West of Canon City.
**Affiliations:** Good Sam; AAA; Colorado Association of Campgrounds, Cabins, and Lodges.
**Contact:** 719-275-2128.
**Amenities:** Dump station, showers, laundry, picnic tables, grills, store, pool, whirlpool, public phone, playground, cabins, movies, meals, miniature golf, hay rides.
**Sites:** 80, 8 full hookups.
**Price per night:** $16.50 to $24.
**Elevation:** 6,350 feet.
**Season:** Year-round.
**Finding the campground:** From Canon City, travel west on U.S. Highway 50 about 9 miles to the campground.

**The campground:** If you're looking for a place that is close to Royal Gorge and has enough activities to keep your kids busy and happy when you aren't out seeing the sights, this is the place. There is always something going on here, from Saturday morning cartoons to steak dinners. And when there isn't a planned activity, the pool is the perfect place to spend warm summer afternoons. The camp has closely spaced sites, but not quite parking-lot close. They are scattered across a piñon-covered hillside. Some have nice views of the mountains to the north. If you can live without hookups, the tent sites at the back of the park are a good choice. Most sites have at least a little shade.

# Additional Campgrounds in the Canon City/Royal Gorge Area

| | Type* | Contact | Location |
|---|---|---|---|
| Buffalo Bill's Royal Gorge Campground | P (44) | 719-269-3211 | Junction of US 50 & Royal Gorge Road |
| Floyd's RV Park | P (30) | 719-372-3385 | 1438 US 50 in Penrose |
| Indian Springs Ranch & Campground | P (30) | 719-372-3907 | N of Canon City off CR 67 |
| Mountain View Campground | P (38) | 719-275-7232 | W of Canon City on US 50 |
| Royal View Campground | P (48) | 719-275-1900 | Off US 50 near the Royal Gorge |
| RV Station Campground | P | 719-815-4576 | E of Canon city on US 50 |

 - * See "Key to Abbreviations" p.22—(# of sites)

# Area 31: Salida

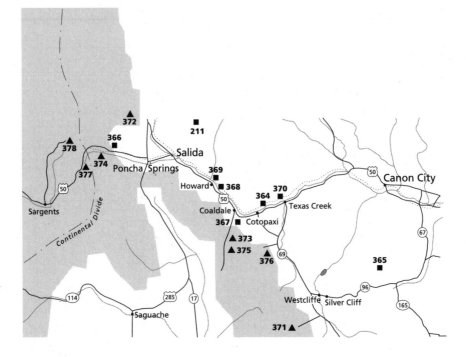

## SALIDA

Salida and Buena Vista are sister towns along the Arkansas River. Salida is larger and has an upscale downtown complete with coffeehouses, brew pubs, and antique shops. Activities here generally center on the river, but there are other things to do.

Hiking along the Rainbow Trail is one of them. The trail stretches 100 miles through the Sangre de Cristos Mountains. Terrain varies from steep mountainsides to flat open stretches of meadowland. Access to the trail is easy from many of the national forest campgrounds south and east of Salida.

After a hike or a float down the river, a soothing swim and soak at Salida's indoor hot-springs complex are a relaxing way to end the day. Other activities include a nine-hole golf course, jeep rentals, and horseback riding.

Camping accommodations include a vast array of RV parks along U.S. Highway 50 as it follows the Arkansas River. These are always crowded. There are a few parks off the river where the crowds are a bit smaller. Rougher camping choices include national forest camps in all directions. All of them are quiet and generally not crowded, but you will have to do a little driving if you plan to enjoy the river.

**For More Information:**

Heart of the Rockies Chamber of Commerce
406 W. Rainbow Boulevard
Salida, CO 81201
719-539-2068 or 800-831-8594

Salida Hot Springs
410 W. Rainbow Boulevard
Salida, CO 81201
719-539-6738

# Commercial

## 364  Arkansas River/Cotopaxi KOA

**Location:** East of Cotopaxi.
**Affiliations:** KOA.
**Contact:** 719-275-9308, fax 719-275-2249.
**Amenities:** Dump station, showers, laundry, picnic tables, grills, fire rings, pool, store, public phone, playground, cabins, river fishing, miniature golf, hayride, movies.
**Sites:** 78, 29 full hookups.
**Price per night:** $17 to $21.
**Elevation:** 6,300 feet.
**Finding the campground:** From Cotopaxi, travel 1.5 miles east on U.S. Highway 50 to the campground.

**The campground:** There are so many choices of campgrounds along this stretch of the Arkansas River that it's nice to have one with a familiar name and a reputation you can rely on. The campground has plenty of activities, and rafting trips can be arranged a short drive away.

## 365  Cross D Bar Trout Ranch

**Location:** East of Westcliff.
**Affiliations:** None.
**Contact:** 719-783-2007, fax 303-733-8859, e-mail dickm@csn.net.
**Amenities:** Dump station, picnic tables, grills, fire rings, fishing ponds, hiking trails, horseback riding.
**Sites:** 38, no full hookups.
**Price per night:** $8 to $14.
**Elevation:** 9,200 feet.
**Season:** Year-round.
**Finding the campground:** From Westcliff, go about 12 miles east on Colorado Highway 96 to County Road 347. Turn south and go about 2 miles, then 0.25 mile on a dirt road; follow the signs.

**The campground:** At Cross D Bar you'll find RV spaces on a working cattle ranch and trout farm. For a fee, you can fish for trophy sized fish (catch-and-release). No state license is required. You can also take fly-fishing lessons geared to your ability. Equipment is available on site. The hosts are so sure you'll want to come here again that they sell memberships.

## 366 Heart of the Rockies

**Location:** West of Poncha Springs.
**Affiliations:** Good Sam; AAA; Colorado Association of Campgrounds, Cabins, and Lodges.
**Contact:** 719-539-4051.
**Reservations:** 800-496-2245.
**Amenities:** Dump station, showers, laundry, picnic tables, grills, store, pool, public phone, playground, rafting, miniature golf, horseback riding, movies.
**Sites:** 68, 25 full hookups.
**Price per night:** $14 to $20.
**Elevation:** 8,200 feet.
**Season:** Year-round.
**Finding the campground:** From the junction of U.S. Highways 285 and 50, travel west on US 50, about 5 miles to the campground.

**The campground:** This hilltop campground near the San Isabel National Forest is a great destination for anyone looking for mountain camping with a few more amenities than those found in the national forest campgrounds. From here you can raft the Arkansas, hike the Colorado Trail, or take a four-wheel-drive jaunt across the Old Monarch Pass. And with the pool, golf course, and horse stable, there is plenty to keep the kids busy when the family isn't out exploring the countryside.

## 367 Hidden Valley Ranch & Campground

**Location:** East of Coaldale.
**Affiliations:** Colorado Association of Campgrounds, Cabins, and Lodges.
**Contact:** 719-942-4171.
**Reservations:** 800-320-4171.
**Amenities:** Dump station, showers, laundry, picnic tables, grills, fire rings, cabins, fishing ponds, store, snack bar.
**Sites:** 46, 25 full hookups.
**Price per night:** $16.50 to $18.50.
**Elevation:** 6,900 feet.
**Season:** Year-round.
**Finding the campground:** From Coaldale, travel east about 1 mile on U.S. Highway 50 to County Road 40. Turn north and go about 0.5 mile to the campground.

**The campground:** For travelers who want to enjoy recreational opportunities on the Arkansas River east of Salida, but who want a quiet place to come home to every evening, this is the only choice. A hill of solid rock between the campground and the river and highway ensures that this campground will be quiet. Sites are spread across a grassy lawn dotted with shade trees. For a fee, you can fish in the on-site ponds, and you can arrange horseback riding next door.

## 368 Pleasant Valley RV Park

**Location:** Howard.
**Affiliations:** Colorado Association of Campgrounds, Cabins, and Lodges.
**Contact:** 719-942-3484.
**Amenities:** Dump station, showers, laundry, picnic tables, grills, public phone, patios, river fishing.
**Sites:** 58, all full hookups.
**Price per night:** $12 to $18.
**Elevation:** 6,640 feet.
**Season:** Year-round.
**Finding the campground:** From Howard, travel east on U.S. Highway 50 to milepost 235. Turn north onto County Road 47 and go across the river to the campground.
**The campground:** This pretty campground has an advantage that most of the campgrounds on the Arkansas River don't: it sits across the river from the highway, escaping much of the traffic noise. The park is grassy with some shaded sites. You can fish the river from camp, and you can arrange rafting trips just a short walk away. Pleasant Valley is a nice destination spot in an area full of good recreational choices.

## 369 Sugarbush General Store & Campground

**Location:** Howard.
**Affiliations:** Colorado Association of Campgrounds, Cabins, and Lodges.
**Contact:** 719-942-3363, www.entertain.com.wedgwood/sugr.html.
**Amenities:** Dump station, showers, laundry, picnic tables, grills, store, public phone, river fishing, movies.
**Sites:** 29, 14 full hookups.
**Price per night:** $12 to $17.
**Elevation:** 6,910 feet.
**Season:** Year-round.
**Finding the campground:** At the center of Howard on U.S. Highway 50.

**The campground:** Sugarbush is one of the smallest parks on the Arkansas River, which adds to its quiet beauty. It has sites set amid shade trees; both a small brook and the river run through camp. Rafting can be arranged nearby, and river fishing is possible right in camp.

## 370 Whispering Pines Resort

**Location:** Texas Creek.
**Affiliations:** Colorado Association of Campgrounds, Cabins, and Lodges.
**Contact:** 719-275-3827.
**Reservations:** 888-275-3827.
**Amenities:** Dump station, showers, laundry, picnic tables, grills, fire rings, cabins, river fishing, float trips.
**Sites:** 32, 20 full hookups.
**Price per night:** $7.50 to $15.
**Elevation:** 7,200 feet.
**Finding the campground:** In the town of Texas Creek, travel west on U.S. Highway 50 to the campground.

**The campground:** Straddling the Arkansas River, this busy campground allows you to enjoy the water as well as attractions east and west along US 50. Rafting trips and fishing are both possible from camp. For families on a budget, this is the lowest priced RV park in the area.

# Public

## 371 Alvarado

**Location:** Southwest of Westcliff.
**Facilities:** Central water, fire rings, picnic tables, vault toilets.
**Sites:** 47.
**Fee:** $9.
**Elevation:** 10,500 feet.
**Road conditions:** two lane, dirt.
**Management:** San Isabel National Forest, 719-275-4119.
**Activities:** Hiking, horseback riding.
**Finding the campground:** From Westcliff, travel 3.5 miles south on Colorado Highway 69 to County Road 140. Turn west and go 6.5 miles to the campground.

**The campground:** Alvarado is a hiker's paradise. Fishing opportunities are limited, which keeps the crowds away. That translates to peace and quiet for hikers. The Rainbow Trail, which is accessible near camp, provides more than 100 miles of hiking along the eastern side of the Sangre de Cristo Range. Trails branch off at numerous points, many leading over the mountains and down into the San Luis Valley on the other side. This is the kind of place to set your adventurous spirit free. The campground itself is a mix of wooded and meadow sites staggered on a hillside. Many have incredible views of Venable Peak.

## 372 | Angel of Shavano

**Location:** Northwest of Salida.
**Facilities:** Central water, fire rings, picnic tables, vault toilets.
**Sites:** 20.
**Fee:** $9.
**Elevation:** 9,200 feet.
**Road conditions:** two lane, dirt.
**Management:** San Isabel National Forest, 719-275-4119.
**Activities:** Hiking, fishing, four-wheel driving.
**Finding the campground:** From Salida, travel west on U.S. Highway 50, about 10 miles to Forest Service Road 240. Turn north and go about 5 miles to the campground.

**The campground:** Named for the silhouette of an angel that appears in the snow remaining in the crags of Mount Shavano in late spring, this pretty campground is just far enough off the highway to thin out the crowd. Even on busy holiday weekends, you'll likely find a spot or two open here. You can access the Colorado Trail from camp, and if that doesn't keep you busy, you can try a little stream fishing. For those with durable transportation, FSR 240 continues northwest to a series of small lakes and a small campground (North Fork Reservoir).

## 373 | Coaldale

**Location:** South of Coaldale.
**Facilities:** Fire rings, picnic tables, vault toilets; no water.
**Sites:** 11.
**Fee:** $7.
**Elevation:** 8,500 feet.
**Road conditions:** Paved.
**Management:** San Isabel National Forest, 719-539-3591.
**Activities:** Fishing, rafting.
**Finding the campground:** From Coaldale, travel 4.1 miles southwest on County Road 6 to the campground.

**The campground:** This is a tent camper's paradise. There is room for only two trailers; the remaining sites are for tents. There is no water, but you can haul it from Hayden Creek (Campground 375) a mile up the road. The sites at Coaldale are on the banks of Hayden Creek in a dense pine forest. This is the closest national forest campground to the playground surrounding the Arkansas River, so rafters can camp here to avoid the crowds at the riverside commercial campgrounds.

## 374 | Garfield

**Location:** West of Salida.
**Facilities:** Central water, fire rings, picnic tables, vault toilets.

**Sites:** 11.
**Fee:** $9.
**Elevation:** 10,000 feet.
**Road conditions:** Paved.
**Management:** San Isabel National Forest, 719-539-3591.
**Activities:** Fishing, hiking, four-wheel driving.
**Finding the campground:** From Salida travel west on U.S. Highway 50, about 18 miles to the campground.

**The campground:** Garfield is the perfect stopover along US 50. In fact, it is one of only two easily accessible camps between Salida and Gunnison. Traffic noise could be a problem, but Garfield is a pretty place to stop for the night.

## 375 Hayden Creek

**Location:** Southwest of Coaldale.
**Facilities:** Central water, fire rings, picnic tables, vault toilets.
**Sites:** 11.
**Fee:** $9.
**Elevation:** 8,000 feet.
**Road conditions:** two lane, gravel.
**Management:** San Isabel National Forest, 719-539-3591.
**Activities:** Hiking, fishing, rafting, four-wheel driving.
**Finding the campground:** From Coaldale, travel 5.1 miles southwest on County Road 6 to the campground.

**The campground:** This could easily be called "Hidden Creek," because in their rush to enjoy the Arkansas River few people seem to notice this little valley just to the south. The campground is small and can get crowded, but there is room for trailers. Access to the Rainbow Trail is nearby, allowing unlimited hiking through the Sangre de Cristos. FSR 6 continues as a four-wheel-drive road over Hayden Pass to Villa Grove for those inclined to see things from a bumpier perspective.

## 376 Lake Creek

**Location:** Northwest of Westcliff.
**Facilities:** Central water, fire rings, picnic tables, vault toilets.
**Sites:** 12.
**Fee:** $9.
**Elevation:** 8,200 feet.
**Road conditions:** two lane, gravel.
**Management:** San Isabel National Forest, 719-275-4119.
**Activities:** Fishing, hiking.
**Finding the campground:** From Westcliff, travel 12.5 miles north on Colorado Highway 69 to County Road 198. Turn west and go about 3 miles to the campground.

**The campground:** Have you ever dreamed of a campground where you could fling the fish directly from the creek into your frying pan? We all wish it were that easy, and the logistics are actually possible at a few of the sites here. The 12 campsites at Lake Creek are widely spaced in a dense oak, pine, and wild rose forest. The camp gets little use, making it an ideal retreat from the rest of the world. Hiking opportunities into the Sangre de Cristos are almost limitless, with the Rainbow Trail passing just above the camp on its winding path along the eastern slope of these beautiful peaks.

## 377 Monarch Park

**Location:** West of Salida.
**Facilities:** Central water, fire rings, picnic tables, vault toilets.
**Sites:** 38.
**Fee:** $10.
**Elevation:** 10,500 feet.
**Road conditions:** two lane, gravel.
**Management:** San Isabel National Forest, 719-539-3591.
**Reservations:** 800-280-CAMP, www.nrrc.com, $8.65 fee.
**Activities:** Fishing, scenic driving, rafting, four-wheel driving.
**Finding the campground:** From Salida, travel 19.5 miles west on U.S. Highway 50 to Forest Service Road 231. Turn south and continue about 1 mile to the camp.

**The campground:** Lying just below the top of Monarch Pass, this peaceful campground draws a large stopover crowd every night, but it makes a very nice destination spot as well. It is far enough off the road to escape the noise from all but the loudest trucks. Most of the campsites are widely spaced. Several beaver dams have been enhanced to create a string of fishing ponds at the eastern end of the campground; they are stocked during the summer months. Other nearby activities include a scenic tram ride at the top of Monarch Pass, rafting on the Arkansas, which can be arranged in Poncha Springs or Salida, and horseback riding from the stable located halfway up the eastern side of the pass. Hiking and biking trails, including the Colorado Trail, are plentiful in the area. The Old Monarch Pass (FSR 237) is ideal for four-wheel driving. Author's tip: Take a close look at site 9; it offers a few surprises.

## 378 Snowblind

**Location:** Northeast of Sargents.
**Facilities:** Central water, fire rings, picnic tables, vault toilets.
**Sites:** 23.
**Fee:** $6.
**Elevation:** 9,800 feet.
**Road conditions:** two lane, gravel.
**Management:** Gunnison National Forest, 970-641-0471.
**Activities:** Fishing, four-wheel driving.

**Finding the campground:** Sargents is located on U.S. Highway 50 west of Monarch Pass. From Sargents, travel northeast on US 50 about 1 mile to Forest Service Road 888. Turn north and continue about 7 miles to the campground.

**The campground:** Snowblind is a pretty camp hidden away in the aspen trees. Usage is fairly low, and the sites are well spaced. If you choose your site wisely, you may spend a week here without seeing another camper. Fishing is possible in Tomichi Creek, both in camp and along the road. FSR 888 continues northward, connecting with several other roads that lead eventually to the Alpine Tunnel on the Continental Divide (the hard way).

## Additional Campgrounds in the Salida Area

| | Type* | Contact | Location |
|---|---|---|---|
| Four Seasons RV | P (60) | 719-539-3084 | E of Salida on US 50 |
| Grape Creek RV Park | P (34) | 719-783-2588 | S of Westcliff on CO 69 |
| Lazy J Resort & Rafting Company | P (35) | 800-678-4274 | Milepost 242 on US 50 |
| Riverside Motel & Campground | P (32) | 800-727-0525 | 7870 W US in Salida |
| North Crestone Creek | NF (13) | 719-655-2553 | N of Crestone on FSR 950 |
| North Fork Reservoir | NF (8) | 719-539-3591 | NW of Poncha Springs on CR 240 |
| DeWeese | SWA DSP | 719-473-2945 | N of Westcliff on Copper Gulch Road |
| Middle Taylor Creek | SWA | 719-473-2945 | W of Westcliff on Hermit Lakes Road |

\-    * See "Key to Abbreviations" p.22—(# of sites)

# Area 32: Pueblo

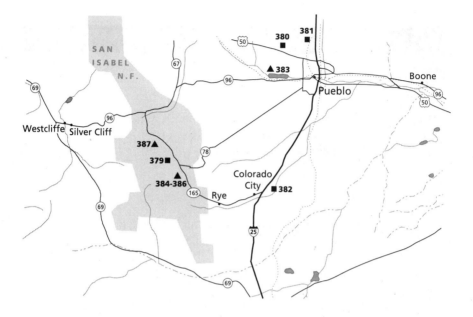

## PUEBLO

Pueblo is the gateway to the Arkansas River. The river and U.S. Highway 50 flow through here, feeding life and tourists into this sprawling town of more than 100,000 people. The community lies more than 1,000 feet lower than the neighboring towns of Walsenburg and Colorado Springs.

The lower elevation means you can visit here earlier or later in the season, with less chance of snow on the ground. Activities in or very near town include indoor ice skating, fishing, golfing, and boating and other water sports. Hiking and biking trails follow the river, and you can rent bicycles. A small zoo is also on the riverfront.

Just a short drive away are the Wet Mountains and their crown jewel, Lake San Isabel. North of the lake, you can visit Bishop's Castle, a monument to hard work. It is one man's way of expressing himself with mortar and stone, and it's worth the stop.

Camping throughout the area includes some very nice interstate RV parks, one mountain RV park, the vast Pueblo Reservoir campgrounds, and wonderful national forest camps at Lake Isabel.

**For More Information**:

The Pueblo Chamber of Commerce
302 N. Santa Fe Avenue
Pueblo, CO 81003

719-542-1704
www.pueblo.org
e-mail: pubcham@usa.net

# Commercial

## 379 Aspen Acres

**Location:** Rye.
**Affiliations:** Colorado Association of Campgrounds, Cabins, and Lodges.
**Contact:** 719-485-3275, fax 719-485-3382.
**Amenities:** Dump station, showers, laundry, picnic tables, grills, fire rings, public phone, meals, church services, cabins.
**Sites:** 66.
**Price per night:** $17.
**Elevation:** 8,800 feet.
**Finding the campground:** From Exit 74 on Interstate 25, travel west on Colorado Highway 165, about 22 miles to the campground.

**The campground:** Billed as "the way Colorado used to be," this quiet campground in the aspens above Lake San Isabel offers a real change of pace from city RV parks. Nearby attractions other than the lake include Bishop's Castle, two golf courses, hiking trails, and stream fishing. This is a very nice place to stay for any length of time, but be prepared to put up with or join in with the Texan jokes. The snow isn't the only thing around here that gets deep from time to time.

## 380 Haggard's RV Park

**Location:** Pueblo.
**Affiliations:** Good Sam; Colorado Association of Campgrounds, Cabins, and Lodges.
**Contact:** 719-547-2101.
**Amenities:** Dump station, showers, laundry, picnic tables, grills, public phone, playground.
**Sites:** 120, 29 full hookups.
**Price per night:** $18 to $21.
**Elevation:** 5,300 feet.
**Season:** Year-round.
**Finding the campground:** From Exit 101 on Interstate 25, travel west on U.S. Highway 50, about 18 miles to the campground.

**The campground:** This parking-lot-style campground is conveniently located, allowing you to enjoy activities in both directions: the Royal Gorge to the west and Pueblo to the east. Sites are open, revealing excellent views of Pikes Peak and the surrounding Sangre de Cristo Mountains.

## 381 Pueblo KOA

**Location:** North of Pueblo.
**Affiliations:** KOA; Colorado Association of Campgrounds, Cabins, and Lodges.
**Contact:** 719-542-2273.
**Reservations:** 800-KOA-PIKE.
**Amenities:** Dump station, showers, laundry, picnic tables, grills, store, pool, public phone, playground, cabins.
**Sites:** 77, 22 full hookups.
**Price per night:** $16 to $23.
**Elevation:** 4,695 feet.
**Season:** Year-round.
**Finding the campground:** From Pueblo, travel north on Interstate 25 to Exit 108, then travel north on the West Frontage Road, about 0.5 mile to the campground.

**The campground:** The Pueblo KOA is an easy-in, easy-out campground with all the usual amenities and amiability. The location makes it possible to enjoy both Pueblo and Colorado Springs attractions from one base. Traffic noise from the interstate may be the only drawback.

## 382 Pueblo South/Colorado City KOA

**Location:** South of Pueblo.
**Affiliations:** KOA; Good Sam; AAA; Family Campers; Airstream Association; Colorado Association of Campgrounds, Cabins, and Lodges.
**Contact:** 719-676-3376.
**Reservations:** 800-KOA-8646.
**Amenities:** Dump station, showers, laundry, picnic tables, grills, store, whirlpool, public phone, playground, cabins, fire rings, hiking trails, movies, meals.
**Sites:** 68, 30 full hookups.
**Price per night:** $15 to $21.
**Elevation:** 6,000 feet.
**Finding the campground:** From Pueblo, travel south on Interstate 25, about 20 miles to Exit 74. The campground is on the east side of the highway.

**The campground:** This KOA is ideally located to allow you to enjoy the wealth of activities available in Pueblo, as well as those found in the nearby San Isabel National Forest. Activities in the immediate vicinity include golf, hiking, and scenic driving. This is also a good stopover along I-25 for those who prefer a country setting over the busier city spots.

| Public |
| --- |

## 383 Pueblo Reservoir State Park

**Location:** West of Pueblo.
**Facilities:** Central water, fire rings, picnic tables, vault toilets, electricity, dump station, laundry, showers, swim beach, bath house, snack bar, boat ramps, marina, boat rentals, personal-watercraft rentals, hiking trails.
**Sites:** 401.
**Fee:** $6 to $10.
**Elevation:** 4,796 feet.
**Road conditions:** Paved.
**Management:** Colorado Department of Parks and Outdoor Recreation, 719-471-0900.
**Reservations:** 800-678-CAMP, $6.75 fee.
**Activities:** Fishing, boating, water sports, hiking, biking, horseback riding.
**Season:** Year-round.
**Finding the campground:** From Pueblo, travel west on U.S. Highway 50 about 4 miles. Turn south on Pueblo Boulevard and go about 4 miles to Thatcher Avenue. Turn west and go about 6 miles to the park entrance.

**The campground:** Pueblo Reservoir is a water sport and fishing haven. It covers 4,646 acres, making it the second largest lake in a state park after Navajo Reservoir. Campsites are spread among five campgrounds, four on the north shore and one near the marina on the south shore. Even with such a huge number of sites available, the park fills quickly on summer weekends, so reservations are recommended. Hikers, bikers, and horseback riders will enjoy the selection of trails, including the Pueblo River Trail, which connects to trails in the city of Pueblo.

## 384 Lake San Isabel: La Vista

**Location:** Southwest of Pueblo.
**Facilities:** Central water, fire rings, picnic tables, vault toilets, electricity.
**Sites:** 29.
**Fee:** $13.
**Elevation:** 8,800 feet.
**Road conditions:** Paved.
**Management:** San Isabel National Forest, 719-275-4119.
**Reservations:** 800-280-CAMP, www.nrrc.com, $8.65 fee.
**Activities:** Fishing, hiking, scenic driving.
**Finding the campground:** From Colorado City (which is south of Pueblo), travel northwest on Colorado Highway 165, about 15 miles to the campground.

**The campground:** Lake San Isabel is worth going out of your way to find if you happen to be in this part of the state. Surrounded by evergreens, it offers excellent fishing throughout the summer months. Each of the three campgrounds at the lake has something special to offer. La Vista is the newest, with 29 sites overlooking the northwest end of the lake. Though shade is sparse, daytime temperatures are moderate, and the incredible view of the lake against a mountain backdrop makes up for the lack of trees.

## 385 Lake San Isabel: Saint Charles

**Location:** Southwest of Pueblo.
**Facilities:** Central water, fire rings, picnic tables, vault toilets.
**Sites:** 15.
**Fee:** $7.50.
**Elevation:** 8,800 feet.
**Road conditions:** Paved.
**Management:** San Isabel National Forest, 719-275-4119.
**Reservations:** 800-280-CAMP, www.nrrc.com, $8.65 fee.
**Activities:** Fishing, hiking, scenic driving.
**Finding the campground:** From Colorado City (south of Pueblo), travel northwest on Colorado Highway 165, about 15 miles to the campground.

**The campground:** Surrounded by lush evergreen forest, these 15 sites border the Saint Charles River. Many sites have access to the stream. Sites are well spaced and often separated by huge boulders. Hiking trails in the area include Cisneros and Saint Charles, both of which lead to peaks in the Wet Mountains. And, of course, you can wet your hook in Lake San Isabel. Bears have been known to raid the campgrounds at the lake at night. So, before you arrive, you may want to review the safety rules for camping in bear country.

## 386 Lake San Isabel: Southside

**Location:** Southwest of Pueblo.
**Facilities:** Central water, fire rings, picnic tables, vault toilets.
**Sites:** 8.
**Fee:** $8.
**Elevation:** 8,800 feet.
**Road conditions:** Paved.
**Management:** San Isabel National Forest, 719-275-4119.
**Reservations:** 800-280-CAMP, www.nrrc.com, $8.65 fee.
**Activities:** Fishing, hiking, scenic driving.
**Finding the campground:** From Colorado City (south of Pueblo), travel northwest on Colorado Highway 165, about 15 miles to the campground.

**The campground:** The smallest campground at Lake San Isabel is Southside. Though its sites are tightly spaced in parking-lot style, it offers the easiest access to the lakeshore and may be preferred by anglers.

## 387 Ophir Creek

**Location:** Southwest of Pueblo.
**Facilities:** Central water, fire rings, picnic tables, vault toilets.
**Sites:** 31.
**Fee:** $7.
**Elevation:** 8,900 feet.
**Road conditions:** One-and-a-half lane, gravel.
**Management:** San Isabel National Forest, 719-275-4119.
**Activities:** Fishing, hiking, biking, scenic driving, four-wheel driving.
**Finding the campground:** From Colorado City (south of Pueblo), travel northwest on Colorado Highway 165, about 20 miles to Forest Service Road 361. Turn west and go about 0.5 mile to the campground.

**The campground:** Ophir is a very secluded campground and it gets relatively little use due to competition from the camps at Lake San Isabel. Fishing sites are rather limited, but hiking, biking, and four-wheel driving opportunities are almost limitless along the roads and trails that crisscross the Wet Mountains. Keep in mind that the range was named "Wet" for a very good reason. Take your rain gear.

## Additional Campgrounds in the Pueblo Area

| | Type* | Contact | Location |
|---|---|---|---|
| Fort's Mobile Home & RV Park | P (34) | 719-564-2327 | Off I-25, exit 94 |
| Oak Creek | NF (15) | 719-275-4119 | SW of Canon City on CR 143 |

- * See "Key to Abbreviations" p.22—(# of sites)

*West Spanish peak dominates the skyline from Walsenburg to Cuchara.*

# Area 33: Trinidad, Cuchara, and Walsenburg

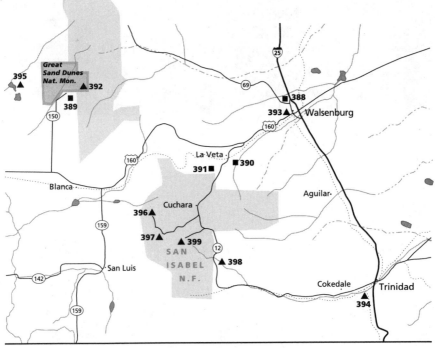

## TRINIDAD, CUCHARA, AND WALSENBURG

The sights along the scenic byway that connects these three towns epitomizes all that is Colorado. It's all here: soaring mountains covered with pines and aspens, fragrant fields of wildflowers, lush green meadows, piñon-covered mesas, and clear mountain lakes and streams filled with trout.

Not only can you see it all, but you can do it all, too. Activities include fishing, boating, hiking, horseback riding, and four-wheel driving. There are hot mineral baths and fine restaurants; there's a ski resort and a championship golf course. What more could you ask for?

Camping choices include several nice RV parks, three state parks, and three incredibly beautiful national forest camps. The only drawback is that when you leave, a piece of your heart is likely to remain here forever.

**For More Information:**

Huerfano Chamber of Commerce
P.O. Box 493
Walsenburg, CO 81089
719-738-1065

Colorado Welcome Center
309 N. Nevada
Trinidad, CO 81082
719-846-9512

Trinidad Chamber of Commerce
719-846-9285

LaVeta/Cuchara Chamber of Commerce
P.O. Box 32
LaVeta, CO 81055
719-742-3676

Grandote Golf Course
719-742-3123

# Commercial

## 388 Dakota Campground

**Location:** Walsenburg.
**Affiliations:** Colorado Association of Campgrounds, Cabins, and Lodges.
**Contact:** 719-738-9912.
**Amenities:** Dump station, showers, laundry, picnic tables, grills, fire rings, playground, public phone.
**Sites:** 72, 52 full hookups.
**Price per night:** $16.50 to $17.
**Elevation:** 6,300 feet.
**Season:** Year-round.
**Finding the campground:** From Exit 52 on Interstate 25, travel south on Business Loop I-25, about 0.75 mile to the campground.

**The campground:** Dakota is a parking-lot-style campground that makes an ideal stopover. So much so, in fact, that you'll usually find it full of Texans headed into or out of the state. It's just far enough off the highway to escape some of the traffic noise, but not so far that access is difficult.

## 389 Great Sand Dunes Oasis Campground & RV Park

**Location:** North of Mosca.
**Affiliations:** Good Sam; AAA; Colorado Association of Campgrounds, Cabins, and Lodges.
**Contact:** 719-378-2222.
**Amenities:** Dump station, showers, laundry, picnic tables, grills, store, public phone, playground, cabins, restaurant, fishing pond.
**Sites:** 120, 20 full hookups.
**Price per night:** $10 to $16.50.
**Elevation:** 8,200 feet.
**Finding the campground:** From the junction of Colorado Highway 150 and U.S. Highway 160, travel north about 16 miles to the campground.

**The campground:** This is the only place that can guarantee you a camping spot near the sand dunes, because the national park campground (Campground 392) doesn't take reservations. RV sites are in an open and level area with a view of the dunes. The hundred tent sites are scattered across a piñon-covered hillside, allowing a bit more privacy. The lodge offers four-wheel-drive tours of the dunes, and there is a bonus in the form of a golf course nearby.

## 390 Mary's Place RV Park

**Location:** La Veta.
**Affiliations:** None.
**Contact:** 719-742-3252.
**Amenities:** Showers, picnic tables.
**Sites:** 28, all full hookups.
**Price per night:** $14 to $16.
**Elevation:** 6,900 feet.
**Finding the campground:** At the corner of Oak and Grand in La Veta.

**The campground:** Mary's Place is the perfect place to stay in La Veta if you want to appreciate fully the tranquility of this interesting town, which has everything from a museum to an art studio to explore. It doesn't hurt that this is also the closest RV park to the award-winning golf course at Grandote Country Club.

## 391 Sulphur Springs Guest Ranch

**Location:** Southwest of La Veta.
**Affiliations:** None.
**Contact:** 719-742-5111.
**Reservations:** 800-946-4111.
**Amenities:** Showers, hot mineral baths, hiking trails, cabins, stream fishing.
**Sites:** Dispersed, no full hookups.
**Price per night:** $10 to $15.

**Elevation:** 7,000 feet.
**Finding the campground:** From La Veta, travel south on Colorado Highway 12 to County Road 421. Turn west and follow the signs to the camp.

**The campground:** Sulphur Springs is a very interesting place to stay. It is primarily a church or group camp, complete with bunkhouses that can accommodate up to 50 campers. But there are also primitive and RV campsites available to individuals. The location allows you to enjoy golfing in La Veta, hiking in the San Isabel National Forest, scenic driving along Colorado Highway 12, or horseback riding in Cuchara. All of this is then topped off by an evening soak in a private hot mineral tub. It doesn't get much better than this.

## Public

### 392 Great Sand Dunes National Monument: Piñon Flats

**Location:** West of Walsenburg.
**Facilities:** Central water, fire rings, picnic tables, vault toilets.
**Sites:** 88.
**Fee:** $6, plus $10 vehicle entrance fee.
**Elevation:** 8,715 feet.
**Road conditions:** Paved.
**Management:** National Park Service, 719-378-2312.
**Activities:** Hiking, photography, four-wheel-driving (not on the dunes).
**Finding the campground:** From Walsenburg, travel west on U.S. Highway 160, about 60 miles to Colorado Highway 150. Turn north and go about 16 miles to the monument entrance.

**The campground:** The Great Sand Dunes is one of those places you have got to see even if you choose to camp elsewhere. The mountains of sand roll like the Sahara in front of the jagged Sangre de Cristos. The size of the dunes is deceptive and becomes apparent only as you begin to trek across the sand. Camping here affords you the best opportunity to play in the sand and experience the magic of the place, but the accommodations are sparse. No reservations are taken, so there is a strong possibility that you could arrive and have no place to stay. Make sure you have an alternative plan, and don't forget the camera, because nobody back home will believe your descriptions without proof.

### 393 Lathrop State Park

**Location:** West of Walsenburg.
**Facilities:** Central water, fire rings, picnic tables, vault toilets, electricity, dump station, laundry, showers, swim beach, bath house, boat ramp, hiking trails, golf course.

**Sites:** 98.
**Fee:** $6 to $10, plus $4 daily or $40 annual vehicle pass.
**Elevation:** 6,410 feet.
**Road conditions:** Paved.
**Management:** Colorado Department of Parks and Outdoor Recreation, 719-471-0900.
**Reservations:** 800-678-CAMP, $7 fee.
**Activities:** Fishing, hiking, golf, water sports.
**Season:** Year-round.
**Finding the campground:** From Walsenburg, travel west on U.S. Highway 160, about 3 miles to the park entrance.

**The campground:** Lathrop makes a nice place to stay in the Spanish Peaks area when the national forest campgrounds are closed in the spring and late fall. It would also be attractive to those who simply prefer a bit more open space. Sites are well spaced on hills dotted with piñons and junipers. Some sites have beautiful views of the peaks.

Martin Lake is the focal point of the park and offers a variety of activities, including water skiing. Golfers will enjoy a round on the nine-hole course, which makes an excellent warm-up for the tougher course near La Veta. The park is also a good stopover point for travelers entering or leaving the state along Interstate 25, but reservations are recommended for weekend nights.

## 394 Trinidad State Park

**Location:** West of Trinidad.
**Facilities:** Central water, fire rings, picnic tables, vault toilets, electricity, dump station, laundry, showers, boat ramps, hiking trails.
**Sites:** 62.
**Fee:** $7 to $10, plus $4 daily or $40 annual vehicle pass.
**Elevation:** 6,276 feet.
**Road conditions:** Paved.
**Management:** Colorado Department of Parks and Outdoor Recreation, 719-471-0900.
**Reservations:** 800-678-CAMP, $7 fee.
**Activities:** Water sports, fishing, hiking.
**Season:** Year-round.
**Finding the campground:** From Trinidad, travel west on Colorado Highway 12 about 3 miles to the campground.

**The campground:** Trinidad Lake is a warm-water sports mecca for the southern portion of the state. Boating and skiing are allowed, but swimming is prohibited because there is no separate swim beach. The campground is well laid out on a hillside overlooking the lake. Sites are moderately spaced amid piñons and junipers, but shade is scarce. Trails run the length of each shore, allowing hikers to enjoy views of the lake and the surrounding terrain.

## 395 San Luis Lakes State Park

**Location:** West of Walsenburg.
**Facilities:** Central water, fire rings, picnic tables, vault toilets, electricity, dump station, laundry, showers, boat ramp, hiking trails.
**Sites:** 51.
**Fee:** $10; Plus $4 daily or $40 for an annual vehicle pass.
**Elevation:** 7,525 feet.
**Road conditions:** Paved.
**Management:** Colorado Department of Parks and Outdoor Recreation, 719-471-0900.
**Reservations:** 800-678-CAMP, $7 fee.
**Activities:** Water sports, fishing, wildlife viewing.
**Finding the campground:** From Walsenburg, travel west on U.S. Highway 160, about 60 miles to Colorado Highway 150. Turn north and go 13.5 miles to Six Mile Lane. Turn left and go about 8 miles, then north 0.1 mile to the park entrance.

**The campground:** San Luis Lakes is a little-known park that is popular with water-sports enthusiasts and avid wildlife watchers. The campground is set in the open on the vast flatland that stretches between the Rio Grande and the Sangre de Cristo Mountains. Water activities are limited to the western end of the lake; the eastern tip is a wildlife refuge that attracts a mix of waterfowl, raptors, and songbirds. Surrounding the lake is a bison ranch, which affords visitors an unusual opportunity to see these magnificent creatures roaming in huge herds, as they did more than a century ago. Views of the mountains are almost overkill at this unusual park.

## 396 Bear Lake

**Location:** South of Cuchara.
**Facilities:** Central water, fire rings, picnic tables, vault toilets.
**Sites:** 14.
**Fee:** $9.
**Elevation:** 10,500 feet.
**Road conditions:** two lane, gravel, rough.
**Management:** San Isabel National Forest, 719-275-4119.
**Activities:** Fishing, hiking, photography, wildlife viewing, scenic driving, horseback riding, golf.
**Finding the campground:** Cuchara is on Colorado Highway 12 southwest of La Veta. From Cuchara, continue south for about 4 miles to Forest Service Road 413. Turn west and go about 5 miles to the campground.

**The campground:** Bear Lake is without a doubt one of the prettiest campgrounds in the state. Unfortunately there are quite a few Texans who are aware of that fact, so getting a site here is difficult. Fishing is usually good, but if the trout aren't cooperating, there are plenty of other ways to occupy your time. One of the best is a pack trip through the southern tip of the Sangre de Cristos.

Arrangements can be made in Cuchara. As a last resort, you can drive to La Veta to play one of the top-ranked golf courses in the state, Grandote.

## 397 | Blue Lake

**Location:** South of Cuchara.
**Facilities:** Central water, fire rings, picnic tables, vault toilets.
**Sites:** 15.
**Fee:** $9.
**Elevation:** 10,500 feet.
**Road conditions:** two lane, gravel, rough.
**Management:** San Isabel National Forest, 719-275-4119.
**Activities:** Fishing, hiking, photography, wildlife viewing, scenic driving, horseback riding.
**Finding the campground:** Cuchara is on Colorado Highway 12 southwest of La Veta. From Cuchara, continue south for about 4 miles to Forest Service Road 413. Turn west and go about 4 miles to the campground.

**The campground:** Blue Lake is the first campground you come to on Forest Service Road 413. Its beauty is unmatched (except perhaps by neighboring Bear Lake). The fishing here is good and there are plenty of trees from which to hang your hammock. If the campgrounds are still open (call first) in mid-September, the prime activity would be scenic driving. Cucharas Pass turns a vivid gold even in years considered poor for color change. Pick a good year and you'll be dazzled. Bring your camera.

## 398 | Monument Lake

**Location:** West of Trinidad.
**Facilities:** Central water, dump station, showers, laundry, picnic tables, grills, fire rings, restaurant, horse rentals, cabins, boat ramp, playground.
**Sites:** 100.
**Fee:** $12 to $16.
**Elevation:** 9,000 feet.
**Road conditions:** Paved.
**Management:** City of Trinidad, 719-868-2226.
**Reservations:** 800-845-8006.
**Activities:** Fishing, hiking, horseback riding, scenic driving.
**Finding the campground:** From Trinidad, travel west on Colorado Highway 12, about 36 miles to the campground.

**The campground:** From fishing to trail riding to fine dining, this family destination spot has something for everyone. The campsites are a bit close together, but with so many things to do, few people actually spend time at camp. The surrounding mountains are beautiful, and a drive north through Cuchara and La Veta is a must while you are in the area.

## 399 Purgatoire

**Location:** South of Cuchara.
**Facilities:** Central water, fire rings, picnic tables, vault toilets.
**Sites:** 23.
**Fee:** $9.
**Elevation:** 9,800 feet.
**Road conditions:** One-and-a-half lane, gravel.
**Management:** San Isabel National Forest, 719-275-4119.
**Activities:** Fishing, hiking.
**Finding the campground:** Cuchara is on Colorado Highway 12 southwest of La Veta. From Cuchara, continue south for about 12 miles to Forest Service Road 411/County Road 34.5. Turn west and go 4.2 miles to the campground.

**The campground:** This beautiful campground allows you to enjoy the beauty of the Sangre de Cristos up close. Fishing is possible in the North Fork Purgatoire River, but it is probably better at North Lake on Colorado Highway 12. The fact that Purgatoire Campground is well off the main road increases your chances of getting a site, even on weekends. The adventurous can hike over to Blue and Bear lakes on Trail 1309.

## Additional Campgrounds in the Trinidad, Cuchara, and Walsenburg Areas

| | Type* | Contact | Location |
|---|---|---|---|
| Biggs RV Park | P (22) | 719-846-3307 | Off I-25, exit 11, in Trinidad |
| Cawthon Campground & Motel | P (42) | 719-846-3303 | Off I-25, exit 13A, in Trinidad |
| Circle the Wagons Resort | P (55) | 719-742-3233 | In La Veta on CO 12 |
| La Veta Motel & RV Park | P (14) | 719-742-5303 | In La Veta on Oak Street |
| Blanca RV Park | P (31) | 719-379-3201 | In Blanca on US 160 |
| Country Host Motel Campground | P (18) | 719-738-3800 | Walsenburg |
| Stonewall Inn & RV | P (14) | 719-868-2294 | CO 12 in Weston |
| Ute Creek Campground | P (24) | 719-376-3238 | Fort Garland |
| Huerfano | SWA DSP | 719-473-2945 | W of Gardener on CR 580 |
| Mountain Home Reservoir | SWA DSP | 970-249-3431 | SE of Fort Garland on Icehouse Road |
| Smith Reservoir | SWA DSP | 970-249-3431 | SW of Blanca on Airport Road |

- * See "Key to Abbreviations" p.22—(# of sites)

# Area 34: East

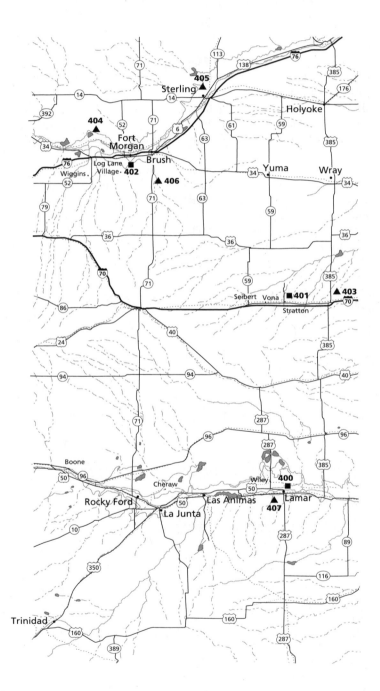

# LAMAR, STRATTON, AND FORT MORGAN

The plains of eastern Colorado are often overlooked by travelers who drive a little faster through here in their rush to get to the mountains. But for those who take the time to ease off the accelerator and get off the highway, even for a moment or two, this part of the state has a few surprises in store.

Three state parks grace the eastern third of the state; all of them feature beautiful lakes. There are twenty-three state wildlife areas, also with beautiful lakes. In the far north and far south, the national grasslands are treasures that allow us a glimpse of the land as the early settlers must have seen it—without telephone poles and asphalt highways, and with nothing but golden prairie blowing in the breeze.

Remnants of the Mountain Branch of the Santa Fe Trail are etched into the plains, and travelers today can follow the route through Prowers, Bent, Otero, and Las Animas counties, stopping to enjoy the historical sites along the way. In Baca County in the far southwest, a short hike into Picture Canyon offers a glimpse of early communication in the form of Indian petroglyphs.

Camping choices here are as vast as the prairie itself. The small towns on major highways almost all have RV parks for weary travelers. The state parks are excellent choices, and if you can stand a complete lack of facilities, dispersed camping is available at all of the state wildlife areas.

## Commercial

### 400 Lamar KOA

**Location:** Lamar.
**Affiliations:** KOA.
**Contact:** 719-336-7625.
**Amenities:** Dump station, showers, laundry, public phone, store, picnic tables, cabins, grills, pool, playground, miniature golf.
**Sites:** 43, 11 full hookups.
**Price per night:** $15 to $20.
**Elevation:** 3,615 feet.
**Season:** Year-round.
**Finding the campground:** From the junction of U.S. Highways 50 and 287 in Lamar, travel 4.25 miles north, and then west to the campground.

**The campground:** The Lamar KOA is a perfect stopover in your travels through eastern Colorado. The people of Lamar are among the friendliest in the state. It seems as if there's some kind of festival or parade almost every weekend, and visitors are always welcome to participate. If you plan to fish at John Martin Reservoir, the KOA is a comfortable place to come back to at the end of the day (especially if you don't want to cook, since there are several good restaurants to choose from in town).

## 401 Trail's End Campground

**Location:** Stratton.
**Affiliations:** Good Sam; AAA; Colorado Association of Campgrounds, Cabins, and Lodges.
**Contact:** 719-348-5529, fax 719-348-5529, e-mail tctravis@iguana.ruralnet.com.
**Reservations:** 800-777-6042.
**Amenities:** Dump station, laundry, showers, pool, public phone, playground, cabins, pool, hot tub, miniature golf, showers, picnic tables, grills.
**Sites:** 36, 30 full hookups.
**Price per night:** $13 to $18.
**Elevation:** 4,400 feet.
**Season:** Year-round.
**Finding the campground:** From Exit 419 on Interstate 70, travel north 1 block to New York Avenue, then east 1 block to the campground.

**The campground:** This small campground along Interstate 70 could serve as either your first or last night's stay in Colorado as you travel the interstate. To help give you sweet dreams of the Colorado Rockies, the hosts deliver homemade cookies to your camp every night during the summer. Now if that isn't hospitality, I don't know what is.

## 402 Wayward Winds Campground

**Location:** Fort Morgan.
**Affiliations:** Good Sam.
**Contact:** 970-867-8948.
**Amenities:** Dump station, laundry, showers, pool, public phone, playground, restaurant, picnic tables.
**Sites:** 55, 48 full hookups.
**Price per night:** $13.39 to $15.75.
**Elevation:** 4,330 feet.
**Season:** Year-round.
**Finding the campground:** From Exit 75 on Interstate 76, take the South Frontage Road west about 100 yards. The campground entrance is behind the Madison Hotel.

**The campground:** Wayward Winds is a grassy campground close to Jackson Lake, which offers all the amenities of town. If you are a music fan, check out the Glen Miller Museum in Fort Morgan.

# Public

## 403 Bonny State Park

**Location:** North of Burlington.
**Facilities:** Dump station, laundry, showers, swimming beach, snack bar, boat ramps, marina, boat rentals, personal-watercraft rentals, trails, picnic tables, fire rings, central water.
**Sites:** 200.
**Fee:** $6 to $10, plus $4 daily or $40 annual vehicle pass.
**Elevation:** 3,700 feet.
**Road conditions:** two lane, dirt.
**Management:** Colorado Department of Parks and Outdoor Recreation, 970-354-7306.
**Reservations:** 800-678-CAMP, $7 fee.
**Activities:** Fishing, water sports, bird watching.
**Season:** Year-round.
**Finding the campground:** From Exit 438 on Interstate 70, travel north about 23 miles on U.S. Highway 385 to County Road 2. Turn right and go 1.5 miles to the entrance. Campgrounds are scattered around the lake.

**The campground:** This park contrasts sharply with the surrounding countryside. It is an oasis hidden upon the rolling plains. The wetlands here host more than 250 species of birds along their migration routes. The campgrounds themselves are varied. Wagon Wheel is the most developed; it boasts 26 sites with electricity. All the sites are set among grassy lawns, with cottonwoods and pines providing the shade. East Beach and North Cove are less developed but offer opportunities to camp closer to the shore. Foster Grove was designed with the nature lover in mind. It sits among a stand of trees near a marsh. This would also be the quietest of the three campgrounds.

## 404 Jackson Lake State Park

**Location:** West of Goodrich.
**Facilities:** Dump station, electricity, laundry, showers, swim beach, snack bar, boat ramps, marina, boat rentals, personal-watercraft rentals, picnic tables, fire rings, central water.
**Sites:** 262.
**Fee:** $7 to $10, plus $4 daily or $40 annual vehicle pass.
**Elevation:** 4,400 feet.
**Road conditions:** two lane, gravel.
**Management:** Colorado Department of Parks and Outdoor Recreation, 970-645-2551.
**Reservations:** 800-678-CAMP, $7 fee.
**Activities:** Fishing, water sports.
**Season:** Year-round.
**Finding the campground:** From Goodrich, travel 2.5 miles west on County Road Y.5 to the park entrance.

**The campground:** Jackson Lake provides a wonderful warm-water retreat northeast of Denver. With water sports taking a close second to hiking as a favorite activity in Colorado, you can expect the lake to be crowded every weekend of the summer. Reservations are recommended. Campsites stretch along the western shore, offering good water access and somewhat reducing the crowded feeling. The park makes a pleasant stopover along Interstate 76 during the week.

## 405 North Sterling State Park

**Location:** Northeast of Sterling.
**Facilities:** Dump station, laundry, showers, swim beach, picnic tables, fire rings, central water, snack bar, boat ramps, marina, boat rentals, personal-watercraft rentals.
**Sites:** 50.
**Fee:** $7, plus $4 daily or $40 annual vehicle pass.
**Elevation:** 4,065 feet.
**Road conditions:** Paved.
**Management:** Colorado Department of Parks and Outdoor Recreation, 970-522-3657.
**Reservations:** 800-678-CAMP, $7 fee.
**Activities:** Fishing, water sports, bird watching.
**Finding the campground:** From Sterling, travel north on County Road 39. The road will make a few zigzags, changing numbers with each one, but if you continue north on this road about 9 miles, it will intersect with CR 46. Turn west and go about 2 miles to CR 33. From there, follow the signs to the park.

**The campground:** North Sterling is yet another of the reservoirs fed by the South Platte River. It is a crystal blue lake on the open prairie. Don't come expecting tree-lined shores like those at Bonny and Jackson state parks. Here the horizon is largely uninterrupted. The lake is just 12 miles from the original Overland Trail. On a quiet day, you can almost hear the rumble of wagon wheels in the wind. The campgrounds are being upgraded and will soon include some sites with electrical hookups. Fishing is primarily for warm-water bass and walleye. Winter birders may get an opportunity to watch a large group of nesting bald eagles.

## 406 Brush Memorial Campground

**Location:** South of Brush.
**Facilities:** Dump station, electricity, picnic tables, swimming pool, wading pool, playground, showers, golf course, tennis courts, water.
**Sites:** 24.
**Fee:** $10.
**Elevation:** 4,100 feet.
**Road conditions:** Paved.
**Management:** City of Brush, 970-842-5001.
**Activities:** Swimming, golf, tennis.

**Finding the campground:** Brush is just off Interstate 76, east of Fort Morgan. In Brush, travel southeast on U.S. Highway 34 to Clayton Street. Turn south and go 4 blocks to the park.

**The campground:** If you find yourself in need of a good stopover along I-76, try this delightful city park in Brush. The kids can splash in the pool, there's golf nearby, and the campground has all the amenities of a commercial RV park.

## 407 John Martin Reservoir/Lake Hasty

**Location:** West of Lamar.
**Facilities:** Dump station, picnic tables, playground, sim beach, wheelchair-accessible sites, central water.
**Sites:** 65.
**Fee:** $7.
**Elevation:** 3.851 feet.
**Road conditions:** Two lane, gravel.
**Management:** U.S. Army Corps of Engineers, 719-336-3476.
**Activities:** Fishing, water sports.
**Finding the campground:** From Lamar, travel west on U.S. Highway 50 to Hasty. Turn south on County Road 24 and go 4 miles to the campground.

**The campground:** There is a very nice campground hidden away on Lake Hasty behind the dam that created John Martin Reservoir. Sites are scattered across a grassy park under towering shade trees. Boats are not allowed on Lake Hasty, but boat ramps for John Martin are just around the east end of the dam. Shore fishing is allowed on Lake Hasty. This campground is an ideal weekend retreat or one-night stopover.

## Additional Campgrounds in the East

|  | Type* | Contact | Location |
|---|---|---|---|
| Buffalo Hills Campground | P (91) | 800-569-1824 | I-76 & US 6 in Sterling |
| Cadillac Joe's Camground & | P (37) | 719-347-2000 | US 24 Calhan |
| Denver East/ Strasburg KOA | P (76) | 303-622-9274 | I-70, exit 310, in Strasburg |
| Gorton's Shady Grove | P (40) | 970-664-2218 | I-70, exit 405, in Seibert |
| Hud's Campground | P (20) | 719-829-4344 | W of McClane on US 50 |
| LaJunta | P (70) | 800-562-9501 | US 50 in LaJunta |
| Limon KOA | P (70) | 719-775-2151 | 575 Colorado Avenue in Limon |
| Little England Motel & RV Park | P (25) | 719-765-4812 | I-70, exit 395, in Flagler |

| | Type* | Contact | Location |
|---|---|---|---|
| Little England Motel & RV Park RV Park | P (25) | 719-765-4812 | I-70, exit 395, in Flagler |
| Marshall Ash Village RV Park | P (39) | 719-34?-???? | In Stratton on Colorado Avenue |
| Meadow Lake Cafe, Motel & RV Park | P (29) | 970-383-2290 | CR S in Limon |
| The Junction RV Park & Campground | P (40) | 719-267-3262 | ????? |
| Crow Valley Recreation Area | NF (5) | 970-553-5004 | NW of Briggsdale on CR 77 |
| Adobe Creek Reservoir | SWA DSP | 719-473-2945 | N of Las Animas on CR 10 |
| Arkansas River | SWA DSP | 719-473-2945 | E of Holly on CR 39 |
| Burchfield | SWA DSP | 719-473-2945 | E of Walsh on CR DD |
| Flagler Reservoir | SWA DSP | 719-473-2945 | E of Flagler on CR 4 |
| Higbee | SWA DSP | 719-473-2945 | E of Lamar off US 50 |
| Holbrook Reservoir | SWA DSP | 719-473-2945 | NE of LaJunta |
| Horse Creek Reservoir | SWA DSP | 719-473-2945 | N of La Junta on CR 33 |
| Hugo | SWA DSP | 719-473-2945 | E of Hugo on CR 21 |
| Jumbo Reservoir | SWA DSP | 970-484-2836 | I-76, exit 138, on CO 138 |
| Karval Reservoir | SWA DSP | 719-473-2945 | S of CO 94 on CR 109 |
| Lake Dorothy | SWA DSP | 719-473-2945 | N of Raton, New Mexico, in Sugarite |
| Lake Henry | SWA DSP | 719-473-2945 | NW of Ordway |
| McClelland | SWA DSP | 719-473-2945 | N of Rocky Ford on CR 266 |
| Meredith Reservoir | SWA DSP | 719-473-2945 | E of Ordway on CR 21 |
| Olney Springs | SWA DSP | 719-473-2945 | NW of Olney Springs on CR 7 |
| Ordway Reservoir | SWA DSP | 719-473-2945 | N of Ordway on CO 71 |
| Prewitt Reservoir | SWA DSP | 970-484-2836 | NE of Brush |
| Queens | SWA DSP | 719-473-2945 | S of Eads on CR C |
| Rocky Ford | SWA DSP | 719-473-2945 | NW of La Junta on CR 80.5 |

| | Type* | Contact | Location |
|---|---|---|---|
| Tamarack Ranch | SWA DSP | 719-473-2945 | I-76, exit 149, on US 55 |
| Thurston Creek | SWA DSP | 719-473-2945 | NW of Lamar on CR 7 |
| Timpas Creek | SWA DSP | 719-473-2945 | S of La Junta on CR Z |
| Two Buttes Reservoir | SWA DSP | 719-473-2945 | NE of Springfield on US 287/385 |

* See "Key to Abbreviations" p.22—(# of sites)

# Appendix 1:
# Group Campgrounds

| | Type* | Contact | Location |
|---|---|---|---|
| Angel of Shavano Group | NF | 719-539-3591 | NW of Poncha Springs |
| Bogan Flats Group | NF | 970-963-2266 | SW of Carbondale |
| Camp Hale Group | NF | 970-827-5715 | NW of Leadville |
| Chapman Group | NF | 970-963-2266 | E of Basalt |
| Chris Park Group | NF | 970-247-4874 | N of Durango |
| Crow Valley Group | NF | 970-353-5004 | N of Briggsdale |
| Cutthroat Bay Group | NF | 970-887-3331 | NW side of Lake Granby |
| Difficult Group | NF | 970-925-3443 | E of Aspen |
| East Elk Creek Group | NP | 970-641-2337 | N side of Curecanti Recreation Area |
| Eggleston Group | NF | 970-242-8211 | Grand Mesa |
| Florida Group | NF | 970-884-2512 | N of Lemon Reservoir |
| Glacier Basin Group | NP | 970-586-1399 | Rocky Mountain National Park |
| House Creek Group | NF | 970-882-7296 | McPhee Reservoir |
| McPhee Group | NF | 970-882-7296 | McPhee Reservoir |
| Meadows Group | NF | 303-275-5610 | SE of Buffalo Creek |
| Mogote Group | NF | 719-274-8971 | W of Antonito |
| Mountain Park Group | NF | 970-498-2770 | E of Rustic |
| North Flow Overflow Group | NF | 970-878-4039 | E of Meeker |
| Pickle Gulch Group | NF | 303-567-2901 | N of Black Hawk |
| Pike Community Group | NF | 719-636-1602 | N of Woodland Park |
| Ponderosa Group | NF | 719-275-4119 | Lake San Isabel |
| Printer Boy Group | NF | 719-486-0749 | Turquoise Reservoir |
| Red Rocks Group | NF | 719-636-1602 | N of Woodland |
| Spruce Group | NF | 719-275-4119 | Lake San Isabel |
| Stewart J. Adam Group House Group | NF | 970-353-5004 | N of Briggsdale |
| Tigiwon Community | NF | 970-827-5715 | S of Dowd |
| Timberline Group | NF | 303-275-5610 | S of Grant |
| Windy Point Group | NF | 970-468-5400 | Dillon Reservoir |
| Ute Group | NF | 970-264-2268 | W of Pagosa Springs |

\* See "Key to Abbreviations" p.22.

# Appendix 2: Additional Information

**Road Conditions:**
Denver area: 303-639-1111
Statewide: 303-639-1234

**Golf:**
Colorado Golf Association
5655 S. Yosemite, Suite 101
Englewood, CO 80111
303-779-4653
e-mail: cologolf@usga.org

**Rafting:**
Colorado River Outfitters Association
P.O. Box 1662
Buena Vista, CO 81211
303-369-4632

**Fishing & Hunting Regulations:**
Colorado Division of Wildlife
6060 Broadway
Denver, CO 80216
303-779-4653

# About the Author

Some of Melinda Crow's earliest memories revolve around camping in Colorado. She caught her first fish at Monument Lake before she could even pronounce the words "rainbow trout." When not in Colorado in a pop-up trailer, she makes her second home in Amarillo, Texas, with her husband, who helps with the driving, photography, and campfire building. Her daughter, at the age of nine, can set up camp faster than most adults.

Crow sincerely hopes that her Colorado friends, both old and new, forgive her for stubbornly remaining at least part Texan. She is author of *The Rockhound's Guide to Texas* and *The Rockhound's Guide to New Mexico*, both by Falcon Publishing.